American Accent Training

A guide to speaking and pronouncing colloquial American English

Second Edition

Ann Cook

Illustrated by Holly Forsyth
Audio by Busy Signal Studios

BARRON'S

This book is dedicated to Nate Cook.

Also, my special thanks for their extensive contributions to my editor, Dimitry Popow, Carolyn Jaeckin, Dr. Maria Bruno, Karina Lombard, Dr. Hyouk-Keun Kim, Ph.D., Karl Althaus, Adrian Wong, Sergey Korshunov, and Jerry Danielson at Busy Signal Studios.

All inquiries should be addressed to:
Barron's Educational Series, Inc.
250 Wireless Boulevard
Hauppauge, NY 11788
http://www.barronseduc.com

International Standard Book No. 0-7641-1429-8

Library of Congress Catalog Card No. 99-75495

PRINTED IN CHINA
20 19 18 17 16 15 14 13 12 11 10

Table of Contents

Read This First

Welcome to *American Accent Training*. This book and CD set is designed to get you started on your American accent. We'll follow the book and go through the 13 lessons and all the exercises step by step. Everything is explained and a complete Answer Key may be found in the back of the text.

What Is Accent?

Accent is a combination of three main components: *intonation* (speech music), *liaisons* (word connections), and *pronunciation* (the spoken sounds of vowels, consonants, and combinations). As you go along, you'll notice that you're being asked to look at accent in a different way. You'll also realize that the grammar you studied before and this accent you're studying now are completely different.

Part of the difference is that grammar and vocabulary are systematic and structured—the *letter* of the language. Accent, on the other hand, is free form, intuitive, and creative—more the *spirit* of the language. So, thinking of music, feeling, and flow, let your mouth relax into the American accent.

Can I Learn a New Accent?

Can a person actually learn a new accent? Many people feel that after a certain age, it's just not possible. Can classical musicians play jazz? If they practice, of course they can! For your American accent, it's just a matter of learning and practicing techniques this book and CD set will teach you. It is up to you to use them or not. How well you do depends mainly on how open and willing you are to sounding different from the way you have sounded all your life.

A very important thing you need to remember is that you can use your accent to say *what* you mean and *how* you mean it. Word stress conveys meaning through tone or feeling, which can be much more important than the actual words that you use. We'll cover the expression of these feelings through intonation in the first lesson.

You may have noticed that I talk fast and often run my words together. You've probably heard enough "English-teacher English"—where … everything … is … pronounced without having to listen too carefully. That's why on the CDs we're going to talk just like the native speakers that we are, in a normal conversational tone.

Native speakers may often tell people who are learning English to "slow down" and to "speak clearly." This is meant with the best of intentions, but it is exactly the opposite of what a student really needs to do. If you speak fairly quickly and with strong intonation, you will be understood more easily. To illustrate this point, you will hear a Vietnamese student first trying to speak slowly and carefully and then repeating the same words quickly and with strong intonation. Studying, this exercise took her only about two minutes to practice, but the difference makes her sound as if she had been in America for many years.

▼　　　　Please listen. You will hear the same words twice.

Hello, my name is Muoi. I'm taking American Accent Training.

You may have to listen to this CD a couple of times to catch everything. To help you, every word on the CD is also written in the book. By seeing and hearing simultaneously, you'll learn to reconcile the differences between the *appearance* of English (spelling) and the *sound* of English (pronunciation and the other aspects of accent).

The CD leaves a rather short pause for you to repeat into. The point of this is to get you responding quickly and without spending too much time thinking about your response.

Accent versus Pronunciation

Many people equate *accent* with *pronunciation*. I don't feel this to be true at all. America is a big country, and while the pronunciation varies from the East Coast to the West Coast, from the southern to the northern states, two components that are uniquely American stay basically the same—the speech music, or *intonation*, and the word connections or *liaisons*. Throughout this program, we will focus on them. In the latter part of the book we will work on pronunciation concepts, such as Cat? Caught? Cut? and Betty Bought a Bit of Better Butter; we also will work our way through some of the difficult sounds, such as TH, the American R, the L, V, and Z.

"Which Accent Is Correct?"

American Accent Training was created to help people "sound American" for lectures, interviews, teaching, business situations, and general daily communication. Although America has many regional pronunciation differences, the accent you will learn is that of standard American English as spoken and understood by the majority of educated native speakers in the United States. Don't worry that you will sound slangy or too casual because you most definitely won't. This is the way a professor lectures to a class, the way a national newscaster broadcasts, the way that is most comfortable and familiar to the majority of native speakers.

"Why Is My Accent So Bad?"

Learners can be seriously hampered by a negative outlook, so I'll address this very important point early. First, your accent is *not* bad; it is nonstandard to the American ear. There is a joke that goes: What do you call a person who can speak three languages? *Trilingual.* What do you call a person who can speak two languages? *Bilingual.* What do you call a person who can only speak one language? *American.*

Every language is equally valid or good, so every accent is *good.* The average American, however, truly does have a hard time understanding a nonstandard accent. George Bernard Shaw said that the English and Americans are two people *divided* by the same language!

Some students learn to overpronounce English because they naturally want to say the word as it is written. Too often an English teacher may allow this, perhaps thinking that colloquial American English is unsophisticated, unrefined, or even incorrect. Not so at all! Just as you don't say the T in *listen*, the TT in *better* is pronounced D, *bedder.* Any other pronunciation will sound foreign, strange, wrong, or different to a native speaker.

Less Than It Appears ... More Than It Appears

As you will see in Exercise 1-21, Squeezed-Out Syllables, on page 18, some words appear to have three or more syllables, but all of them are not actually spoken. For example, *business* is not (*bi*/zi/ness), but rather (*biz*/ness).

Just when you get used to eliminating whole syllables from words, you're going to come across other words that look as if they have only one syllable, but really need to be said with as many as three! In addition, the inserted syllables are filled with letters that are not in the written word. I'll give you two examples of this strange phenomenon. *Pool* looks like a nice, one-syllable word, but if you say it this way, at best, it will sound like *pull*, and at worst will be unintelligible to your listener. For clear comprehension, you need to say three syllables (pu/wuh/luh). Where did that W come from? It's certainly not written down anywhere, but it is there just as definitely as the P is there. The second example is a word like *feel*. If you say just the letters that you see, it will sound more like *fill*. You need to say (fee/yuh/luh). Is that really a Y? Yes. These mysterious semivowels are explained under Liaisons in Chapter 2. They can appear either inside a word as you have seen, or between words as you will learn.

Language Is Fluent and Fluid

Just like your own language, conversational English has a very smooth, fluid sound. Imagine that you are walking along a dry riverbed with your eyes closed. Every time you come to a rock, you trip over it, stop, continue, and trip over the next rock. This is how the average foreigner speaks English. It is slow, awkward, and even painful. Now imagine that you are a great river rushing through that same riverbed—rocks are no problem, are they? You just slide over and around them without ever breaking your smooth flow. It is *this* feeling that I want you to capture in English.

Changing your old speech habits is very similar to changing from a stick shift to an automatic transmission. Yes, you continue to reach for the gearshift for a while and your foot still tries to find the clutch pedal, but this soon phases itself out. In the same way, you may still say "telephone **call**" (kohl) instead of (kahl) for a while, but this too will soon pass.

You will also have to think about your speech more than you do now. In the same way that you were very aware and self-conscious when you first learned to drive, you will eventually relax and deal with the various components simultaneously.

A new accent is an adventure. Be bold! Exaggerate wildly! You may worry that Americans will laugh at you for putting on an accent, but I guarantee you, they won't even notice. They'll just think that you've finally learned to "talk right." Good luck with your new accent!

A Few Words On Pronunciation

CD 1 Track 2

I'd like to introduce you to the pronunciation guide outlines in the following chart. There aren't too many characters that are different from the standard alphabet, but just so you'll be familiar with them, look at the chart. It shows eight *tense* vowels and six *lax* vowels and semivowels.

Tense Vowels? Lax Vowels?

In some books, tense vowels are called *long* and lax vowels are called *short*. Since you will be learning how to lengthen vowels when they come before a voiced consonant, it would be confusing to say that *hen* has a long, short vowel. It is more descriptive to say that it has a lax vowel that is doubled or lengthened.

Tense Vowels				**Lax Vowels**			
Symbol	**Sound**	**Spelling**	**Example**	**Symbol**	**Sound**	**Spelling**	**Example**
ā	ɛi	take	[tak]	ɛ	eh	get	[gɛt]
ē	ee	eat	[et]	i	ih	it	[it]
ī	äi	ice	[is]	ü	ih + uh	took	[tük]
ō	ou	hope	[hop]	ə	uh	some	[səm]
ū	ooh	smooth	[smuth]				
ä	ah	caught	[kät]		**Semivowels**		
æ	ä + ɛ	cat	[kæt]	ər	er	her	[hər]
æo	æ + o	down	[dæon]	ᵊl	ul	dull	[dəᵊl]

Although this may look like a lot of characters to learn, there are really only four new ones: æ, ä, ə, and ü. Under Tense Vowels, you'll notice that the vowels that say their own name simply have a line over them: [ā], [ē], [ī], [ō], [ū]. There are three other tense vowels. First, [ä], is pronounced like the sound you make when the doctor wants to see your throat, or when you loosen a tight belt and sit down in a soft chair—*aaaaaaaah*! Next, you'll find [æ], a combination of the tense vowel [ä] and the lax vowel [ɛ]. It is similar to the noise that a goat or a lamb makes. The last one is [æo], a combination of [æ] and [o]. This is a very common sound, usually written as *ow* or *ou* in words like *down* or *round*.

    A *tense vowel* requires you to use a lot of facial muscles to produce it. If you say [ē], you must stretch your lips back; for [ū] you must round your lips forward; for [ä] you drop your jaw down; for [æ] you will drop your jaw far down and back; for [ā] bring your lips back and drop your jaw a bit; for [ī] drop your jaw for the *ah* part of the sound and pull it back up for the *ee* part; and for [ō] round the lips, drop the jaw and pull back up into [ū]. An American [ō] is really [ōū].

    ▼ Now you try it. Repeat after me. [ē], [ū], [ā], [æ], [ä], [ī], [ō].

A *lax vowel*, on the other hand, is very reduced. In fact, you don't need to move your face at all. You only need to move the back of your tongue and your throat. These sounds are very different from most other languages.

Under Lax Vowels, there are four reduced vowel sounds, starting with the Greek letter epsilon [ɛ], pronounced *eh*; [i] pronounced *ih*, and [ü] pronounced *ü*, which is a combination of *ih* and *uh*, and the schwa, [ə], pronounced *uh*—the softest, most reduced, most relaxed sound that we can produce. *It is also the most common sound in English.* The semivowels are the American R (pronounced *er*, which is the schwa plus R) and the American L (which is the schwa plus L). Vowels will be covered in greater detail in Chapters 3, 8, and 11.

Voiced Consonants? Unvoiced Consonants?

A consonant is a sound that causes two points of your mouth to come into contact, in three locations—the *lips*, the *tip of the tongue*, and the *throat*. A consonant can either be *unvoiced* (whispered) or *voiced* (spoken), and it can appear at the beginning, middle, or end of a word. You'll notice that for some categories, a particular sound doesn't exist in English.

Initial		Medial		Final	
Unvoiced	**Voiced**	**Unvoiced**	**Voiced**	**Unvoiced**	**Voiced**
parry	bury	apple	able	mop	mob
ferry	very	afraid	avoid	off	of
stew	zoo	races	raises	face	phase
sheet		pressure	pleasure	crush	garage
two	do	petal	pedal	not	nod
choke	joke	gaucho	gouger	rich	ridge
think	that	ether	either	tooth	smooth
come	gum	bicker	bigger	pick	pig
		accent	exit	tax	tags
	yes		player		day
	wool		shower		now
his		ahead			
	late		collect		towel
	rate		correct		tower
	me		swimmer		same
	next		connect		man
			finger		ring

Pronunciation Points

1. In many dictionaries, you may find a character that looks like an upside down V, [ʌ] and another character that is an upside-down *e* [ə], the *schwa*. There is a linguistic distinction between the two, but they are *pronounced* exactly the same. Since you can't hear the difference between these two sounds, we'll just be using the upside-down *e* to indicate the schwa sound. It is pronounced *uh*.

2. The second point is that we do not differentiate between [ä] and [ɔ]. The [ä] is pronounced *ah*. The backwards C [ɔ] is more or less pronounced *aw*. This *aw* sound has a "back East" sound to it, and as it's not common to the entire United States, it won't be included here.

3. R can be considered a *semivowel*. One characteristic of a vowel is that nothing in the mouth touches anything else. R definitely falls into that category. So in the exercises throughout the book it will be treated not so much as a consonant, but as a vowel.

4. The *ow* sound is usually indicated by [äu], which would be *ah + ooh*. This may have been accurate at some point in some locations, but the sound is now generally [æo]. *Town* is [tæon], *how* is [hæo], *loud* is [læod], and so on.

5. Besides *voiced* and *unvoiced*, there are two words that come up in pronunciation. These are *sibilant* and *plosive*. When you say the [s] sound, you can feel the air *sliding* out over the tip of your tongue—this is a sibilant. When you say the [p] sound, you can feel the air *popping* out from between your lips—this is a plosive. Be aware that there are two sounds that are sometimes mistakenly taught as sibilants, but are actually plosives: [th] and [v].

6. For particular points of pronunciation that pertain to your own language, refer to the Nationality Guides on page 172.

> Throughout this text, we will be using three symbols to indicate three separate actions:
>
> ▼   Indicates a command or a suggestion.
>
> ✜   Indicates the beep tone.
>
> ✖   Indicates that you need to turn the CD on or off, back up, or pause.

Telephone Tutoring

Preliminary Diagnostic Analysis

CD 1 Track 3

This is a speech analysis to identify the strengths and weaknesses of your American accent. If you are studying American Accent Training on your own, please contact toll-free (800) 457-4255 or www.americanaccent.com for a referral to a qualified telephone analyst. The diagnostic analysis is designed to evaluate your current speech patterns to let you know where your accent is standard and nonstandard.

> Hello, my name is _____. I'm taking American Accent Training. There's a lot to learn, but I hope to make it as enjoyable as possible. I should pick up on the American intonation pattern pretty easily, although the only way to get it is to practice all of the time.

1. all, long, caught
2. cat, matter, laugh
3. take, say, fail
4. get, egg, any
5. ice, I'll, sky
6. it, milk, sin
7. eat, me, seen
8. work, girl, bird
9. come, front, indicate
10. smooth, too, shoe
11. took, full, would
12. told, so, roll
13. out, house, round
14. boy, oil, toy

A	B	C	D	E	F
1. pit	1. bit	1. staple	1. stable	1. cap	1. cab
2. fear	2. veer	2. refers	2. reverse	2. half	2. have
3. sue	3. zoo	3. faces	3. phases	3. race	3. raise
4. sheer	4. din	4. cashew	4. casual	4. rush	4. rouge
5. tin	5. gin	5. metal	5. medal	5. hat	5. had
6. chin	6. then	6. catcher	6. cadger	6. rich	6. ridge
7. thin	7. gut	7. ether	7. either	7. bath	7. bathe
8. cut	8. race	8. bicker	8. bigger	8. tack	8. tag
9. yellow	9. breed	9. million	9. correction	9. say	9. sore
10. would	10. man	10. coward	10. surprise	10. how	10. peeper
11. him	11. name	11. reheat	11. summer	11. soul	11. palm
12. lace		12. collection	12. runner	12. people	12. can
13. bleed		13. supplies	13. kingdom		13. sing

1. Go upstairs.
2. I am going to the other room.
3. My name is Ann.
4. It is the end of the bad years.
5. Give it to his owner.

1. Go⁽ʷ⁾upstairs.
2. I⁽ʸ⁾am going t' thee⁽ʸ⁾əther room.
3. My nay mi Zæn.
4. Idiz the⁽ʸ⁾en d'v th' bæ dyearz.
5. G' v' to⁽ʷ⁾i zon'r.

1. Betty bought a bit of better butter.

2. Beddy bada bida bedder budder.

3. Italian	Italy
4. attack	attic
5. atomic	atom
6. photography	photograph

| 7. bet | bed |

Chapter 1

American Intonation

The American Speech Music

CD 1 Track 4

What to Do with Your Mouth to Sound American

One of the main differences between the way an American talks and the way the rest of the world talks is that we don't really move our lips. (So, when an American says, "Read my lips!" what does he *really* mean?) We create most of our sounds in the throat, using our tongue very actively. If you hold your fingers over your lips or clench your jaws when you practice speaking American English, you will find yourself much closer to native-sounding speech than if you try to pronounce every … single … sound … very … carefully.

If you can relate American English to music, remember that the indigenous music is jazz. Listen to their speech music, and you will hear that Americans have a melodic, jazzy way of producing sounds. Imagine the sound of a cello when you say, *Beddy bada bida bedder budder* (Betty bought a bit of better butter) and you'll be close to the native way of saying it.

Because most Americans came from somewhere else, American English reflects the accent contributions of many lands. The speech music has become much more exaggerated than British English, developing a strong and distinctive intonation. If you use this intonation, not only will you be easier to understand, but you will sound much more confident, dynamic, and persuasive.

Intonation, or speech music, is the sound that you hear when a conversation is too far away to be clearly audible but close enough for you to tell the nationality of the speakers. The American intonation *dictates* liaisons and pronunciation, and it *indicates* mood and meaning. Without intonation, your speech would be flat, mechanical, and very confusing for your listener. What *is* the American intonation pattern? How is it different from other languages? *Foa egzampuru, eefu you hea ah Jahpahneezu pahsohn speakingu Ingurishu,* the sound would be very choppy, mechanical, and unemotional to an American. *Za sem vey vis Cheuman pipples*, it sounds too stiff. *A mahn frohm Paree ohn zee ahzer ahnd, eez intonashon goes up at zee end ov evree sentence*, and has such a strong intonation that he sounds romantic and highly emotional, but this may not be appropriate for a lecture or a business meeting in English.

American Intonation Do's and Don'ts

Do Not Speak Word by Word

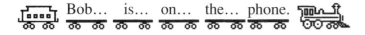
Bob... is... on... the... phone.

Connect Words to Form Sound Groups

bä bizän the foun.

Use Staircase Intonation

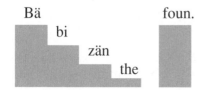

Start a new staircase
when you want to emphasize
that information, generally a *noun*.

❖ **Do not speak word by word.**
If you speak word by word, as many people who learned "printed" English do, you'll end up sounding mechanical and foreign. You may have noticed the same thing happens in your own language: When someone reads a speech, even a native speaker, it sounds stiff and stilted, quite different from a normal conversational tone.

❖ **Connect words to form sound groups.**
This is where you're going to start doing something *completely different* than what you have done in your previous English studies. This part is the most difficult for many people because it goes against everything they've been taught. Instead of thinking of each word as a unit, think of *sound units*. These sound units may or may not correspond to a word written on a page. Native speakers don't say *Bob is on the phone*, but say [bäbizän the foun]. Sound units make a sentence flow smoothly, like peanut butter—never really ending and never really starting, just flowing along. Even chunky peanut butter is acceptable. So long as you don't try to put plain peanuts directly onto your bread, you'll be OK.

❖ **Use staircase intonation.**

Let those sound groups floating on the wavy river in the figure flow downhill and you'll get the staircase. Staircase intonation not only gives you that American sound, it also makes you sound much more confident. Not every American uses the downward staircase. A certain segment of the population uses rising staircases—generally, teenagers on their way to a shopping mall: *"Hi, my name is Tiffany. I live in La Cañada. I'm on the pep squad."*

What Exactly Is Staircase Intonation?

In saying your words, imagine that they come out as if they were bounding lightly down a flight of stairs. Every so often, one jumps up to another level, and then starts down again. Americans tend to stretch out their sounds longer than you may think is natural. So to lengthen your vowel sounds, put them on two stairsteps instead of just one.

The sound of an American speaking a foreign language is very distinctive, because we double sounds that should be single. For example, in Japanese or Spanish, the word *no* is, to our ear, clipped or abbreviated.

Clipped   *Standard American*

When you have a word ending in an *unvoiced consonant*—one that you "whisper" (t, k, s, x, f, sh)—you will notice that the preceding vowel is said quite quickly, and on a single stairstep. When a word ends in a vowel or a *voiced consonant*—one that you "say" (b, d, g, z, v, zh, j), the preceding vowel is said more slowly, and on a double stairstep.

Unvoiced   *Voiced*

There are two main consequences of not doubling the second category of words: Either your listener will hear the wrong word, or even worse, you will always sound upset.

Consider that the words *curt*, *short*, *terse*, *abrupt*, and *clipped* all literally mean *short*. When applied to a person or to language, they take on the meaning of *upset* or *rude*. For example, in the expressions "*His curt reply …,*" "*Her terse response...,*" or "*He was very short with me*" all indicate a less than sunny situation.

Three Ways to Make Intonation

About this time, you're coming to the point where you may be wondering, what exactly are the mechanics of intonation? What changes when you go to the top of the staircase or when you put stress on a word? There are three ways to stress a word.

❖ The first way is to just get *louder* or raise the volume. This is not a very sophisticated way of doing it, but it will definitely command attention.

❖ The second way is to *streeeeetch* the word out or lengthen the word that you want to draw attention to (which sounds very insinuating).

❖ The third way, which is the most refined, is to change *pitch*. Although pausing just before changing the pitch is effective, you don't want to do it every time, because then it becomes an obvious technique. However, it will make your audience stop and listen because they think you're going to say something interesting.

Exercise 1-1: Rubber Band Practice with Nonsense Syllables   CD 1 Track 5

Take a rubber band and hold it with your two thumbs. Every time you want to stress a word by changing pitch, pull on the rubber band. Stretch it out gently, don't jerk it sharply. Make a looping ∞ figure with it and do the same with your voice. Use the rubber band and stretch it out every time you change pitch. Read first across, then down.

A	B	C	D
1. **duh** duh **duh**	1. **la** la **la**	1. **mee** mee **mee**	1. **ho** ho **ho**
2. duh duh **duh**	2. la la **la**	2. mee mee **mee**	2. ho ho **ho**
3. duh **duh** duh	3. la **la** la	3. mee **mee** mee	3. ho **ho** ho
4. **duh** duh duh	4. **la** la la	4. **mee** mee mee	4. **ho** ho ho

Read each column down, keeping the same intonation pattern.

A	B	C	D
1. **duh** duh **duh**	1. duh duh **duh**	1. duh **duh** duh	1. **duh** duh duh
2. A B C	2. impre**cise**	2. con**di**tion	2. **al**phabet
3. 1 2 3	3. a hot **dog**	3. a **hot** dog	3. **hot** dog stand
4. **Dogs** eat **bones.**	4. They eat **bones.**	4. They **eat** them.	4. **Give** me one.

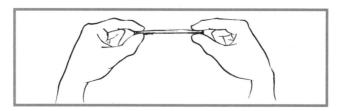

Staircase Intonation

CD 1 Track 6

So what is intonation in American English? What do Americans do? We go up and down staircases. We start high and end low.

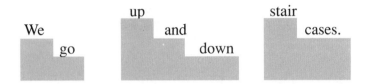

Every time we want to stress a word or an idea, we just start a new staircase. That sounds simple enough, but when and where do you start a new staircase?

Statement Intonation with Nouns

Intonation or pitch change is primarily used to introduce *new information*. This means that when you are making a statement for the first time, you will stress the *nouns*.

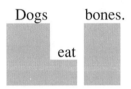

Exercise 1-2: Noun Intonation

CD 1 Track 7

Practice the noun stress pattern after me, using pitch change. Add your own examples.

1. **Dogs** eat **bones.**
2. **Mike** likes **bikes.**
3. **Elsa** wants a **book.**
4. **Adam** plays **pool.**
5. **Bobby** needs some **money.**
6. **Susie** combs her **hair.**
7. **John** lives in **France.**
8. **Nelly** teaches **French.**
9. **Ben** writes **articles.**
10. **Keys** open **locks.**
11. **Jerry** makes **music.**
12. **Jean** sells some **apples.**
13. **Carol** paints the **car.**
14. **Bill** and I fix the **bikes.**
15. Ann and **Ed** call the **kids.**
16. The **kids** like the **candy.**
17. The **girls** have a **choice.**
18. The **boys** need some **help.**
19. _____
20. _____

✖ Pause the CD.
▼ Practice the patterns five more times on your own, using your rubber band.

5

Statement Intonation with Pronouns CD 1 Track 8

When you replace the nouns with pronouns (i.e., *old information*), stress the verb.

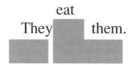

As we have seen, *nouns* are *new* information; *pronouns* are *old* information. In a nutshell, these are the two basic intonation patterns:

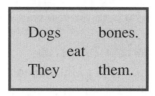

Exercise 1-3: Noun and Pronoun Intonation CD 1 Track 9

In the first column, stress the nouns. In the second column, stress the verb. Fill in your own examples at the bottom.

1. **Bob** sees **Betty**.	1. He **sees** her.
2. **Betty** knows **Bob**.	2. She **knows** him.
3. Ann and **Ed** call the **kids**.	3. They **call** them.
4. **Jan** sells some **apples**.	4. She **sells** some.
5. **Jean** sells **cars**.	5. She **sells** them.
6. **Bill** and I fix the **bikes**.	6. We **fix** them.
7. **Carl** hears **Bob** and me.	7. He **hears** us.
8. **Dogs** eat **bones**.	8. They **eat** them.
9. The **girls** have a **choice**.	9. They **have** one.
10. The **kids** like the **candy**.	10. They **like** it.
11. The **boys** need some **help**.	11. They **need** something.
12. **Ellen** should call her **sister**.	12. She should **call** someone.
13. The **murderer** killed the **plumber**.	13. He **killed** a man.
14. The **tourists** went **shopping**.	14. They **bought** stuff.
15. _____	15. _____
16. _____	16. _____
17. _____	17. _____
18. _____	18. _____
19. _____	19. _____
20. _____	20. _____

Statement Versus Question Intonation CD 1 Track 10

You may have learned at some point that questions have a rising intonation. They do, but usually a question will step upward until the very end, where it takes one quick little downward step. A question rises a little higher than a statement with the same intonation pattern.

"Here is my **car**."

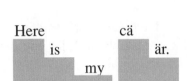

"Where is my **car**?"

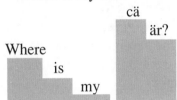

Emotional or Rhetorical Question Intonation

If you know that your car is parked outside, however, and someone doesn't see it and asks you where it is, you might think that it has been stolen and your emotion will show in your intonation as you repeat the question. As your feelings rise in an emotional situation, your intonation rises up along with them.

"Where is my **car**?"

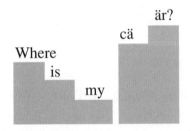

"**Why**? Is it **gone**?"

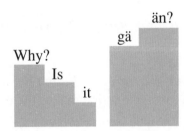

Exercise 1-4: Sentence Intonation Test CD 1 Track 11

Pause the CD and underline or highlight the words that you think should be stressed. Check Answer Key, beginning on page 193.

1. Sam sees Bill.
2. She wants one.
3. Betty likes English.
4. They play with them.
5. Children play with toys.
6. Bob and I call you and Bill.
7. You and Bill read the news.
8. It tells one.
9. Bernard works in a restaurant.
10. He works in one.
11. He sees him.
12. Mary wants a car.
13. She likes it.
14. They eat some.
15. Len and Joe eat some pizza.
16. We call you.
17. You read it.
18. The news tells a story.
19. Mark lived in France.
20. He lived there.

Exercise 1-5: Four Main Reasons for Intonation   CD 1 Track 12

Depending on the situation, a word may be stressed for any of the following reasons:

New Information   **Opinion**   **Contrast**   **"Can't"**

1. New Information
*It sounds like **rain**.*

Rain is the new information. It's the most important word in that sentence and you could replace everything else with *duh-duh-duh*. *Duh-duh-duh **rain*** will still let you get your point across.

▼   Repeat: *Duh-duh-duh **rain** / It sounds like **rain**.*

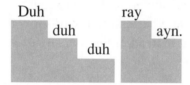

▼   Make *rain* very musical and put it on two notes: *ray-ayn.*

*Duh-duh-duh **ray-ayn** / It sounds like **ray-ayn**.*

2. Opinion
*It **sounds** like rain, but I don't think it **is**.*

In this case, intonation makes the meaning the opposite of what the words say: *It **looks** like a diamond, but I think it's a **zircon**. It **smells** like Chanel, but at that price, it's a **knock**-off. It **feels** like... It **tastes** like...* These examples all give the impression that you mean the *opposite* of what your senses tell you.

▼   Practice the intonation difference between new information and opinion:

     *It sounds like **rain**.* (It's rain.)
     *It **sounds** like rain.* (but it's not.)

3. Contrast
*He **likes** rain, but he **hates** snow.*

Like and *hate* are contrasted and are the stronger words in the sentence.

4. Can't
*It **can't rain** when there're no **clouds**.*

Contractions (*shouldn't, wouldn't*) and negatives (*no, not, never*) are important words since they totally negate the meaning of a sentence, but they are not usually stressed. *Can't* is the exception.

Exercise 1-6: Pitch and Meaning Change

Practice saying the four sentences after me. Pay close attention to the changes in pitch that you must make to convey the different meanings intended. The words to be stressed are indicated in bold face.

1. It sounds like **rain**.

2. It **sounds** like rain.

3. He **likes** rain, but he **hates** snow.

4. It **can't rain** on my **parade**! He **can't do** it. (*See also Ex. 1-43 for negatives.*)

Exercise 1-7: Individual Practice

Practice saying the sentences after the suggestion and the beep tone ✜. *You will be given only a **short** time in which to reply so that you won't have the leisure to overthink. Start speaking as soon as you hear the tone because I'll be saying the sentence only a few seconds later.*

1. Convey the information that it really does sound as if rain is falling. ✜

2. Convey the opinion that although it has the sound of rain, it may be something else. ✜

3. Convey the different feelings that someone has about rain and snow. ✜

4. Convey the fact that rain is an impossibility right now. ✜

✖ Pause the CD.
▼ Practice the four sentences on your own ten times.
✖ Once you're familiar with moving the stress around and feeling how the meaning changes, turn the CD on to continue with the next exercise.

Exercise 1-8: Meaning of "Pretty"

Native speakers make a clear distinction between pretty **easily** *(easily) and* **pretty** easily *(a little difficult). Repeat the answers after me paying close attention to your stress.*

Question: How did you like the movie?
Answer: 1. *It was pretty **good**.* (She liked it.)
        2. *It was **pretty** good.* (She didn't like it much.)

Exercise 1-9: Inflection

CD 1 Track 16

Notice how the meaning changes, while the actual words stay the same.

1. **I** didn't say he stole the money. Someone **else** said it.

2. I **didn't** say he stole the money. **That's** not true at **all**.

3. I didn't **say** he stole the money. I only **suggested** the **possibility**.

4. I didn't say **he** stole the money. I think someone **else** took it.

5. I didn't say he **stole** the money. Maybe he just **borrowed** it.

6. I didn't say he stole **the** money, but rather some **other** money.

7. I didn't say he stole the **money**. He may have taken some **jewelry**.

I	**I** didn't say he stole the money. Someone **else** said it. It's true that somebody said it, but I wasn't that person.
Didn't	I **didn't** say he stole the money. **That's** not true at **all**. Someone has accused me and I'm protesting my innocence.
Say	I didn't **say** he stole the money. I only **suggested** the **possibility**. Maybe I hinted it. Maybe I wrote it. In some way, I indicated that he stole the money, *but* I didn't say it.
He	I didn't say **he** stole the money. I think someone **else** took it. I think someone stole the money, only not the person you suspect did it.
Stole	I didn't say he **stole** the money. Maybe he just **borrowed** it. I agree that he took it, but I think his motive was different.
The	I didn't say he stole **the** money, but rather some **other** money. We agree that he stole some money, but I don't think it's this money.
Money	I didn't say he stole the **money**. He may have taken some **jewelry**. We agree that he's a thief, but we think he stole different things.

Notice that in the first half of these sentences nothing changes but the intonation.

▼ Repeat after me.

Exercise 1-10: Individual Practice　　　　　　　　　CD 1 Track 17

Now, let's see what you can do with the same sentence, just by changing the stress around to different words. I'll tell you which meaning to express. When you hear the tone ❖, say the sentence as quickly as you can, then I'll say the sentence for you. To test your ear, I'm going to repeat the sentences in random order. Try to determine which word I'm stressing. The answers are given in parentheses, but don't look unless you really have to. Here we go.

    1. Indicate that he borrowed the money and didn't steal it. (5) ❖
    2. Indicate that you are denying having said that he stole it. (2) ❖
    3. Indicate that you think he stole something besides money. (7) ❖
    4. Indicate that you were not the person to say it. (1) ❖
    5. Indicate that you don't think that he was the person who stole it. (4) ❖
    6. Indicate that you didn't say it outright, but did suggest it in some way. (3) ❖
    7. Indicate that he many have stolen a different amount of money. (6) ❖

Overdo It

Practice these sentences on your own, really exaggerating the word that you think should be stressed. In the beginning, you're going to feel that this is ridiculous. (*Nobody stresses this hard! Nobody talks like this! People are going to laugh at me!*) Yet as much as you may stress, you're probably only going to be stressing about half as much as you should.

✖ Pause the CD and practice the sentences in random order ten times.

Another reason you must overexaggerate is because when you get tired, emotional, or relaxed, you will stop paying attention. When this happens, like a rubber band, you're going to snap back to the way you originally were sounding (10 percent). So, if you just stretch yourself to the exact position where you ideally want to be, you'll go back almost completely to the old way when you relax. For practice, then, stretch yourself far *beyond* the normal range of intonation (150 percent), so when you relax, you relax back to a standard American sound (100 percent).

We All Do It

Possibly about this time you're thinking, *Well, maybe you do this in English, but in* **my** *language, I just really don't think that we do this.* I'd like you to try a little exercise.

Exercise 1-11: Translation　　　　　　　　　CD 1 Track 18

Take the sentence **I didn't say he stole the money** *and translate it into your native language. Write it down below, using whatever letters or characters you use in your language.*

Now that you have written your sentence down, try shifting the stress around in your own language by going through the stress patterns 1-7 in Exercise 1-9. Don't try to put on a particularly American or other accent; just concentrate on stressing a different word in the sentence each time you say it.

For example, if your language is German, *Ich habe nicht gesagt daß er das Geld gestohlen hat*, you would change the stress to: ***Ich** habe nicht gesagt daß er das Geld gestohlen hat*, or *Ich habe **nicht** gesagt daß er das Geld gestohlen hat*.

If you translated it into French, you would say, *Je **n'ai pas** dit qu'il a volé l'argent*, or *Je n' pas dit qu'il a **volé** l'argent*.

In Japanese, many people think that there are no intonation changes, but if you hear someone say, *wak**ka**nai*, you'll realize that it has similarities to every other language. *Watashi wa **kare** ga okane o nusunda to wa iimasen deshita*. Or perhaps, *Watashi wa kare ga okane o nusunda to wa **iimasen** deshita*.

No matter how strange it may sound to you, stress each different word several times in your language. You may notice that with some words it sounds perfectly normal, but with other words it sounds very strange. Or you may find that in your language, rather than stressing a word, you prefer to change the word order or substitute another word. Whatever you do is fine, as long as you realize where your language patterns are similar to and different from the American English intonation patterns. Then, when you do it again, in English, it will be much easier.

Note *An excellent exercise is to practice speaking your native language with an American accent. If you can sound like an American speaking your native language, imagine how easy it would be to speak English with an American accent.*

✖ Pause the CD and practice shifting the stressed words in your native language.

Intonation Contrast

Below are two sentences—the first is stressed on the most common, everyday word, *book*. Nine times out of ten, people will stress the sentence in this way. The second sentence has a less common, but perfectly acceptable intonation, since we are making a distinction between two possible locations.

Normal intonation	Where's the **book**? It's on the **table**.
Changed intonation	Is the book **on** the table or **under** it? It's **on** the table.

✖ Pause the CD and repeat the sentences.

Exercise 1-12: Create Your Own Intonation Contrast　　　CD 1 Track 19

Write a short sentence and indicate where you think the most normal intonation would be placed. Then, change the meaning of the sentence slightly and change the intonation accordingly.

Normal intonation _____

Changed intonation _____

Exercise 1-13: Variable Stress   CD 1 Track 20

Notice how the meaning of the following sentence changes each time we change the stress pattern. You should be starting to feel in control of your sentences now.

1. *What would you **like**?*
   This is the most common version of the sentence, and it is just a simple request for information.

2. *What would **you** like?*
   This is to single out an individual from a group.

3. *What **would** you like?*
   You've been discussing the kinds of things he might like and you want to determine his specific desires: *"Now that you mention it, what **would** you like?"*
   or
   He has rejected several things and a little exasperated, you ask, *"If you don't want any of these, what **would** you like?"*

4. ***What** would you like?*
   You didn't hear and you would like the speaker to repeat herself.
   or
   You can't believe what you heard: *"I'd like strawberry jam on my asparagus."*—
   *"**What** would you like?"*

✖ Turn off the CD and repeat the four sentences.

Exercise 1-14: Make a Variable Stress Sentence   CD 1 Track 21

*Now **you** decide which words should be emphasized. Write a normal, everyday sentence with at least seven words and put it through as many changes as possible. Try to make a pitch change for each word in the sentence and think about how it changes the meaning of the entire sentence.*

1._____

2._____

3._____

4._____

5._____

6._____

7._____

Application of Intonation

There is always at least one stressed word in a sentence and frequently you can have quite a few if you are introducing a lot of new information or if you want to contrast several things. Look at the paragraph in Exercise 1-15. Take a pencil and mark every word that you think should be stressed or sound stronger than the words around it. I'd like you to make just an accent mark (´) to indicate a word you think should sound stronger than others around it.

Reminder The three ways to change your voice for intonation are: (1) **Volume** (speak louder), (2) **Length** (stretch out a word), and (3) **Pitch** (change your tone).

✖ Pause the CD and work on the paragraph below.

Exercise 1-15: Application of Stress

Mark every word or syllable with ´ where you think that the sound is stressed. Use the first sentence as your example. Check Answer Key, beginning on page 193. Pause the CD.

Héllo, my´ name is _____. I'm taking American Accent Training. There's a lot to learn, but I hope to make it as enjoyable as possible. I should pick up on the American intonation pattern pretty easily, although the only way to get it is to practice all of the time. I use the up and down, or peaks and valleys, intonation more than I used to. I've been paying attention to pitch, too. It's like walking down a staircase. I've been talking to a lot of Americans lately, and they tell me that I'm easier to understand. Anyway, I could go on and on, but the important thing is to listen well and sound good. Well, what do you think? Do I?

▼ Listen and re-mark the stressed words with your marker. After you've put in the accent marks where you think they belong, take one of the colored translucent markers and as I read very slowly, mark the words that I stress. I am going to exaggerate the words far more than you'd normally hear in a normal reading of the paragraph. You can mark either the whole word or just the strong syllable, whichever you prefer, so that you have a bright spot of color for where the stress should fall.

Note *If you do the exercise only in pencil, your eye and mind will tend to skip over the accent marks. The spots of color, however, will register as "different" and thereby encourage your pitch change. This may strike you as unusual, but trust me, it works.*

✖ Pause the CD and practice reading the paragraph out loud three times on your own.

How You *Talk* Indicates to People How You *Are*   CD 1 Track 24

Beware of "Revealing" a Personality that You Don't Have!

There is no absolute right or wrong in regard to intonation because a case can be made for stressing just about any word or syllable, but you actually reveal a lot about yourself by the elements you choose to emphasize. For example, if you say, *Hello*, this intonation would indicate doubt. This is why you say, *Hello?* when answering the telephone because you don't know who is on the other end. Or when you go into a house and you don't know who's there because you don't see anyone. But if you're giving a speech or making a presentation and you stand up in front of a crowd and say, *Hello*, the people would probably laugh because it sounds so uncertain. This is where you'd confidently want to say **Hello, my** *name is So-and-so*.

A second example is, **my** *name is*—as opposed to *my* **name** *is*. If you stress *name*, it sounds as if you are going to continue with more personal information: *My* **name** *is So-and-so, my* **address** *is such-and-such, my* **blood** *type is O*. Since it may not be your intention to give all that information, stay with the standard—**Hello, my** *name is So-and-so*.

If you stress *I* every time, it will seem that you have a very high opinion of yourself. Try it: *I'm* *taking American Accent Training.* *I've* *been paying attention to pitch, too.* *I think I'm quite wonderful.*

An earnest, hard-working person might emphasize words this way: *I'm* **taking** *American Accent Training* (Can I learn this stuff?). *I hope to* **make** *it as enjoyable as possible* (I'll force myself to enjoy it if I have to). *Although the only way to get it is to practice* **all** *the time* (24 hours a day).

A Doubting Thomas would show up with: *I* **should** *pick up on* (but I might not) *the American intonation pattern* **pretty** *easily*, (but it looks pretty hard, too). *I've been talking to a lot of Americans lately, and they* **tell** *me that I'm easier to understand* (but I think they're just being polite).

Exercise 1-16: Paragraph Intonation Practice   CD 1 Track 25

▼ From your color-marked copy, read each sentence of the paragraph in Exercise 1-15 after me. Use your rubber band, give a clear pitch change to the highlighted words, and think about the meaning that the pitch is conveying.

✖ Back up the CD and practice this paragraph three times.

✖ Pause the CD and practice three times on your own.

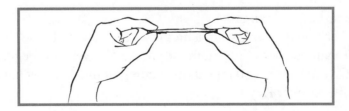

Exercise 1-17: Staircase Intonation Practice

Draw one step of the staircase for each word of the paragraph. Start a new staircase for every stressed word. There usually is more than one staircase in a sentence. New sentences don't have to start new staircases; they can continue from the previous sentence until you come to a stressed word. I'll read the beginning sentences. Check the first sentence against the example. Then put the words of the second sentence on a staircase, based on the way I read it. Remember, I'm exaggerating to make a point.

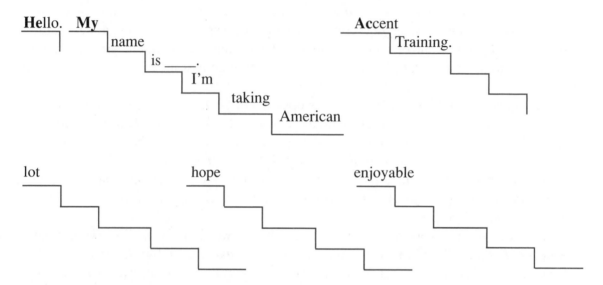

▼   Write out the rest of the staircases.

✖   Turn the CD back on to check your staircases with the way I read the paragraph.

✖   Pause the CD again to check your staircases in the Answer Key, beginning on page 193.

✖   Back up the CD, and listen and repeat my reading of the paragraph while following the staircases in the Answer Key.

Exercise 1-18: Reading with Staircase Intonation   CD 1 Track 27

Read the following with clear intonation where marked.

Hello, **my** name is_____. I'm taking American **Accent** Training. There's a **lot** to learn, but I **hope** to make it as **enjoyable** as possible. I should pick **up** on the American **intonation** pattern pretty **easily**, although the **only** way to **get** it is to **practice** all of the time. I use the **up** and down, or **peaks** and valleys, **intonation** more than I **used** to. I've been paying attention to **pitch**, **too**. It's like **walking** down a **stair**case. I've been **talking** to a lot of **Americans** lately, and they tell me that I'm **easier** to under**stand**. **Any**way, I could go **on** and on, but the **important** thing is to **listen** well and sound **good**. Well, what do you **think**? **Do** I?

Exercise 1-19: Spelling and Numbers   CD 1 Track 28

Just as there is stress in words or phrases, there is intonation in spelling and numbers. Americans seem to spell things out much more than other people. In any bureaucratic situation, you'll be asked to spell names and give all kinds of numbers—your phone number, your birth date, and so on. There is a distinct stress and rhythm pattern to both spelling and numbers—usually in groups of three or four letters or numbers, with the stress falling on the last member of the group. Acronyms (phrases that are represented by the first letter of each word) and initials are usually stressed on the last letter. Just listen to the words as I say them, then repeat the spelling after me.

Acronym	Pronunciation
IBM	Eye Bee **Em**
MIT	Em Eye **Tee**
Ph.D.	Pee Aitch **Dee**
MBA	Em Bee **ɛi**
LA	Eh **Lay**
IQ	Eye **Kyu**
RSVP	Are Ess Vee **Pee**
TV	Tee **Vee**
USA	You Ess **ɛi**
ASAP	**ɛi** Ess **ɛi** **Pee**
CIA	See Eye **ɛi**
FBI	Eff Bee **Eye**
USMC	You Ess Em **See**
COD	See Oh **Dee**
SOS	Ess Oh **Ess**
X,Y,Z	Ex, Why, **Zee**

Spelling	Pronunciation
Box	Bee Oh **Ex**
Cook	See Oh Oh **Kay**
Wilson	Dubba You Eye **El**, Ess Oh **En**

Numbers	Pronunciation
Area Code	213
Zip Code	9470**8**
Date	9/6/**62**
Phone Number	555-91**32**

Exercise 1-20: Sound/Meaning Shifts

CD 1 Track 29

Intonation is powerful. It can change meaning and pronunciation. Here you will get the chance to play with the sounds. Remember, in the beginning, the meaning isn't that important—just work on getting control of your pitch changes. Use your rubber band for each stressed word.

my **tie**	**mai**-tai	**Might** I?
my **keys**	**Mi**key's	My **keys**?
inn key	in **key**	**ink**y
my **tea**	**migh**ty	My **D**
I have **two**.	**I** have, **too**.	I **have** to.

How many **kids** do you have?	I have **two**.
I've been to **Europe**.	**I** have, **too**.
Why do you **work** so hard?	I **have** to.

Exercise 1-21: Squeezed-Out Syllables

CD 1 Track 30

Intonation can also completely get rid of certain entire syllables. Some longer words that are stressed on the first syllable squeeze weak syllables right out. Cover up the regular columns and read the words between the brackets.

actually	[**æk**•chully]	every	[**ɛv**ree]
average	[**ævr**'j]	family	[**fæm**lee]
aspirin	[**æs**prin]	finally	[**fyn**•lee]
broccoli	[**brä**klee]	general	[**jɛn**r'l]
business	[**biz**ness]	groceries	[**gross**reez]
camera	[**kæm**ruh]	interest	[**intr**'st]
chocolate	[**chäk**l't]	jewelry	[**jool**ree]
comfortable	[**k'mf**•t'bl]	mathematics	[**mæth**mædix]
corporal	[**cor**pr'l]	memory	[**mem**ree]
desperate	[**des**pr't]	orange	[**ornj**]
diamond	[**däim**'nd]	probably	[**präb**lee]
diaper	[**däi**per]	restaurant	[**res**tränt]
different	[**diffr**'nt]	separate	[**sep**r't]
emerald	[**ɛmr**'ld]	several	[**sɛvr**'l]
vegetable	[**vej**•t'bl]	liberal	[**libr**'l]
beverage	[**bev**•r'j]	conference	[**cänf**rns]
bakery	[**bā**•kree]	coverage	[**c'vr**'j]
catholic	[**cæth**•l'k]	history	[**hiss**tree]
nursery	[**nr**sree]	accidentally	[**æk**•sə•**dent**•lee]
onion	[**ən**y'n]	basically	[**ba**•sə•klee]

Note *The ~**cally** ending is always pronounced ~**klee**.*

Syllable Stress

CD 1 Track 31

Syllable Count Intonation Patterns

In spoken English, if you stress the wrong syllable, you can totally lose the meaning of a word: "MA-sheen" is hardly recognizable as "ma-SHEEN" or *machine*.

At this point, we won't be concerned with *why* we are stressing a particular syllable—that understanding will come later.

Exercise 1-22: Syllable Patterns   CD 1 Track 32

In order to practice accurate pitch change, repeat the following column. Each syllable will count as one musical note. Remember that words that end in a vowel or a voiced consonant will be longer than ones ending in an unvoiced consonant.

1 Syllable
Pattern 1a

A	B	C
la!	get	stop
cat	quick	which
jump	choice	bit
box	loss	beat

Pattern 1b

A	B	C
la-a	law	bid
dog	goes	bead
see	choose	car
plan	lose	know

2 Syllables
Pattern 2a

A	B	C
la-**la**	Bob **Smith**	for **you**
a **dog**	my **car**	Who **knows**?
a **cat**	some **more**	cas**sette**
des**troy**	red **tape**	bal**let**
a **pen**	en**close**	va**let**
pre**tend**	con**sume**	to **do**
your **job**	my **choice**	to**day**
pea **soup**	How's **work**?	to**night**

Pattern 2b

A	B	C
la-la	**wrist**watch	**phone** book
hot dog	**text**book	**door**knob
icy	**book**shelf	**note**book
suitcase	**sun**shine	**house** key
project	**place**mat	**ballot**
sunset	**stapler**	**valid**
Get one!	**mo**dern	**dog** show
Do it!	**mo**dem	**want** ad

> *a hot **dog** is an overheated canine*
> *a **hot** dog is a frankfurter*

American Accent Training

Exercise 1-22: Syllable Patterns *continued*   CD 1 Track 32

3 Syllables

	A	**B**	**C**
Pattern 3a	la-la-la Bob's hot **dog** Bob won't **know.** Sam's the **boss.** Susie's **nice.** **Bill** went **home.** **Cats** don't **care.** **Stocks** can **fall.** **School** is **fun.**	**Worms** eat **dirt.** **Inchworms inch.** **Pets** need **care.** **Ed's** too **late.** **Paul** threw **up.** **Wool** can **itch.** **Birds** sing **songs.** **Spot** has **fleas.** **Nick's** a **punk.**	**Joe** has **three.** **Bob** has **eight.** **Al** jumped **up.** **Glen** sat **down.** **Tom** made **lunch.** **Kids** should **play.** **Mom** said, "**No!**" **Mars** is **red.** **Ned** sells **cars.**
Pattern 3b	la-la-**la** a hot **dog** I don't **know.** He's the **boss.** We cleaned **up.** in the **bag** for a **while** I went **home.** We don't **care.** It's in **March.**	Make a **cake.** He for**got.** Take a **bath.** We're too **late.** I love **you.** over **here** What a **jerk!** How's your **job?** How'd it **go?** Who'd you **meet?**	IBM a good **time** Use your **head!** How are **you?** We came **home.** on the **bus** engi**neer** She fell **down.** They called **back.** You goofed **up.**
Pattern 3c	la-la-la a **hot** dog I **don't** know! Jim **killed** it. to**mor**row a **fruit**cake the **en**gine a **wine**glass po**ta**to what**ev**er	per**cen**tage (%) ad**van**tage It's **star**ting. Let's **try** it. fi**nan**cial I **thought** so. on **Wednes**day in **A**pril I **love** you. Let's **tell** him.	O**hi**o his **foot**ball They're **leav**ing. How **are** you? em**phat**ic Dale **planned** it. You **took** it. ex**ter**nal a **bar**gain Don't **touch** it.
Pattern 3d	la-la-la **hot** dog stand **I** don't know. **an**alyze **ar**ticle **din**nertime **di**gital **an**alog **cell** structure	**al**phabet **pos**sible **Show** me one. **a**rea **punc**tuate **em**phasis **syl**lable **Post**It note **Ro**lodex	**phone** number **think** about **com**fortable **wai**ting for **pit**iful **ev**erything **or**chestra **ig**norant **Ru**bbermaid

20

Exercise 1-22: Syllable Patterns *continued*   CD 1 Track 32

4 Syllables

	A	**B**	**C**

Pattern 4a

A	B	C
la-la-la-**la**	**Nate** needs a **break.**	**Max** wants to **know.**
Spot's a hot **dog.**	**Ed** took my **car.**	**Al's** kitchen **floor**
Jim killed a **snake.**	**Jill** ate a **steak.**	**Bill's** halfway **there.**
Joe doesn't **know.**	**Spain's** really **far.**	**Roses** are **red,**
Nate bought a **book.**	**Jake's** in the **lake.**	**Violets** are **blue,**
Al brought some **ice.**	**Sam's** in a **bar.**	**Candy** is **sweet,**
		and so are you.

Pattern 4b

A	B	C
la-la-la-**la**	She asked for **help.**	I want to **know.**
It's a hot **dog.**	We took my **car.**	the kitchen **floor**
He killed a **snake.**	We need a **break.**	We watched **TV.**
He doesn't **know.**	It's really **far.**	She's halfway **there.**
We came back **in.**	I love you, **too.**	We played all **day.**
He bought a **book.**	They got a**way.**	Please show me **how.**

Pattern 4c

A	B	C
la-la-la-la	**Boys** ring **door**bells.	**Phil** knows **mail**men.
Bob likes **hot** dogs.	**Bill** ate **break**fast.	**Joe** grew **egg**plants.
Ann eats **pan**cakes.	**Guns** are **le**thal.	**Hump**ty **Dump**ty
Cats eat **fish** bones.	**Inch**worms **bug** me.	**Hawks** are **vi**cious.
Bears are **fuzz**y.	**Rag**tops **cost** more.	**Home**work **bores** them.
Planets **ro**tate.	**Sales**men **sell** things.	**Mike** can **hear** you.

Pattern 4d

A	B	C
la-la-**la**-la	an a**larm** clock	He said "**light**bulb."
It's my **hot** dog.	I don't **need** one.	What does "**box**" mean?
imi**ta**tion	Ring the **door**bell.	Put your **hands** up.
ana**ly**tic	What's the **mat**ter?	Where's the **mail**man?
We like **sci**ence.	intro**duc**tion	an as**sem**bly
my to-**do** list	my re**port** card	defi**ni**tion

Pattern 4e

A	B	C
la-**la**-la-la	po**ta**to chip	What **time** is it?
a **hot** dog stand	Whose **turn** is it?	my **phone** number
Jim **killed** a man.	We **worked** on it.	Let's **eat** something.
a**nal**ysis	How **tall** are you?	How **old** are you?
in**vis**ible	in**san**ity	un**touch**able
a **plat**ypus	a**bil**ity	a **ma**niac

Pattern 4f

A	B	C
la-la-la-la	**su**pervisor	**light**house keeper
permanently	**win**dow cleaner	**cough** medicine
demonstrated	**race** car driver	**bus**iness meeting
category	**Jan**uary (jæn•yə•wery)	**Feb**ruary (feb•yə•wery)
office supplies	**prog**ress report	**ba**by-sitter
educator	**thing**amajig	**dic**tionary

Exercise 1-23: Syllable Count Test   CD 1 Track 33

Put the following words into the proper category based on the syllable count intonation.
Write the pattern number in the space provided. Check Answer Key, beginning on p. 193.

Single Words
1. stop __	5. analyze (*v*) __	9. believe __
2. go __	6. analysis (*n*) __	10. director __
3. sympathy __	7. analytic (*adj*) __	11. indicator __
4. sympathetic __	8. mistake __	12. technology __

Noun Phrases
1. tech support __	5. English test __	9. a fire engine __
2. software program __	6. airline pilot __	10. sports fanatic __
3. the truth __	7. Y2K __	11. the kitchen floor __
4. notebook __	8. Santa Claus __	12. computer disk __

Phrases
1. on the table __	5. for sure __	9. on the way __
2. in your dreams __	6. OK __	10. like a princess __
3. last Monday __	7. thank you __	11. to pick up __
4. for a while __	8. back to back __	12. a pickup __

Sentences
1. Al gets T-shirts. __	5. I don't know. __	9. She has head lice. __
2. I went too fast. __	6. Bob works hard. __	10. Gail has head lice. __
3. Get up! __	7. It's in the back. __	11. Sue's working hard. __
4. Get one! __	8. Buy us some! __	12. I want some more. __

Mixed
1. Do it again. __	8. in the middle __	15. Make up your mind! __
2. Joe was upset. __	9. It's a good trick. __	16. Tom has frostbite. __
3. banana __	10. specifically __	17. Sam's a champ. __
4. banana split __	11. Bill needs it. __	18. He's a winner. __
5. categorize __	12. jump around __	19. He likes to win. __
6. child support __	13. on my own __	20. Al hates pork chops. __
7. Mexican food __	14. by myself __	21. He likes ground beef. __

Make up your own examples, one of each pattern. Make up more on your own.

1. _____	2a	5. _____	3c	9. _____	4c
2. _____	2b	6. _____	3d	10. _____	4d
3. _____	3a	7. _____	4a	11. _____	4e
4. _____	3b	8. _____	4b	12. _____	4f

Complex Intonation

Word Count Intonation Patterns

This is the beginning of an extremely important part of spoken American English—the rhythms and intonation patterns of the long streams of nouns and adjectives that are so commonly used. These exercises will tie in the intonation patterns of **adjectives** (*nice, old, best*, etc.), **nouns** (*dog, house, surgeon*, etc.), and **adverbs** (*very, really, amazingly*, etc.)

One way of approaching sentence intonation is not to build each sentence from scratch. Instead, use patterns, with each pattern similar to a mathematical formula. Instead of plugging in numbers, however, plug in words.

In Exercise 1-2, we looked at simple noun•verb•noun patterns, and in Exercise 1-22 and 1-23, the syllable-count intonation patterns were covered and tested. In Exercises 1-24 to 1-37, we'll examine intonation patterns in two word phrases.

It's important to note that there's a major difference between *syllable stress* and *compound noun stress* patterns. In the syllable count exercises, each *syllable* was represented by a single musical note. In the noun phrases, each individual *word* will be represented by a single musical note—no matter how many total syllables there may be.

At times, what appears to be a single syllable word will have a "longer" sound to it—*seed* takes longer to say than *seat* for example. This was introduced on page 3, where you learned that a final voiced consonant causes the previous vowel to double.

Exercise 1-24: Single-Word Phrases

Repeat the following noun and adjective sentences.

Noun	Adjective
1. It's a **nail**.	It's **short**.
2. It's a **cake**.	It's **chocolate**. [chäkl't]
3. It's a **tub**.	It's **hot**. [hät]
4. It's a **drive**.	It's **härd**.
5. It's a **door**.	It's in **back**. [bæk]
6. It's a **cärd**.	There are **four**.
7. It's a **spot**. [spät]	It's **smäll**.
8. It's a **book**. [bük]	It's **good**.[güd]

Write your own noun and adjective sentences below. You will be using these examples throughout this series of exercises.

9. It's a _____ It's_____
10. It's a _____ It's_____
11. It's a _____ It's_____

Two-Word Phrases

Descriptive Phrases

CD 1 Track 36

Nouns are "heavier" than adjectives; they carry the weight of the new information. An adjective and a noun combination is called a *descriptive phrase*, and in the absence of contrast or other secondary changes, the stress will always fall naturally on the noun. In the absence of a noun, you will stress the adjective, but as soon as a noun appears on the scene, it takes immediate precedence—and should be stressed.

Exercise 1-25: Sentence Stress with Descriptive Phrases   CD 1 Track 37

Repeat the following phrases.

Adjective	**Noun and Adjective**
1. It's **short**.	It's a short **nail**.
2. It's **chocolate**.	It's a chocolate **cake**.
3. It's **good**.	It's a good **plan**.
4. It's **guarded**.	It's a guarded **gate**.
5. It's **wide**.	It's a wide **river**.
6. There're **four**.	There're four **cards**.
7. It was **small**.	It was a small **spot**.
8. It's the **best**.	It's the best **book**.

Pause the CD and write your own adjective and noun/adjective sentences. Use the same words from Ex. 1-24.

9.	It's _____	It's a _____
10.	It's _____	It's a _____
11.	It's _____	It's a _____

Exercise 1-26: Two Types of Descriptive Phrases   CD 1 Track 38

Repeat.

Adjective Noun	**Adverb Adjective**
1. It's a short **nail**.	It's really **short**.
2. It's a chocolate **cake**.	It's dark **chocolate**.
3. It's a hot **bath**.	It's too **hot**.
4. It's a hard **drive**.	It's extremely **hard**.

Exercise 1-26: Two Types of Descriptive Phrases *continued*　　CD 1 Track 38

5.	It's the back **door**.	It's far **back**.
6.	There are four **cards**.	There are only **four**.
7.	It's a small **spot**.	It's laughably **small**.
8.	It's a good **book**.	It's amazingly **good**.

Pause the CD and write your own adjective/noun and adverb/adjective sentences, carrying over Ex. 1-25.

9. It's a _____　　It's_____
10. It's a _____　　It's_____
11. It's a _____　　It's_____

Exercise 1-27: Descriptive Phrase Story—The Ugly Duckling　　CD 1 Track 39

The following well-known story has been rewritten to contain only descriptions. Stress the second word of each phrase. Repeat after me.

There is a *mother duck*. She lays *three eggs*. Soon, there are three *baby birds*. Two of the birds are *very beautiful*. One of them is *quite ugly*. The *beautiful ducklings* make fun of their *ugly brother*. The *poor thing* is *very unhappy*. As the *three birds* grow older, the *ugly duckling* begins to change. His *gray feathers* turn *snowy white*. His *gangly neck* becomes *beautifully smooth*.

In *early spring*, the *ugly duckling* is swimming in a *small pond* in the *back yard* of the *old farm*. He sees his *shimmering reflection* in the *clear water*. What a *great surprise*! He is no longer an *ugly duckling*. He has grown into a *lovely swan*.

Set Phrases　　CD 1 Track 40

A Cultural Indoctrination to American Norms

When I learned the alphabet as a child, I heard it before I saw it. I heard that the last four letters were *dubba-you, ex, why, zee*. I thought that *dubba-you* was a long, strange name for a letter, but I didn't question it any more than I did *aitch*. It was just a name. Many years later, it struck me that it was a *double U*. Of course, a W is really UU. I had such a funny feeling, though, when I realized that something I had taken for granted for so many years had a background meaning that I had completely overlooked. This "funny feeling" is exactly what most native speakers get when a two-word phrase is stressed on the wrong word. When two individual words go through the cultural process of becoming a set phrase, the original sense of each word is more or less forgotten and the new meaning completely takes over. When we hear the word *painkiller*, we think *anesthetic*. If, however, someone says *painkiller*, it brings up the strength and almost unrelated meaning of *kill*.

　　When you have a two-word phrase, you have to either stress on the first word, or on the second word. If you stress both or neither, it's not clear what you are trying to say. Stress on the first word is more noticeable and one of the most important concepts of intonation that you are going to study. At first glance, it doesn't seem significant, but the more you look at this concept, the more you are going to realize that it reflects how we Americans think, what concepts we have adopted as our own, and what things we consider important.

Set phrases are our "cultural icons," or word images; they are indicators of a *determined use* that we have internalized. These set phrases, with stress on the first word, have been taken into everyday English from descriptive phrases, with stress on the second word. As soon as a descriptive phrase becomes a set phrase, the emphasis shifts from the *second* word to the *first*. The original sense of each word is more or less forgotten and the new meaning takes over.

Set phrases indicate that we have internalized this phrase as an *image*, that we all agree on a concrete idea that this phrase represents. A hundred years or so ago, when Levi Strauss first came out with his denim pants, they were described as *blue **jeans***. Now that we all agree on the image, however, they are ***blue*** *jeans*.

A more recent example would be the descriptive phrase, *He's a real party animal.* This slang expression refers to someone who has a great time at a party. When it first became popular, the people using it needed to explain (with their intonation) that he was an *animal* at a *party*. As time passed, the expression became cliché and we changed the intonation to *He's a real **party** animal* because "everyone knew" what it meant.

Clichés are hard to recognize in a new language because what may be an old and tired expression to a native speaker may be fresh and exciting to a newcomer. One way to look at English from the inside out, rather than always looking from the outside in, is to get a feel for what Americans have already accepted and internalized. This starts out as a purely language phenomenon, but you will notice that as you progress and undergo the relentless cultural indoctrination of standard intonation patterns, you will find yourself expressing yourself with the language cues and signals that will mark you as an insider—not an outsider.

When the interpreter was translating for the former Russian President Gorbachev about his trip to San Francisco in 1990, his pronunciation was good, but he placed himself on the outside by repeatedly saying, *cable **car***. The phrase ***cable*** *car* is an image, an established entity, and it was very noticeable to hear it stressed on the second word as a mere description.

An important point that I would like to make is that the "rules" you are given here are not meant to be memorized. This discussion is only an introduction to give you a starting point in understanding this phenomenon and in recognizing what to listen for. Read it over; think about it; then listen, try it out, listen some more, and try it out again.

As you become familiar with intonation, you will become more comfortable with American norms, thus the cultural orientation, or even cultural indoctrination, aspect of the following examples.

Note *When you get the impression that a two-word description could be hyphenated or even made into one word, it is a signal that it could be a set phrase—for example, **flash** light, **flash**-light, **flash**light. Also, stress the first word with Street (**Main** Street) and nationalities of food and people (**Mexican** food, **Chinese** girls).*

Exercise 1-28: Sentence Stress with Set Phrases   CD 1 Track 41

Repeat the following sentences.

	Noun	**Noun/Adj.**	**Set Phrase**
1.	It's a **finger**.	It's a **nail**.	It's a **finger**nail.
2.	It's a **pan**.	It's a **cake**.	It's a **pan**cake.
3.	It's a **tub**.	It's **hot**.	It's a **hot** tub. (*Jacuzzi*)
4.	It's a **drive**.	It's **hard**.	It's a **hard** drive.
5.	It's a **bone**.	It's in **back**.	It's the **back**bone. (*spine*)
6.	It's a **card**.	It's a **trick**.	It's a **card** trick.
7.	It's a **spot**.	It's a **light**.	It's a **spot**light.
8.	It's a **book**.	It's a **phone**.	It's a **phone** book.

Pause the CD and write your own noun and set phrase sentences, carrying over the same nouns you used in Exercise 1-25. Remember, when you use a noun, include the article (a, an, the); when you use an adjective, you don't need an article.

9.	It's a _____	It's a _____	It's a _____
10.	It's a _____	It's a _____	It's a _____
11.	It's a _____	It's a _____	It's a _____

Exercise 1-29: Making Set Phrases   CD 1 Track 42

Pause the CD and add a noun to each word as indicated by the picture. Check Answer Key, beginning on page 193.

1.	a **chair** + _a chairman_		11.	a wrist _____
2.	a **phone** _____		12.	a beer _____
3.	a house _____		13.	a high _____
4.	a base _____		14.	a hunting _____
5.	a door _____		15.	a dump _____
6.	The White _____		16.	a jelly _____
7.	a movie _____		17.	a love _____
8.	The Bullet _____		18.	a thumb _____
9.	a race _____		19.	a lightning _____
10	a coffee _____		20.	a pad _____

Exercise 1-30: Set Phrase Story—The Little Match Girl　　　CD 1 Track 43

The following story contains only set phrases, as opposed to the descriptive story in Exercise 1-27. Stress the first word of each phrase.

The little *match girl* was out in a *snowstorm*. Her feet were like *ice cubes* and her *fingertips* had *frostbite*. She hadn't sold any matches since *daybreak*, and she had a *stomachache* from the *hunger pangs*, but her *stepmother* would beat her with a *broomstick* if she came home with an empty *coin purse*. Looking into the bright *living rooms*, she saw *Christmas trees* and warm *fireplaces*. Out on the *snowbank*, she lit a match and saw the image of a grand *dinner table* of food before her. As the *matchstick* burned, the illusion slowly faded. She lit *another one* and saw a room full of happy *family members*. On the last match, her *grandmother* came down and carried her home. In the morning, the *passersby* saw the little *match girl*. She had frozen during the *nighttime*, but she had a smile on her face.

Contrasting a Description and a Set Phrase

We now have two main intonation patterns—*first word stress* and *second word stress*. In the following exercise, we will contrast the two.

Exercise 1-31: Contrasting Descriptive and Set Phrases　　　CD 1 Track 44

Repeat after me.

Descriptive Phrase	**Set Phrase**
1. It's a short **nail**.	It's a **finger**nail.
2. It's a chocolate **cake**.	It's a **pan**cake.
3. It's a hot **bath**.	It's a **hot** tub.
4. It's a long **drive**.	It's a **hard** drive.
5. It's the back **door**.	It's the **back**bone.
6. There are four **cards**.	It's a **card** trick.
7. It's a small **spot**.	It's a **spot**light.
8. It's a good **book**.	It's a **phone** book.

Pause the CD and rewrite your descriptive phrases (Ex. 1-25) and set phrases (Ex. 1-28).

9. It's a _____	It's a _____
10. It's a _____	It's a _____
11. It's a _____	It's a _____

Exercise 1-32: Two-Word Stress

Repeat the following pairs.

Descriptive Phrase	Set Phrase
a light **bulb**	a **light** bulb
blue **pants**	**blue** jeans
a cold **fish**	a **gold**fish
a gray **hound**	a **grey**hound
an old **key**	an **inn** key
a white **house**	The **White** House
a nice **watch**	a **wrist**watch
a sticky **web**	a **spider** web
a clean **cup**	a **coffee** cup
a sharp **knife**	a **steak** knife
a baby **alligator**	a **baby** bottle
a shiny **tack**	**thumb**tacks
a wire **brush**	a **hair**brush
a new **ball**	a **foot**ball
a toy **gun**	a **machine** gun
a silk **bow**	a **Band**-Aid
a bright **star**	a **fire**cracker
Mary **Jones**	a **mail**box
Bob **Smith**	a **spray** can
foreign **affairs**	a **wine**glass
down **payment**	a **foot**print
New **York**	a **straw**berry
Social **Security**	a **fig** leaf
City **Hall**	an **ice** cream

Summary of Stress in Two-Word Phrases

First Word	set phrases	**light** *bulb*
	streets	**Main** *Street*
	Co. or Corp.	**Xerox** *Corporation*
	nationalities of food	**Chinese** *food*
	nationalities of people	**French** *guy*

Second Word	descriptive phrases	*new* **information**
	road designations	*Fifth* **Avenue**
	modified adjectives	*really* **big**
	place names and parks	*New* **York**, *Central* **Park**
	institutions, or Inc.	*Oakland* **Museum**, *Xerox* **Inc**.
	personal names and titles	*Bob* **Smith**, *Assistant* **Manager**
	personal pronouns and possessives	*his* **car**, *Bob's* **brother**
	articles	*the* **bus**, *a* **week**, *an* **hour**
	initials and acronyms	*U.S., IQ*
	chemical compounds	*zinc* **oxide**
	colors and numbers	*red* **orange**, *26*
	most compound verbs	*go* **away**, *sit* **down**, *fall* **off**
	percent and dollar	*10* **percent**, *50* **dollars**
	hyphenated nationalities	*African-***American**
	descriptive nationalities	*Mexican* **restaurant**

Nationalities

When you are in a foreign country, the subject of nationalities naturally comes up a lot. It would be nice if there were a simple rule that said that all the words using nationalities are stressed on the first word. There isn't, of course. Take this preliminary quiz to see if you need to do this exercise. For simplicity's sake, we will stick with one nationality—American.

Exercise 1-33: Nationality Intonation Quiz   CD 2 Track 1

Pause the CD and stress one word in each of the following examples. Repeat after me.

1. an American guy
2. an American restaurant
3. American food
4. an American teacher
5. an English teacher

When you first look at it, the stress shifts may seem arbitrary, but let's examine the logic behind these five examples and use it to go on to other, similar cases.

1. an Américan guy

The operative word is *American*; *guy* could even be left out without changing the meaning of the phrase. Compare *I saw two **American** guys yesterday*, with *I saw two **Americans** yesterday*. Words like *guy, man, kid, lady, people* are de facto pronouns in an anthropocentric language. A strong noun, on the other hand, would be stressed—*They flew an American **flag***. This is why you have the pattern change in Exercise 1-22: 4e, *Jim **killed** a man*; but 4b, *He killed a **snake***.

2. an American réstaurant

Don't be sidetracked by an ordinary descriptive phrase that happens to have a nationality in it. You are describing the restaurant, *We went to a good **restaurant** yesterday* or *We went to an American **restaurant** yesterday*. You would use the same pattern where the nationality is more or less incidental in *I had French **toast** for breakfast*. ***French** fry*, on the other hand, has become a set phrase.

3. Américan food

Food is a weak word. *I never ate **American** food when I lived in Japan. Let's have **Chinese** food for dinner.*

4. an American téacher

This is a description, so the stress is on *teacher*.

5. an Énglish teacher

This is a set phrase. The stress is on the subject being taught, not the nationality of the teacher: *a **French** teacher, a **Spanish** teacher, a **history** teacher*.

Exercise 1-34: Contrasting Descriptive and Set Phrases   CD 2 Track 2

Repeat the following pairs.

Set Phrase	Descriptive Phrase
An **English** teacher……teaches English.	An English **teacher**……is from England.
An **English** book……teaches the English language.	An English **book**…is on any subject, but it came from England.
An **English** test……tests a student on the English language.	An English **test**…is on any subject, but it deals with or came from England.
English food……is kippers for breakfast.	An English **restaurant**……serves kippers for breakfast.

Intonation can indicate completely different meanings for otherwise similar words or phrases. For example, an *English* teacher teaches English, but an *English* **teacher** is from England; *French* class is where you study French, but *French* **class** is Gallic style and sophistication; an *orange* tree grows oranges, but an *orange* **tree** is any kind of tree that has been painted orange. To have your intonation tested, call (800) 457-4255.

Exercise 1-35: Contrast of Compound Nouns   CD 2 Track 3

In the following list of words, underline the element that should be stressed. Pause the CD. Afterwards, check the Answer Key, beginning on page 193. Repeat after me.

1. The **White** House	21. convenience store	41. a doorknob
2. a white **house**	22. convenient store	42. a glass door
3. a darkroom	23. to pick up	43. a locked door
4. a dark room	24. a pickup truck	44. ice cream
5. Fifth Avenue	25. six years old	45. I scream.
6. Main Street	26. a six-year-old	46. elementary
7. a main street	27. six and a half	47. a lemon tree
8. a hot dog 🐕	28. a sugar bowl	48. Watergate
9. a hot dog 🍴	29. a wooden bowl	49. the back gate
10. a baby blanket	30. a large bowl	50. the final year
11. a baby's blanket	31. a mixing bowl	51. a yearbook
12. a baby bird	32. a top hat	52. United States
13. a blackbird	33. a nice hat	53. New York
14. a black bird	34. a straw hat	54. Long Beach
15. a greenhouse	35. a chairperson	55. Central Park
16. a green house	36. Ph.D.	56. a raw deal
17. a green thumb	37. IBM	57. a deal breaker
18. a parking ticket	38. MIT	58. the bottom line
19. a one-way ticket	39. USA	59. a bottom feeder
20. an unpaid ticket	40. ASAP	60. a new low

Exercise 1-36: Description and Set Phrase Test CD 2 Track 4

Let's check and see if the concepts are clear. Pause the CD and underline or highlight the stressed word. Check Answer Key, beginning on page 193. Repeat after me.

1. He's a **nice guy**.

2. He's an **American guy** from **San Francisco**.

3. The **cheerleader** needs a **rubber band** to hold her **ponytail**.

4. The **executive assistant** needs a **paper clip** for the **final report**.

5. The **law student** took an **English test** in a **foreign country**.

6. The **policeman** saw a **red car** on the **freeway** in **Los Angeles**.

7. My **old dog** has **long ears** and a **flea problem**.

8. The **new teacher** broke his **coffee cup** on the **first day**.

9. His **best friend** has a **broken cup** in his **other office**.

10. Let's play **football** on the **weekend** in **New York**.

11. "**Jingle Bells**" is a **nice song**.

12. Where are my **new shoes**?

13. Where are my **tennis shoes**?

14. I have a **headache** from the **heat wave** in **South Carolina**.

15. The **newlyweds** took a **long walk** in **Long Beach**.

16. The **little dog** was sitting on the **sidewalk**.

17. The **famous athlete** changed clothes in the **locker room**.

18. The **art exhibit** was held in an **empty room**.

19. There was a **class reunion** at the **high school**.

20. The **headlines** indicated a **new policy**.

21. We got **on line** and went to americanaccent **dot com**.

22. The **stock options** were listed in the **company directory**.

23. All the **second-graders** were out on the **playground**.

Exercise 1-37: Descriptions and Set Phrases—Goldilocks   CD 2 Track 5

*Read the story and stress the indicated words. Notice if they are a **description**, a **set phrase** or **contrast**. For the next level of this topic, go to page 111. Repeat after me.*

There is a *little **girl***. Her name is ***Goldilocks***. She is in a *sunny **forest***. She sees a *small* **house**. She ***knocks*** *on* the door, but ***no one*** answers. She *goes **inside**.* In the *large **room***, there are *three **chairs***. ***Goldilocks*** sits on the ***biggest*** *chair*, but it is *too **high***. She sits on the ***middle-sized*** one, but it is *too **low***. She sits on the ***small*** *chair* and it is *just **right***. On the table, there are *three **bowls***. There is *hot **porridge*** in the bowls. She tries the ***first*** *one*, but it is *too **hot***; the ***second*** one is *too **cold***, and the ***third*** one is *just **right***, so she eats it all. ***After*** *that*, she *goes **upstairs***. She *looks **around***. There are *three **beds***, so she *sits **down***. The ***biggest*** *bed* is *too **hard***. The ***middle-sized*** bed is *too **soft***. The ***little*** one is *just **right***, so she *lies **down***. Soon, she *falls **asleep***. In the ***meantime***, the family of *three **bears*** comes home — the ***Papa*** *bear*, the ***Mama*** *bear*, and the ***Baby*** *bear*. They *look **around***. They say, "Who's been sitting in our chairs and eating our porridge?" Then they *run **upstairs***. They say, "Who's been sleeping in our beds?" ***Goldilocks*** *wakes **up***. She is *very* **scared**. She *runs **away***. ***Goldilocks*** never *comes **back***.

Note *Up to this point, we have gone into great detail on the intonation patterns of* **nouns**. *We shall now examine the intonation patterns of* **verbs**.

Grammar in a Nutshell

CD 2 Track 6

Everything You Ever Wanted to Know About Grammar ... But Were Afraid to Use

English is a chronological language. We just love to know when something happened, and this is indicated by the range and depth of our verb tenses.

> I *had* already *seen* it by the time she *brought* it in.

As you probably learned in your grammar studies, "the past perfect is an action in the past that occurred before a separate action in the past." Whew! Not all languages do this. For example, Japanese is fairly casual about when things happened, but being a hierarchical language, it is very important to know what *relationship* the two people involved had. A high-level person with a low-level one, two peers, a man and a woman, all these things show up in Japanese grammar. Grammatically speaking, English is democratic.

The confusing part is that in English the verb tenses are very important, but instead of putting them up on the *peaks* of a sentence, we throw them all deep down in the *valleys*! Therefore, two sentences with strong intonation—such as, "***Dogs eat bones***" and "*The **dogs**'ll've eaten the **bones**"* sound amazingly similar. Why? Because it takes the same amount of time to say both sentences since they have the same number of stresses. The three original words and the rhythm stay the same in these sentences, but the meaning changes as you add more stressed words. Articles and verb tense changes are usually not stressed.

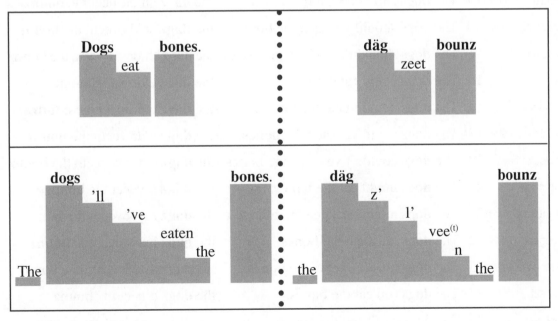

Now let's see how this works in the exercises that follow.

Exercise 1-38: Consistent Noun Stress in Changing Verb Tenses   CD 2 Track 7

This is a condensed exercise for you to practice simple intonation with a wide range of verb tenses. When you do the exercise the first time, go through stressing only the nouns **Dogs** *eat* **bones**. *Practice this until you are quite comfortable with the intonation. The pronunciation and word connections are on the right, and the full verb tenses are on the far left.*

eat	1. The **dogs** eat the **bones**.	the **däg** zeet the **bounz**
ate	2. The **dogs** ate the **bones**.	the **däg** zɛit the **bounz**
are eating	3. The **dogs**'re eating the **bones**.	the **däg** zr reeding the **bounz**
will eat	4. The **dogs**'ll eat the **bones** *(if...)*	the **däg** zə leet the **bounz** *(if...)*
would eat	5. The **dogs**'d eat the **bones** *(if..)*	the **däg** zə deet the **bounz** *(if...)*
would have eaten	6. The **dogs**'d've eaten the **bones** *(if..)*	the **däg** zədə veetn the **bounz** *(if...)*
that have eaten	7. The **dogs** that've eaten the **bones** *(are..)*	the **däg** zədə veetn the **bounz** *(are...)*
have eaten	8. The **dogs**'ve eaten the **bones**.	the **däg** zə veetn the **bounz**
had eaten	9. The **dogs**'d eaten the **bones**.	the **däg** zə deetn the **bounz**
will have eaten	10. The **dogs**'ll've eaten the **bones**.	the **däg** zələ veetn the **bounz**
ought to eat	11. The **dogs** ought to eat the **bones**.	the **däg** zädə eat the **bounz**
should eat	12. The **dogs** should eat the **bones**.	the **dägz** sh'deet the **bounz**
should not eat	13. The **dogs** shouldn't eat the **bones**.	the **dägz** sh'dn•neet the **bounz**
should have eaten	14. The **dogs** should've eaten the **bones**.	the **dägz** sh'də veetn the **bounz**
should not have	15. The **dogs** shouldn't've eaten the **bones**.	the **dägz** sh'dn•nə veetn the **bounz**
could eat	16. The **dogs** could eat the **bones**.	the **dägz** c'deet the **bounz**
could not eat	17. The **dogs** couldn't eat the **bones**.	the **dägz** c'dn•neet the **bounz**
could have eaten	18. The **dogs** could've eaten the **bones**.	the **dägz** c'də veetn the **bounz**
could not have	19. The **dogs** couldn't've eaten the **bones**.	the **dägz** c'dn•nə veetn the **bounz**
might eat	20. The **dogs** might eat the **bones**.	the **dägz** mydeet the **bounz**
might have eaten	21. The **dogs** might've eaten the **bones**.	the **dägz** mydəveetn the **bounz**
must eat	22. The **dogs** must eat the **bones**.	the **dägz** məss deet the **bounz**
must have eaten	23. The **dogs** must've eaten the **bones**.	the **dägz** məsdəveetn the **bounz**
can eat	24. The **dogs** can eat the **bones**.	the **dägz** c'neet the **bounz**
can't eat	25. The dogs **can't eat** the bones.	the dägz **cæn**[(d)]**eet** the **bounz**

Exercise 1-39: Consistent Pronoun Stress in Changing Verb Tenses

CD 2 Track 8

This is the same as the previous exercise, except you now stress the verbs: They **eat** them.
*Practice this until you are quite comfortable with the intonation. Notice that in fluent speech,
the **th** of **them** is frequently dropped (as is the **h** in the other object pronouns, **him**, **her**). The
pronunciation and word connections are on the right, and the tense name is on the far left.*

present	1. They **eat** them.	the**yeed**'m
past	2. They **ate** them.	the**yeid**'m
continuous	3. They're **eating** them.	the**ree**ding'm
future	4. They'll **eat** them *(if...)*	the**leed**'m *(if...)*
present conditional	5. They'd **eat** them *(if...)*	they **deed**'m *(if...)*
past conditional	6. They'd've **eaten** them *(if...)*	they də**veetn**'m *(if...)*
relative pronoun	7. The ones that've **eaten** them *(are...)*	the wənzədə**veetn**'m *(are...)*
present perfect	8. They've **eaten** them *(many times).*	they **veetn**'m *(many times)*
past perfect	9. They'd **eaten** them *(before...)*	they **deetn**'m *(before...)*
future perfect	10. They'll have **eaten** them *(by...)*	they lə**veetn**'m *(by...)*
obligation	11. They ought to **eat** them.	they ädə**eed**'m
obligation	12. They should **eat** them.	they sh'**deed**'m
obligation	13. They shouldn't **eat** them.	they sh'dn•**need**'m
obligation	14. They should have **eaten** them.	they sh'də**veetn**'m
obligation	15. They shouldn't've **eaten** them.	they sh'dn•nə**veetn**'m
possibility/ability	16. They could **eat** them.	they c'**deed**'m
possibility/ability	17. They couldn't **eat** them.	they c'dn•**need**'m
possibility/ability	18. They could have **eaten** them.	they c'də **veetn**'m
possibility/ability	19. They couldn't have **eaten** them.	they c'dn•nə **veetn**'m
possibility	20. They might **eat** them.	they my**deed**'m
possibility	21. They might have **eaten** them.	they mydə**veetn**'m
probability	22. They must **eat** them.	they məss **deed**'m
probability	23. They must have **eaten** them.	they məsdə**veetn**'m
ability	24. They can **eat** them.	they c'**need**'m
ability	25. They **can't eat** them.	they **cæn**[(d)]**eed**'m

Exercise 1-40: Intonation in Your Own Sentence

On the first of the numbered lines below, write a three-word sentence that you frequently use, such as "Computers organize information" or "Lawyers sign contracts" and put it through the 25 changes. This exercise will take you quite a bit of time and it will force you to rethink your perceptions of word sounds as related to spelling. It helps to use a plural noun that ends in a [z] sound (boyz, dogz) rather than an [s] sound (hats, books). Also, your sentence will flow better if your verb begins with a vowel sound (earns, owes, offers). When you have finished filling in all the upper lines of this exercise with your new sentence, use the guidelines from Ex. 1-38 for the phonetic transcription. Remember, don't rely on spelling. Turn off the CD.

eat   1. _____   _____   _____

               _____ • _____ • _____

ate   2. _____   _____   _____

               _____ • _____ • _____

are eating   3. _____   _____   _____

               _____ • _____ • _____

will eat   4. _____   _____   _____

               _____ • _____ • _____

would eat   5. _____   _____   _____

               _____ • _____ • _____

would have eaten 6. _____   _____   _____

               _____ • _____ • _____

that have eaten   7. _____   _____   _____

               _____ • _____ • _____

have eaten   8. _____   _____   _____

               _____ • _____ • _____

had eaten   9. _____   _____   _____

               _____ • _____ • _____

will have eaten 10. _____   _____   _____

               _____ • _____ • _____

Exercise 1-40: Intonation in Your Own Sentence *continued* CD 2 Track 9

ought to eat 11. _____ _____ _____

_____ • _____ • _____

should eat 12. _____ _____ _____

_____ • _____ • _____

should not eat 13. _____ _____ _____

_____ • _____ • _____

should have eaten 14. _____ _____ _____

_____ • _____ • _____

should not have 15. _____ _____ _____

eaten _____ • _____ • _____

could eat 16. _____ _____ _____

_____ • _____ • _____

could not eat 17. _____ _____ _____

_____ • _____ • _____

could have eaten 18. _____ _____ _____

_____ • _____ • _____

could not have 19. _____ _____ _____

_____ • _____ • _____

might eat 20. _____ _____ _____

_____ • _____ • _____

might have eaten 21. _____ _____ _____

_____ • _____ • _____

must eat 22. _____ _____ _____

_____ • _____ • _____

Exercise 1-40: Intonation in Your Own Sentence *continued*   CD 2 Track 9

must have eaten   23. _____   _____   _____

                   _____ • _____ • _____

can eat   24. _____   _____   _____

                   _____ • _____ • _____

can't eat   25. _____   _____   _____

                   _____ • _____ • _____

Exercise 1-41: Supporting Words   CD 2 Track 10

For this next part of the intonation of grammatical elements, each sentence has a few extra words to help you get the meaning. Keep the same strong intonation that you used before and add the new stress where you see the bold face. Use your rubber band.

1. The **dogs** eat the **bones** every **day**.   th' **däg** zeet th' **bounz**evree **day**

2. The **dogs** ate the **bones** last **week**.   th' **däg** zɛit th' **bounz**læss **dweek**

3. The **dogs**'re eating the **bones** right now.   th' **däg** zr reeding th' **bounz** räit næo

4. The **dogs**'ll eat the **bones**   th' **däg** zə leet th' **bounz**if
   if they're **here**.   thɛr **hir**

5. The **dogs**'d eat the **bones**   th' **däg** zə deet th' **bounz**if
   if they were **here**.   they wr **hir**

6. The **dogs**'d've eaten the **bones**   th' **däg** zədə veetn th' **bounz**if
   if they'd **been** here.   theyd **bin** hir

7. The **dogs** that've eaten the **bones** are **sick**.   th' **däg** zədə veetn th' **bounz**r **sick**

8. The **dogs**'ve eaten the **bones** every **day**.   th' **däg** zə veetn th' **bounz**ɛvry **day**

9. The **dogs**'d eaten the **bones**   th' **däg** zə deetn th' **bounz**
   by the time we **got** there.   by th' time we **gät** thɛr

10. The **dogs**'ll have eaten the **bones**   th' **däg** zələ veetn th' **bounz**
    by the time we **get** there.   by th' time we **get** thɛr

Exercise 1-42: Contrast Practice CD 2 Track 11

*Now, let's work with contrast. For example, **The dogs'd eat the bones**, and **The dogs'd eaten the bones**, are so close in sound, yet so far apart in meaning, that you need to make a special point of recognizing the difference by listening for content. Repeat each group of sentences using sound and intonation for contrast.*

would eat	5. The **dogs**'d eat the **bones**.	the **däg** zə deet the **bounz**
had eaten	9. The **dogs**'d eaten the **bones**.	the **däg** zə deetn the **bounz**
would have eaten	6. The **dogs**'d've eaten the **bones**.	the **däg** zədə veetn the **bounz**
that have eaten	7. The **dogs** that've eaten the **bones**.	the **däg** zədə veetn the **bounz**
will eat	4. The **dogs**'ll eat the **bones**.	the **däg** zə leet the **bounz**
would eat	5. The **dogs**'d eat the **bones**.	the **däg** zə deet the **bounz**
would have eaten	6. The **dogs**'d've eaten the **bones**.	the **däg** zədə veetn the **bounz**
have eaten	8. The **dogs**'ve eaten the **bones**.	the **däg** zə veetn the **bounz**
had eaten	9. The **dogs**'d eaten the **bones**.	the **däg** zə deetn the **bounz**
will have eaten	10. The **dogs**'ll have eaten the **bones**.	the **däg** zələ veetn the **bounz**
would eat	5. The **dogs**'d eat the **bones**.	the **däg** zə deet the **bounz**
ought to eat	11. The **dogs** ought to eat the **bones**.	the **däg** zädə eat the **bounz**
can eat	24. The **dogs** can eat the **bones**.	the **dägz** c'neet the **bounz**
can't eat	25. The dogs **can't eat** the bones.	the dägz **cæn**(d)**eet** the **bounz**

Exercise 1-43: Yes, You *Can* or No, You *Can't*? CD 2 Track 12

Next you use a combination of intonation and pronunciation to make the difference between **can** *and* **can't**. *Reduce the positive* **can** *to [k'n] and stress the verb. Make the negative* **can't** *([kæn*(t)*]) sound very short and stress both* **can't** *and the verb. This will contrast with the positive, emphasized* **can**, *which is doubled—and the verb is not stressed. If you have trouble with* **can't** *before a word that starts with a vowel, such as* **open**, *put in a very small [*(d)*]— The keys* **kæn**(d)**open** *the locks. Repeat.*

I can **do** it.	[I k'n **do** it]	*positive*
I **can't do** it.	[I **kæn**(t)**do** it]	*negative*
I **can** do it.	[I **kææn** do it]	*extra positive*
I **can't** do it.	[I **kæn**(t)do it]	*extra negative*

Exercise 1-44: Building an Intonation Sentence　　CD 2 Track 13

Repeat after me the sentences listed in the following groups.

1. I bought a **sand**wich.
2. I **said** I bought a **sand**wich.
3. I **said** I think I bought a **sand**wich.
4. I said I **really** think I bought a **sand**wich.
5. I said I **really** think I bought a chicken **sand**wich.
6. I said I **really** think I bought a **chicken** salad **sand**wich.
7. I said I **really** think I bought a **half** a chicken salad **sand**wich.
8. I said I **really** think I bought a **half** a chicken salad **sand**wich this after**noon**.
9. I **actually** said I **really** think I bought a **half** a chicken salad **sand**wich this after**noon**.
10. I **actually** said I **really** think I bought another **half** a chicken salad **sand**wich this after**noon**.
11. Can you **believe** I **actually** said I **really** think I bought another **half** a chicken salad **sand**wich this after**noon**?

1. I **did** it.
2. I did it **again**.
3. I already **did** it again.
4. I think I already **did** it again.
5. I **said** I think I already **did** it again.
6. I **said** I think I already **did** it again **yesterday**.
7. I **said** I think I already **did** it again the day before **yesterday**.

1. I want a **ball**.
2. I want a large **ball**.
3. I want a **large**, red **ball**.
4. I want a **large**, red, bouncy **ball**.
5. I want a **large**, red bouncy rubber **ball**.
6. I want a **large**, red bouncy rubber **basket**ball.

1. I want a **raise**.
2. I want a big **raise**.
3. I want a **big**, impressive **raise**.
4. I want a **big**, impressive, annual **raise**.
5. I want a **big**, impressive, annual cost of **living** raise.

Exercise 1-45: Building Your Own Intonation Sentences

CD 2 Track 14

*Build your own sentence, using everyday words and phrases, such as **think**, **hope**, **nice**, **really**, **actually**, **even**, **this afternoon**, **big**, **small**, **pretty**, and so on.*

1. _____

2. _____

3. _____

4. _____

5. _____

6. _____

7. _____

8. _____

9. _____

10. _____

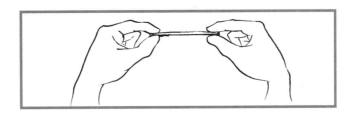

Exercise 1-46: Regular Transitions of Nouns and Verbs   CD 2 Track 15

In the list below, change the stress from the first syllable for nouns to the second syllable for verbs. This is a regular, consistent change. Intonation is so powerful that you'll notice that when the stress changes, the pronunciation of the vowels do, too.

Nouns		Verbs	
an accent	[**æk**s'nt]	to accent	[æk**sɛnt**]
a concert	[**kän**sert]	to concert	[k'n**sert**]
a conflict	[**kän**flikt]	to conflict	[k'n**flikt**]
a contest	[**kän**test]	to contest	[k'n**test**]
a contract	[**kän**træct]	to contract	[k'n**trækt**]
a contrast	[**kän**træst]	to contrast	[k'n**træst**]
a convert	[**kän**vert]	to convert	[k'n**vert**]
a convict	[**kän**vikt]	to convict	[k'n**vict**]
a default	[**dee**fält]	to default	[d'**fält**]
a desert*	[**dɛz**'rt]	to desert	[d'**z'rt**]
a discharge	[**dis**chärj]	to discharge	[d'**schärj**]
an envelope	[**änv**'lop]	to envelop	[envel'**p**]
an incline	[**in**kline]	to incline	[in**kline**]
an influence	[**in**flu(w)'ns]	to influence	[in**flu**(w)ns]†
an insert	[**in**sert]	to insert	[in**sert**]
an insult	[**in**s'lt]	to insult	[in**səlt**]
an object	[**äb**ject]	to object	[ə**bject**]
perfect	[**prf**'ct]	to perfect	[pr**fekt**]
a permit	[**pr**mit]	to permit	[pr**mit**]
a present	[**prɛz**'nt]	to present	[pr'**zɛnt**]
produce	[**pro**duce]	to produce	[pr'**duce**]
progress	[**prägr**'s]	to progress	[pr'**grɛss**]
a project	[**präj**ect]	to project	[pr'**jɛct**]
a pronoun	[**pro**noun]	to pronounce	[pr'**nounce**]
a protest	[**pro**test]	to protest	[pr'**test**]
a rebel	[**rɛb**əl]	to rebel	[r'**bɛl**]
a recall	[**ree**käll]	to recall	[r'**käll**]
a record	[**rɛk**'rd]	to record	[r'**cord**]
a reject	[**re**ject]	to reject	[r'**jɛct**]
research	[**res**'rch]	to research	[r'**srch**]
a subject	[**s'b**jekt]	to subject	[s'**bjekt**]
a survey	[**s'r**vei]	to survey	[s'**rvei**]
a suspect	[**s's**pekt]	to suspect	[s's**pekt**]

** The **désert** is hot and dry. A **dessért** is ice cream. To **desért** is to abandon.*

† Pronunciation symbols (w) and (y) represent a glide sound. This is explained on page 63.

Exercise 1-47: Regular Transitions of Adjectives and Verbs   CD 2 Track 16

*A different change occurs when you go from an adjective or a noun to a verb. The stress stays in the same place, but the -**mate** in an adjective is completely reduced [-m't], whereas in a verb, it is a full [a] sound [-mɛit].*

Nouns/Adjectives		Verbs	
advocate	[**æd**v'k't]	to advocate	[**æd**v'kɛit]
animate	[**æn**'m't]	to animate	[**æn**'mɛit]
alternate	[**äl**tern't]	to alternate	[**äl**ternɛit]
appropriate	[ə**pro**pre⁽ʸ⁾'t]	to appropriate	[ə**pro**pre⁽ʸ⁾ɛit]
approximate	[ə**präks**'m't]	to approximate	[ə**präks**'mɛit]
articulate	[är**tic**yul't]	to articulate	[är**tic**yəlɛit]
associate	[ə**sso**sey't]	to associate	[ə**sso**seyɛit]
deliberate	[d'**libr**'t]	to deliberate	[d'**libe**rɛit]
discriminate	[d'**skrim**'n't]	to descriminate	[d'**skrim**'nɛit]
duplicate	[**dupl**'k't]	to duplicate	[**dupl**'kɛit]
elaborate	[e**læbr**'t]	to elaborate	[ə**læbe**rɛit]
an estimate	[**est**'m't]	to estimate	[**est**'mɛit]
graduate	[**græjyu**⁽ʷ⁾'t]	to graduate	[**græjyu**⁽ʷ⁾ɛit]
intimate	[**int**'m't]	to intimate	[**int**'mɛit]
moderate	[**mäd**er't]	to moderate	[**mäd**erɛit]
predicate	[**prɛd**'k't]	to predicate	[**prɛd**'kɛit]
separate	[**sɛp**r't]	to separate	[**sɛp**erɛit]

Exercise 1-48: Regular Transitions of Adjectives and Verbs   CD 2 Track 17

Mark the intonation or indicate the long vowel on the italicized word, depending which part of speech it is. Pause the CD and mark the proper syllables. See Answer Key, beginning on page 193.

1. You need to *insert* a paragraph here on this newspaper *insert*.
2. How can you *object* to this *object*?
3. I'd like to *present* you with this *present*.
4. Would you care to *elaborate* on his *elaborate* explanation?
5. The manufacturer couldn't *recall* if there'd been a *recall*.
6. The religious *convert* wanted to *convert* the world.
7. The political *rebels* wanted to *rebel* against the world.
8. The mogul wanted to *record* a new *record* for his latest artist.
9. If you *perfect* your intonation, your accent will be *perfect*.
10. Due to the drought, the fields didn't *produce* much *produce* this year.
11. Unfortunately, City Hall wouldn't *permit* them to get a *permit*.
12. Have you heard that your *associate* is known to *associate* with gangsters?
13. How much do you *estimate* that the *estimate* will be?
14. The facilitator wanted to *separate* the general topic into *separate* categories.

The Miracle Technique

Regaining Long-Lost Listening Skills

The trouble with starting accent training after you know a great deal of English is that you know a great deal *about* English. You have a lot of preconceptions and, unfortunately, misconceptions about the sound of English.

A Child Can Learn Any Language

Every sound of every language is within every child. So, what happens with adults? People learn their native language and stop listening for the sounds that they never hear; then they lose the ability to hear those sounds. Later, when you study a foreign language, you learn a lot of spelling rules that take you still further away from the real sound of that language—in this case, English.

What we are going to do here is teach you to *hear* again. So many times, you've heard what a native speaker said, translated it into your own accent, and repeated it with your accent. Why? Because you "knew" how to say it.

<table>
<tr><th colspan="4">Tense Vowels</th><th colspan="4">Lax Vowels</th></tr>
<tr><th>Symbol</th><th>Sound</th><th>Spelling</th><th>Example</th><th>Symbol</th><th>Sound</th><th>Spelling</th><th>Example</th></tr>
<tr><td>ā</td><td>ɛi</td><td>take</td><td>[tak]</td><td>ɛ</td><td>eh</td><td>get</td><td>[gɛt]</td></tr>
<tr><td>ē</td><td>ee</td><td>eat</td><td>[et]</td><td>i</td><td>ih</td><td>it</td><td>[it]</td></tr>
<tr><td>ī</td><td>äi</td><td>ice</td><td>[is]</td><td>ü</td><td>ih + uh</td><td>took</td><td>[tük]</td></tr>
<tr><td>ō</td><td>ou</td><td>hope</td><td>[hop]</td><td>ə</td><td>uh</td><td>some</td><td>[səm]</td></tr>
<tr><td>ū</td><td>ooh</td><td>smooth</td><td>[smuth]</td><td colspan="4"></td></tr>
<tr><td>ä</td><td>ah</td><td>caught</td><td>[kät]</td><td colspan="4" align="center">Semivowels</td></tr>
<tr><td>æ</td><td>ä + ɛ</td><td>cat</td><td>[kæt]</td><td>ər</td><td>er</td><td>her</td><td>[hər]</td></tr>
<tr><td>æo</td><td>æ + o</td><td>down</td><td>[dæon]</td><td>ᵊl</td><td>ul</td><td>dull</td><td>[dəᵊl]</td></tr>
</table>

Exercise 1-49: Tell Me Wədai Say!　　　　　　　　　　　　　　　　**CD 2 Track 19**

*The first thing you're going to do is write down exactly what I say. It will be nonsense to you for two reasons: First, because I will be saying **sound units**, not **word units**. Second, because I will be starting at the **end** of the sentence instead of the **beginning**. Listen carefully and write down exactly what you hear, regardless of meaning. The first sound is given to you—**cher**.*

CD 2 Track 20

```
   ／          ／          ／              ／          ／
___  ___  ___  ___  ___  ___  ___  ___  ___  ___  ___cher.
```

▼ Once you have written it down, check with the version below.

ár	diz	mǽn	zuh	témp	tu	wím	pru	vǽn	náy	cher

▼ Read it out loud to yourself and try to hear what the regular English is. Don't look ahead until you've figured out the sense of it.

Art is man's attempt to improve on nature.

Frequently, people will mistakenly hear *Are these…* [är thez] instead of *Art is…* [är diz]. Not only are the two pronunciations different, but the intonation and meaning would also be different:

*Art is man's **attempt** to improve on **nature**.*
*Are **these** man's **attempts** to improve on **nature**?*

Exercise 1-50: Listening for Pure Sounds   CD 2 Track 21

Again, listen carefully and write the sounds you hear. The answers are below.

1. _____ _____ _____ _____ _____ _____ _____ sən(t). ◀ *Start here*
2. _____ _____ _____ _____ _____ ər(t).
3. _____ _____ _____ _____ _____ _____ gɛn.

Exercise 1-51: Extended Listening Practice   CD 2 Track 22

Let's do a few more pure sound exercises to fine-tune your ear. Remember, start at the end and fill in the blanks right to left, then read them back left to right. Write whichever symbols are easiest for you to read back. There are clues sprinkled around for you and all the answers are in the Answer Key, beginning on page 193.   **CD 2 Track 23**

1. _____ dláik _____ _____ _____ _____ _____, _____ _____ _____ _____ _____ bəl.
2. _____ _____ _____ _____ _____ _____ _____ .
3. _____ _____ _____ _____ _____ _____ gɛn .
4. _____ _____ pwü _____ _____ _____ _____ _____ _____ rǽwer.
5. _____ _____ _____ _____ wi(th) the _____ _____ _____ _____ _____ _____ .
6. _____ _____ kǽon _____ _____ _____ _____ _____ .
7. _____ _____ _____ _____ _____ _____ _____ bləm.
8. _____ _____ vən_____ _____ _____ _____ .
9. _____ _____ pi _____ _____ _____ .
10. _____ _____ _____ pwü _____ _____ _____ _____ fiu _____ _____ _____ _____ .

---

1. **lǽf**dr hǽzno **fourə næks**'nt	2. **Wr** kwell **də** ni **zärt**	3. T' **tee** chiz t' lr nə **gen**
Laughter has no foreign accent.	Work well done is art.	To teach is to learn again.

Reduced Sounds

The Down Side of Intonation

Reduced sounds are all those extra sounds created by an absence of lip, tongue, jaw, and throat movement. They are a principal function of intonation and are truly indicative of the American sound.

Reduced Sounds Are "Valleys"

American intonation is made up of peaks and valleys—tops of staircases and bottoms of staircases. To have strong *peaks*, you will have to develop deep *valleys*. These deep valleys should be filled with all kinds of reduced vowels, one in particular—the completely neutral *schwa*. Ignore spelling. Since you probably first became acquainted with English through the printed word, this is going to be quite a challenge. The position of a syllable is more important than spelling as an indication of correct pronunciation. For example, the words *photograph* and *photography* each have two O's and an A. The first word is stressed on the first syllable so **pho**tograph sounds like [fod'græf]. The second word is stressed on the second syllable, pho**to**graphy, so the word comes out [f'**tah**gr'fee]. You can see here that their spelling doesn't tell you how they sound. Word stress or intonation will determine the pronunciation. Work on listening to words. Concentrate on hearing the pure sounds, not in trying to make the word fit a familiar spelling. Otherwise, you will be taking the long way around and giving yourself both a lot of extra work and an accent!

Syllables that are perched atop a peak or a staircase are strong sounds; that is, they maintain their original pronunciation. On the other hand, syllables that fall in the valleys or on a lower stairstep are weak sounds; thus they are reduced. Some vowels are reduced completely to schwas, a very relaxed sound, while others are only toned down. In the following exercises, we will be dealing with these "toned down" sounds.

In the Introduction ("Read This First," page iv) I talked about *overpronouncing*. This section will handle that overpronunciation. You're going to skim over words; you're going to dash through certain sounds. Your peaks are going to be quite strong, but your valleys, blurry—a very intuitive aspect of intonation that this practice will help you develop.

Articles (such as *the*, *a*) are usually very reduced sounds. Before a consonant, *the* and *a* are both schwa sounds, which are reduced. Before a vowel, however, you'll notice a change—the schwa of *the* turns into a long [e] plus a connecting (y)—*Th' book* changes to *thee(y)only book*; *A hat* becomes *a nugly hat*. The article *a* becomes *an*. Think of [ə•nornj] rather than *an orange*; [ə•nopening], [ə•neye], [ə•nimaginary animal].

Exercise 1-52: Reducing Articles

Consonants		Vowels	
the man	a girl	thee(y)apple	an orange [ə•nornj]
the best	a banana	thee(y)egg	an opening [ə•nop'ning]
the last one	a computer	thee(y)easy way	an interview [ə•ninerview]

When you used the rubber band with [**Däg** zeet **bounz**] and when you built your own sentence, you saw that intonation reduces the unstressed words. Intonation is the peak and reduced sounds are the valleys. In the beginning, you should make extra-high peaks and long, deep valleys. When you are not sure, reduce. In the following exercise, work with this idea. Small words such as articles, prepositions, pronouns, conjunctions, relative pronouns, and auxiliary verbs are lightly skimmed over and almost not pronounced.

You have seen how intonation changes the meaning in words and sentences. Inside a one-syllable word, it distinguishes between a final voiced or unvoiced consonant *be-ed* and *bet*. Inside a longer word, *éunuch* vs *uníque*, the pronunciation and meaning change in terms of vocabulary. In a sentence (He seems **nice**; He **seems** nice.), the meaning changes in terms of intent.

In a sentence, intonation can also make a clear vowel sound disappear. When a vowel is *stressed*, it has a certain sound; when it is *not stressed*, it usually sounds like *uh*, pronounced [ə]. Small words like **to**, **at**, or **as** are usually not stressed, so the vowel disappears.

Exercise 1-53: Reduced Sounds   CD 2 Track 26

Read aloud from the right-hand column. The intonation is marked for you.

To	**Looks Like...**	**Sounds Like...**
	today	[t'**day**]
The preposition *to*	tonight	[t'**night**]
usually reduces so	tomorrow	[t'**märou**]
much that it's like	to work	[t'**wrk**]
dropping the vowel.	to school	[t'**school**]
Use a *t'* or *tə*	to the store	[t' th'**store**]
sound to replace	We have to go now.	[we hæftə **go** næo]
to.	He went to work	[he wentə **work**]
	They hope to find it.	[they houptə **fine** dit]
	I can't wait to find out.	[äi **cæn**⁽ᵗ⁾wai⁽ᵗ⁾tə fine **dæot**]
	We don't know what to do.	[we dont know w'⁽ᵗ⁾t' **do**]
	Don't jump to conclusions.	[dont j'm t' c'n**cloozh**'nz]
	To be or not to be...	[t'**bee**⁽ʸ⁾r **nät** t' bee]
	He didn't get to go.	[he din ge⁽ᵗ⁾tə **gou**]
If that same *to*	He told me to help.	[he told meedə **help**]
follows a vowel	She told you to get it.	[she tol joodə **geddit**]
sound, it will	I go to work	[äi goudə **wrk**]
become *d'* or *də*.	at a quarter to two	[ædə kworder də **two**]
	The only way to get it is...	[thee⁽ʸ⁾only waydə **geddidiz**]
	You've got to pay to get it.	[yoov gäddə paydə **geddit**]
	We plan to do it.	[we plæn də **do** it]
	Let's go to lunch.	[lets goudə **lunch**]
	The score was 4 ~ 6	[th' score w'z for də **six**]

To	**Looks Like...**	**Sounds Like...**
	It's the only way to do it.	[its thee⁽ʸ⁾**ounly** weidə **do**⁽ʷ⁾'t]
	So to speak...	[soda **speak**]
	I don't know how to say it.	[äi don⁽ᵗ⁾know hæwdə **say**⁽ʸ⁾it]
	Go to page 8.	[goudə pay **jate**]
	Show me how to get it.	[show me hæodə **ged**dit]
	You need to know when to do it.	[you nee⁽ᵈ⁾də nou wendə **do**⁽ʷ⁾it]
	Who's to blame?	[hooz də **blame**]

At	We're at home.	[wir°t **home**]
At is just the	I'll see you at lunch.	[äiyəl see you⁽ʷ⁾ət **lunch**]
opposite of *to*.	Dinner's at five.	[d'nnerz°⁽ᵗ⁾ **five**]
It's a small grunt	Leave them at the door.	[leev°m°⁽ᵗ⁾th° **door**]
followed by	The meeting's at one.	[th' meeding z't **w'n**]
a reduced [t].	He's at the post office.	[heez°⁽ᵗ⁾the **pouss**däff°s]
	They're at the bank.	[thɛr°⁽ᵗ⁾th' **bænk**]
	I'm at school.	[äim°⁽ᵗ⁾**school**]

If *at* is followed	I'll see you at eleven.	[äiyəl see you⁽ʷ⁾ədə **lɛv'n**]
by a vowel sound,	He's at a meeting.	[heez'də **meeding**]
it will become	She laughed at his idea.	[she **læf** dədi zy **deey**ə]
'*d* or ə*d*.	One at a time	[wənədə **time**]
	We got it at an auction.	[we gädidədə **näk**sh'n]
	The show started at eight.	[th' **show** stardədə **date**]
	The dog jumped out at us.	[th' däg jump **dæo** dədəs]
	I was at a friend's house.	[äi w'z'd' **frenz** hæos]

It	Can you do it?	[k'niu **do**⁽ʷ⁾'t]
It and *at* sound	Give it to me.	[g'v'⁽ᵗ⁾t' me]
the same in	Buy it tomorrow.	[bäi⁽ʸ⁾ə⁽ᵗ⁾t'**märrow**]
context—['t]	It can wait.	['t c'n **wait**]
	Read it twice.	[ree d'⁽ᵗ⁾**twice**]
	Forget about it!	[frgedd' **bæo**dit]

...and they both	Give it a try.	[givdə **try**]
turn to '*d* or ə*d*	Let it alone.	[ledidə **lone**]
between vowels	Take it away.	[tay kidə **way**]
or voiced	I got it in London.	[äi gädidin **l'n**d'n]
consonants.	What is it about?	[w'd'z'd'**bæot**]
	Let's try it again.	[lets try'd'**gen**]
	Look! There it is!	[**lük** there'd'**z**]

Exercise 1-53: Reduced Sounds *continued* — CD 2 Track 26

For	Looks Like...	Sounds Like...
	This is for you.	[th's'z fr **you**]
	It's for my friend.	[ts fr my **friend**]
	A table for four, please.	[ə table fr **four**, pleeze]
	We planned it for later.	[we **plan** dit fr **layd'r**]
	For example, for instance	[fregg **zæmple**] [**frin** st'nss]
	What is this for?	[w'd'z **this** for] (*for is not reduced at*
	What did you do it for?	[w'j' **do**(w)it for] *the end of a sentence*)
	Who did you get it for?	[hoojya **geddit** for]

From		
	It's from the IRS.	[ts frm thee(y)äi(y)ä **ress**]
	I'm from Arkansas.	[äim fr'm **ärk**'nsä]
	There's a call from Bob.	[therzə **cäll** fr'm **Bäb**]
	This letter's from Alaska!	[this **ledderz** frəmə **læskə**]
	Who's it from?	[hoozit **frəm**]
	Where are you from?	[wher'r you **frəm**]

In		
	It's in the bag.	[tsin thə **bæg**]
	What's in it?	[w'**ts**'n't]
	I'll be back in a minute.	[äiyəl be **bæk**'nə **m'n't**]
	This movie? Who's in it?	[this **movie** ... hooz'**n't**]
	Come in.	[c'**min**]
	He's in America.	[heez'nə **mɛrəkə**]

An		
	He's an American.	[heez'nə **mɛrəkən**]
	I got an A in English.	[äi gäddə **nay** ih **nin**glish]
	He got an F in Algebra.	[hee gäddə **neffinæl** jəbrə]
	He had an accident.	[he hædə **næk**səd'nt]
	We want an orange.	[we want'n **nornj**]
	He didn't have an excuse.	[he didnt hævə neks **kyooss**]
	I'll be there in an instant.	[äi(y)'l be there inə **nin**stnt]
	It's an easy mistake to make.	[itsə **nee**zee m'stake t' **make**]

And		
	ham and eggs	[hæmə **neggz**]
	bread and butter	[bredn **buddr**]
	Coffee? With cream and sugar?	[**käffee** ... with creem'n **sh'g'r**]
	No, lemon and sugar.	[**nou** ... **lem**'n'n sh'g'r]
	... And some more cookies?	['n smore **cükeez**]
	They kept going back and forth.	[they kep going bækn **forth**]
	We watched it again and again.	[we **wäch** didə **gen**'n' **gen**]
	He did it over and over.	[he di di **dovɛrə novɛr**]
	We learned by trial and error.	[we lrnd by tryələ**nerər**]

Exercise 1-53: Reduced Sounds *continued*		CD 2 Track 26

Or	**Looks Like...**	**Sounds Like...**
	Soup or salad?	[super **salad**]
	now or later	[næ⁽ʷ⁾r **lay**dr]
	more or less	[**mor**'r less]
	left or right	[**left**er **right**]
	For here or to go?	[f'r **hir**'r d'**go**]
	Are you going up or down?	[are you going **úp**per **dówn**]

*This is an either / or question (**Up? Down?**) Notice how the intonation is different from "Cream and **sugar**?", which is a **yes / no** question.*

Are		
	What are you doing?	[w'dr you **do**ing]
	Where are you going?	[wer'r you **go**ing]
	What're you planning on doing?	[w'dr yü planning än **do**ing]
	How are you?	[hæwr **you**]
	Those are no good.	[thozer no **good**]
	How are you doing?	[hæwer you **do**ing]
	The kids are still asleep.	[the **kid**zer stillə **sleep**]

Your		
	How's your family?	[hæozhier **fæm**lee]
	Where're your keys?	[wher'r y'r **keez**]
	You're American, aren't you?	[yrə **mer**'k'n, arn choo]
	Tell me when you're ready.	[tell me wen yr **red**dy]
	Is this your car?	[izzis y'r **cär**]
	You're late again, Bob.	[yer lay də **gen**, Bäb]
	Which one is yours?	[which w'n'z **y'rz**]

One		
	Which one is better?	[which w'n'z **bed**der]
	One of them is broken.	[w'n'v'm'z **brok**'n]
	I'll use the other one.	[æl yuz thee⁽ʸ⁾**ə**ther w'n]
	I like the red one, Edwin.	[äi like the **red**w'n, edw'n]
	That's the last one.	[thæts th' lass **dw'n**]
	The next one'll be better.	[the **necks** dw'n'll be **bedd'r**]
	Here's one for you.	[**hir** zw'n f'r **you**]
	Let them go one by one.	[led'm gou w'n by w'n]

The		
	It's the best.	[ts th' **best**]
	What's the matter?	[w'ts th' **mad**der]
	What's the problem?	[w'tsə **präbl**'m]
	I have to go to the bathroom.	[äi hæf t' go d' th' **bæth**room]
	Who's the boss around here?	[hoozə **bäss** səræond hir]
	Give it to the dog.	[g'v'⁽ᵗ⁾tə th' **däg**]
	Put it in the drawer.	[püdidin th' **dror**]

Exercise 1-53: Reduced Sounds *continued*   CD 2 Track 26

A	Looks Like...	Sounds Like...
	It's a present.	[tsə **pre**znt]
	You need a break.	[you needə **break**]
	Give him a chance.	[g'v'mə **chæns**]
	Let's get a new pair of shoes.	[lets geddə new perə **shooz**]
	Can I have a Coke, please?	[c'nai hævə **kouk**, pleez]
	Is that a computer?	[izzædə k'm**pyoo**dr]
	Where's a public telephone?	[wherzə pəblic **tel**əfoun]

Of		
	It's the top of the line.	[tsə täp'v th' **line**]
	It's a state of the art printer.	[tsə **stay** də thee⁽ʸ⁾ärt **prin**ner]
	As a matter of fact, …	[z'mæddərə **fækt**]
	Get out of here.	[ged**dæow** də hir]
	Practice all of the time.	[**præk**t'säll'v th' time]
	Today's the first of May.	[t'**dayz** th' frss d'v **May**]
	What's the name of that movie?	[w'ts th' **nay** m'v thæt **movie**]
	That's the best of all!	[**thæts** th' bess d'**väll**]
	some of them	[səməvəm]
	all of them	[**äll**əvəm]
	most of them	[**mos**dəvəm]
	none of them	[**nən**əvəm]
	any of them	[**enn**yəvəm]
	the rest of them	[th' **res**dəvəm]

Can		
	Can you speak English?	[k'new spee **king**lish]
	I can only do it on Wednesday.	[äi k'**non**ly du⁽ʷ⁾idän **wenz**day]
	A can opener can open cans.	[ə **kæn**opener k'nopen **kænz**]
	Can I help you?	[k'näi **hel** piu]
	Can you do it?	[k'niu **do**⁽ʷ⁾'t]
	We can try it later.	[we k'n **try** it **layder**]
	I hope you can sell it.	[äi **hou** piu k'n **sell**'t]
	No one can fix it.	[nou w'n k'n **fick** sit]
	Let me know if you can find it.	[lemme no⁽ʷ⁾'few k'n **fine** dit]

Had		
	Jack had had enough.	[jæk'd hæd' n'f]
	Bill had forgotten again.	[bil'd frgä⁽ᵗ⁾n nə gen]
	What had he done to deserve it?	[w'd'dee d'nd'd'**zr** vit]
	We'd already seen it.	[weedäl reddy **see** nit]
	He'd never been there.	[heed never **bin** there]
	Had you ever had one?	[h'jou⁽ʷ⁾ever **hæd**w'n]
	Where had he hidden it?	[wer dee **hidn**•nit]
	Bob said he'd looked into it.	[bäb sedeed lük**din** tu⁽ʷ⁾it]

Exercise 1-53: Reduced Sounds *continued* — CD 2 Track 26

Would	Looks Like...	Sounds Like...
	He would have helped, if …	[he wüdə **help** dif …]
	Would he like one?	[woody **lye** kw'n]
	Do you think he'd do it?	[dyiu thing keed **du**[(w)]'t]
	Why would I tell her?	[why wüdäi **tell**er]
	We'd see it again, if…	[weed see[(y)]idəgen, if…]
	He'd never be there on time.	[heed never **be** therän time]
	Would you ever have one?	[w'jou[(w)]ever **hæv**w'n]

Was		
	He was only trying to help.	[he w'zounly trying də **help**]
	Mark was American.	[**mär** kw'z'**mer**'k'n]
	Where was it?	[wer **w'z**'t]
	How was it?	[hæo**w'z**'t]
	That was great!	[thæt w'z **great**]
	Who was with you?	[hoow'z **with** you]
	She was very clear.	[she w'z very **clear**]
	When was the war of 1812?	[wen w'z th' **wor**'v ei[(t)]teen **twelv**]

What		
	What time is it?	[w't **tye** m'z't]
	What's up?	[w'**ts'p**]
	What's on your agenda?	[w'tsänyrə **jen**də]
	What do you mean?	[w'd'y' **mean**]
	What did you mean?	[w'j'**mean**]
	What did you do about it?	[w'j' **du**[(w)]əbæodit]
	What took so long?	[w't **tük** so läng]
	What do you think of this?	[w'ddyə thing k'v **this**]
	What did you do then?	[w'jiu do **then**]
	I don't know what he wants.	[I dont know wədee **wänts**]

Some		
	Some are better than others.	[s'mr beddr thə **nəth**erz]
	There are some leftovers.	[ther'r s'm **lef** doverz]
	Let's buy some ice cream.	[let spy s'**mice** creem]
	Could we get some other ones?	[kwee get s'**mother** w'nz]
	Take some of mine.	[**take** səməv **mine**]
	Would you like some more?	[w'joo like s'**more**]
	(or very casually)	[jlike **smore**]
	Do you have some ice?	[dyü hæv sə**mice**]
	Do you have some mice?	[dyü hæv sə**mice**]

"You can fool some of the people some of the time, but you can't fool all of the people all of the time."
[yuk'n **fool** səmə thə peep°l **səmə** thə time, b'choo **kænt fool** älləthə peep°l **ällə**thə time]

Exercise 1-54: Intonation and Pronunciation of "That"   CD 2 Track 27

*That is a special case because it serves three different grammatical functions. The **relative pronoun** and the **conjunction** are reducible. The **demonstrative pronoun** cannot be reduced to a schwa sound. It must stay [æ].*

Relative Pronoun	The car that she ordered is red.	[the **car** th't she order diz **red**]
Conjunction	He said that he liked it.	[he sed the dee **läik**dit.]
Demonstrative	Why did you do that?	[why dijoo **do** thæt?]
Combination	I know that he'll read that book that I told you about.	[äi **know** the dill read thæt **bük** the dai **tol**joo$^{(w)}$' bæot.]

Exercise 1-55: Crossing Out Reduced Sounds   CD 2 Track 28

Pause the CD and cross out any sound that is not clearly pronounced, including to, for, and, that, than, the, a, the soft [ð], and unstressed syllables that do not have strong vowel sounds.

Hello, **my** name's_____. I'm taking American Accent Training. There's a **lot** to learn, but I **hope** to make it as en**joy**able as possible. I should pick **up** on the American into**na**tion pattern pretty **ea**sily, although the **only** way to **get** it is to **prac**tice all of the time. I use the **up** and down, or **peaks** and valleys, intonation more than I **used** to. I've been paying attention to **pitch**, **too**. It's like **walk**ing down a **stair**case. I've been **talk**ing to a lot of **Ameri**cans lately, and they tell me that I'm **ea**sier to under**stand**. **Any**way, I could go **on** and on, but the im**port**ant thing is to **lis**ten well and sound **good**. **Well**, what do you **think**? **Do** I?

Exercise 1-56: Reading Reduced Sounds   CD 2 Track 29

Repeat the paragraph after me. Although you're getting rid of the vowel sounds, you want to maintain a strong intonation and let the sounds flow together. For the first reading of this paragraph, it is helpful to keep your teeth clenched together to reduce excess jaw and lip movement. Let's begin.

Hello, **my** name'z _____. I'm taking 'mer'k'n **Acc**'nt Train'ng. Therez' **lott**' learn, b't I **hope** t' make 't'z '**njoy**'bl'z poss'bl. I sh'd p'ck '**p** on the 'mer'k'n 'nt'**na**sh'n pattern pretty **ea**s'ly, although the **only** way t' **get** 't 'z t' **prac**t's all 'v th' time. I use the '**p**'n down, or **peaks** 'n valleys, 'nt'**nash**'n more th'n I **used** to. Ive b'n pay'ng 'ttensh'n t' **p'ch**, **too**. 'Ts like **walk**'ng down' **stair**case. Ive b'n **talk**'ng to' lot 'v'**mer**'k'ns lately, 'n they tell me th't Im **ea**sier to 'nder**stand**. **Any**way, I k'd go **on** 'n on, b't the '**mport**'nt th'ng 'z t' **l's**'n wel'n sound **g'd**. **W'll**, wh' d'y' **th'nk**? **Do** I?

Word Groups and Phrasing CD 2 Track 30

Pauses for Related Thoughts, Ideas, or for Breathing

By now you've begun developing a strong intonation, with clear peaks and reduced valleys, so you're ready for the next step. You may find yourself reading the paragraph in Exercise 1-15 like this: ***HellomynameisSo-and-SoI'mtakingAmericanAccent**Training. **There'salot**tolearnbut**Ihope**tomakeitasenjoyableaspossible.* If so, your audience won't completely comprehend or enjoy your presentation.

In addition to intonation, there is another aspect of speech that indicates meaning. This can be called *phrasing* or *tone*. Have you ever caught just a snippet of a conversation in your own language, and somehow known how to piece together what came before or after the part you heard? This has to do with phrasing.

In a sentence, phrasing tells the listener where the speaker is at the moment, where the speaker is going, and if the speaker is finished or not. Notice that the intonation stays on the nouns.

Exercise 1-57: Phrasing   CD 2 Track 31

Repeat after me.

Statement	**Dogs** eat **bones**.
Clauses	**Dogs** eat **bones**, but **cats** eat **fish**. *or* As we all **know**, **dogs** eat **bones**.
Listing	**Dogs** eat **bones**, **kibbles**, and **meat**.
Question	Do **dogs** eat **bones**?
Repeated Question	Do **dogs** eat **bones**?!!
Tag Question	**Dogs** eat **bones**, **don't** they?
Tag Statement	**Dogs** eat **bones**, **DON'T** they!
Indirect Speech	He asked if **dogs** ate **bones**.
Direct Speech	"Do **dogs** eat **bones**?" he **asked**.

For clarity, break your sentences with pauses between natural word groups of related thoughts or ideas. Of course, you will have to break at every comma and every period, but besides those breaks, add other little pauses to let your listeners catch up with you or think over the last burst of information and to allow you time to take a breath. Let's work on this technique. In doing the following exercise, you should think of using *breath groups* and *idea groups*.

Exercise 1-58: Creating Word Groups   CD 2 Track 32

Break the paragraph into natural word groups. Mark every place where you think a pause is needed with a slash.

Hello, **my** name is _____. I'm taking American **Accent** Training. There's a **lot** to learn, but I **hope** to make it as **enjoyable** as possible. I should pick **up** on the American **intonation** pattern pretty **easily**, although the **only** way to **get** it is to **practice** all of the time. I use the **up** and down, or **peaks** and valleys **intonation** more than I **used** to. I've been paying attention to **pitch, too**. It's like **walking** down a **stair**case. I've been **talking** to a lot of **Americans** lately, and they tell me that I'm **easier** to under**stand**. **Any**way, I could go **on** and on, but the **important** thing is to **listen** well and sound **good**. **Well**, what do you **think**? **Do** I?

Note *In the beginning, your word groups should be very short. It'll be a sign of your growing sophistication when they get longer.*

✖ Pause the CD to do your marking.

Exercise 1-59: Practicing Word Groups   CD 2 Track 33

When I read the paragraph this time, I will exaggerate the pauses. Although we're working on word groups here, remember, I don't want you to lose your intonation. Repeat each sentence group after me.

Hello, **my** name is _____. I'm taking American **Accent** Training. There's a **lot** to learn, but I **hope** to make it as **enjoyable** as possible. I should pick **up** on the American **intonation** pattern pretty **easily**, although the **only** way to **get** it is to **practice** all of the time. I use the **up** and down, or **peaks** and valleys **intonation** more than I **used** to. I've been paying attention to **pitch, too**. It's like **walking** down a **stair**case. I've been **talking** to a lot of **Americans** lately, and they tell me that I'm **easier** to understand. **Any**way, I could go **on** and on, but the **important** thing is to **listen** well and sound **good**. **Well**, what do you **think**? **Do** I?

✖ Next, back up the CD and practice the word groups three times using strong intonation. Then, pause the CD and practice three more times on your own. When reading, your pauses should be neither long nor dramatic—just enough to give your listener time to digest what you're saying.

Exercise 1-60: Tag Endings CD 2 Track 34

Pause the CD and complete each sentence with a tag ending. Use the same verb, but with the opposite polarity—positive becomes negative, and negative becomes positive. Then, repeat after me. Check Answer Key, beginning on page 193.

<table>
<tr><td>

Intonation

With a *query*, the intonation rises.

With *confirmation*, the intonation drops.

Pronunciation

Did he?	**Di**dee?
Does he?	**Du**zzy?
Was he?	**Wu**zzy?
Has he?	**Ha**zzy?
Is he?	**I**zzy?
Will he?	**Wi**lly?
Would he?	**Woo**dy?
Can he?	**Ca**nny?
Wouldn't you?	**Wooden** chew?
Shouldn't I?	**Shü**dn näi?
Won't he?	**Woe** knee?
Didn't he?	**Didn** knee?
Hasn't he?	**Has** a knee?
Wouldn't he?	**Wooden** knee?
Isn't he?	**Is** a knee?
Isn't it?	**Is** a nit?
Doesn't it?	**Duzz**a nit?
Aren't I?	**Are** näi?
Won't you?	**Wone** chew?
Don't you?	**Done** chew?
Can't you?	**Can** chew?
Could you?	**Cü**joo?
Would you?	**Wü**joo?

</td><td>

1. The new **clerk** is very **slow**, <u>isn't he</u>!
2. But he can **impróve**, _____?
3. She doesn't **type** very well, _____!
4. They lost their **way**, _____?
5. You don't **think** so, _____!
6. I don't think it's **easy**, _____?
7. I'm your **friend**, _____?
8. You won't be **coming**, _____!
9. He keeps the **books**, _____!
10. We have to close the **office**, _____?
11. We have closed the **office**, _____?
12. We had to close the **office**, _____!
13. We had the **office** closed, _____?
14. We had already closed the **office**, _____?
15. We'd better close the **office**, _____!
16. We'd rather close the **office**, _____?
17. The office has **closed**, _____?
18. You couldn't **tell**, _____!
19. You'll be working **late** tonight, _____?
20. He should have **been** here by now, _____!
21. He should be **promoted**, _____!
22. I didn't send the **fax**, _____?
23. I won't get a **raise** this year, _____?
24. You use the **computer**, _____?
25. You're used to the **computer**, _____!
26. You used to use the **computer**, _____?
27. You never **used** to work **Saturdays**, _____?
28. That's **better**, _____!

</td></tr>
</table>

The basic techniques introduced in this chapter are *pitch*, *stress*, the *staircase* and *musical notes*, *reduced sounds*, and *word groups* and *phrasing*. In chapters 2 through 13, we refine and expand this knowledge to cover every sound of the American accent.

Chapter 2

Word Connections

CD 2 Track 35

As mentioned in the previous chapter, in American English, words are not pronounced one by one. Usually, the end of one word attaches to the beginning of the next word. This is also true for initials, numbers, and spelling. Part of the glue that connects sentences is an underlying hum or drone that only breaks when you come to a period, and sometimes not even then. You have this underlying hum in your own language and it helps a great deal toward making you sound like a native speaker.

Once you have a strong intonation, you need to connect all those stairsteps together so that each sentence sounds like one long word. This chapter is going to introduce you to the idea of liaisons, the connections between words, which allow us to speak in sound groups rather than in individual words. Just as we went over where to put an intonation, here you're going to learn how to connect words. Once you understand and learn to use this technique, you can make the important leap from this practice book to other materials and your own conversation.

To make it easier for you to read, liaisons are written like this: **They tell me the dai measier**. (You've already encountered some liaisons in Exercises 1-38, 1-49, 1-53.) It could also be written **theytellmethedaimeasier**, but it would be too hard to read.

Exercise 2-1: Spelling and Pronunciation   CD 2 Track 36

*Read the following sentences. The last two sentences should be pronounced exactly the same, no matter how they are written. It is the **sound** that is important, not the spelling.*

The dime.
The dime easier.
They tell me the dime easier.
They tell me **the dime** easier to understand.
They tell me **that I'm** easier to understand.

Words are connected in four main situations:

1 Consonant / Vowel
2 Consonant / Consonant
3 Vowel / Vowel
4 T, D, S, or Z + Y

Liaison Rule 1: Consonant / Vowel

Words are connected when a word ends in a consonant sound and the next word starts with a vowel sound, including the semivowels W, Y, and R.

Exercise 2-2: Word Connections	CD 2 Track 37

My name is...	[my nay•miz]
because I've	[b'k'zäiv]
pick up on the American intonation	[pi•kə pän the(y)əmer'kə ninətənashən]

In the preceding example, the word *name* ends in a consonant sound [m] (the *e* is silent and doesn't count), and *is* starts with a vowel sound [i], so *naymiz* just naturally flows together. In *because I've*, the [z] sound at the end of *because* and the [äi] sound of *I* blend together smoothly. When you say the last line [pi•kəpän the(y)əmer'kəninətənashən], you can feel each sound pushing into the next.

Exercise 2-3: Spelling and Number Connections	CD 2 Track 38

You also use liaisons in spelling and numbers:

| LA (Los Angeles) | [eh•lay] |
| 902-5050 | [nai•no•too fai•vo•fai•vo] |

What's the Difference Between a Vowel and a Consonant?

In pronunciation, a consonant touches at some point in the mouth. Try saying [p] with your mouth open—you can't do it because your lips must come together to make the [p] sound. A vowel, on the other hand, doesn't touch anywhere. You can easily say [e] without any part of the mouth, tongue, or lips coming into contact with any other part. This is why we are calling W, Y, and R semivowels, or glides.

Exercise 2-4: Consonant / Vowel Liaison Practice	CD 2 Track 39

Pause the CD and reconnect the following words. On personal pronouns, it is common to drop the H. See Answer Key, beginning on page 193. Repeat.

hold on	[hol don]
turn over	[tur nover]
tell her I miss her	[tellerI misser]

1. read only   _____
2. fall off   _____

Exercise 2-4: Consonant / Vowel Liaison Practice *continued*   CD 2 Track 39

3. follow up on   _____
4. come in   _____
5. call him   _____
6. sell it   _____
7. take out   _____
8. fade away   _____
9. 6-0   _____
10. MA   _____

Liaison Rule 2: Consonant / Consonant

Words are connected when a word ends in a consonant sound and the next word starts with a consonant that is in a similar position. What is a similar position? Let's find out.

Exercise 2-5: Consonant / Consonant Liaisons   CD 2 Track 40

Say the sound of each group of letters out loud (the sound of the letter, not the name: [b] is [buh] not [bee]). There are three general locations—the lips, behind the teeth, or in the throat. If a word ends with a sound created in the throat and the next word starts with a sound from that same general location, these words are going to be linked together. The same with the other two locations. Repeat after me.

Behind the teeth

unvoiced	voiced
t	d
ch	j
—	l
—	n
s	z
sh	zh
—	y

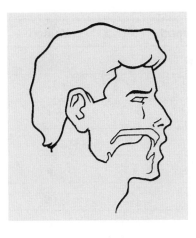

At the lips

unvoiced	voiced
p	b
f	v
—	m
—	w

In the throat

unvoiced	voiced
k	g
h	—
—	ng
—	r

Exercise 2-6: Consonant / Consonant Liaisons

I just didn't get the chance.   [I•jusdidn't•ge⁽ᵗ⁾the•chance.]
I've been late twice.   [I'vbinla⁽ᵗ⁾twice.]

In the preceding examples you can see that because the ending [st] of *just* and the beginning [d] of *didn't* are so near each other in the mouth, it's not worth the effort to start the sound all over again, so they just flow into each other. You don't say *I justə didn'tə getə the chance*, but do say *Ijusdidn't ge⁽ᵗ⁾the chance*. In the same way, it's too much work to say *I'və beenə lateə twice*, so you say it almost as if it were a single word, *I'vbinla⁽ᵗ⁾twice*.

The sound of TH is a special case. It is a floater between areas. The sound is sometimes created by the tongue popping out from between the teeth and other times on the back of the top teeth, combining with various letters to form a new composite sound. For instance, [s] moves forward and the [th] moves back to meet at the mid-point between the two.

Note *Each of the categories in the drawing contains two labels—voiced and unvoiced. What does that mean? Put your thumb and index fingers on your throat and say [z]; you should feel a vibration from your throat in your fingers. If you whisper that same sound, you end up with [s] and you feel that your fingers don't vibrate. So, [z] is a voiced sound, [s], unvoiced. The consonants in the two left columns are paired like that.*

Consonants

Voiced	Unvoiced	Voiced	Unvoiced
b	p		h
d	t	l	
v	f	r	
g	k	m	
j	ch	n	
z	s	ng	
th	th	y	
zh	sh	w	

Exercise 2-7: Liaisons with TH Combination   CD 2 Track 42

When the TH combination connects with certain sounds, the two sounds blend together to form a composite sound. In the following examples, see how the TH moves back and the L moves forward, to meet in a new middle position. Repeat after me.

th + l	with lemon	th + ch	both charges
th + n	with nachos	th + j	with juice
th + t	both times		
th + d	with delivery	n + th	in the
th + s	both sizes	z + th	was that
th + z	with zeal	d + th	hid those

Exercise 2-8: Consonant / Consonant Liaison Practice   CD 2 Track 43

Pause the CD and reconnect the following words as shown in the models. Check Answer Key, beginning on page 193. Repeat.

hard times	[hardtimes]
with luck	[withluck]

1. business deal   _____
2. credit check   _____
3. the top file   _____
4. sell nine new cars   _____
5. sit down   _____
6. some plans need luck   _____
7. check cashing   _____
8. let them make conditions   _____
9. had the   _____
10. both days   _____

Liaison Rule 3: Vowel / Vowel

When a word ending in a *vowel* sound is next to one beginning with a *vowel* sound, they are connected with a glide between the two vowels. A glide is either a slight [y] sound or a slight [w] sound. How do you know which one to use? This will take care of itself—the position your lips are in will dictate either [y] or [w].

Go away.	Go$^{(w)}$away.
I also need the other one.	I$^{(y)}$also need thee$^{(y)}$other one.

For example, if a word ends in [o] your lips are going to be in the forward position, so a [w] quite naturally leads into the next vowel sound—[Go$^{(w)}$away]. You don't want to say

Go...away and break the undercurrent of your voice. Run it all together: [Go⁽ʷ⁾away].

After a long [ē] sound, your lips will be pulled back far enough to create a [y] glide or liaison: [I⁽ʸ⁾also need the⁽ʸ⁾other one]. Don't force this sound too much, though. It's not a strong pushing sound. [I(y) also need the(y)other one] would sound really weird.

Exercise 2-9: Vowel / Vowel Liaison Practice   CD 2 Track 44

Pause the CD and reconnect the following words as shown in the models. Add a (y) glide after an [e] sound, and a (w) glide after an [u] sound. Don't forget that the sound of the American O is really [ou]. Check Answer Key, beginning on page 193.

> she isn't [she⁽ʸ⁾isn't]
> who is   [who⁽ʷ⁾iz]

1. go anywhere   _____
2. so honest   _____
3. through our   _____
4. you are   _____
5. he is   _____
6. do I?   _____
7. I asked   _____
8. to open   _____
9. she always   _____
10. too often   _____

Liaison Rule 4: T, D, S, or Z + Y

When the letter or sound of T, D, S, or Z is followed by a word that starts with Y, or its sound, both sounds are connected. These letters and sounds connect not only with Y, but they do so as well with the initial unwritten [y].

Exercise 2-10: T, D, S, or Z + Y Liaisons   CD 2 Track 45

Repeat the following.

T + Y = CH

What's your **name**?	[wǝcher **name**]
Can't you **do** it?	[kænt chew **do**⁽ʷ⁾it]
Actually	[æk•chully]
Don't you **like** it?	[dont chew **lye** kit]
Wouldn't you?	[**wood**en chew]
Haven't you? No, not **yet**.	[**hæv**en chew? nou, nä **chet**]
I'll let you **know**.	[I'll letcha **know**]
Can I get you a **drink**?	[k'näi getchewǝ **drink**]

Exercise 2-10: T, D, S, or Z + Y Liaisons *continued* CD 2 Track 45

We thought you weren't **coming**.	[we thä chew wrnt **kə**ming]
I'll bet you **ten** bucks he for**got**.	[æl betcha **ten** buxee fr**gät**]
Is **that** your final **answer**?	[is **thæ**chr fin'**læn** sr]
natural	[**næch**rəl]
per**pet**ual	[perpechə(w)əl]
virtual	[**vr**chə(w)əl]

D + Y = J

Did you **see** it?	[didjə **see**(y)it]
How did you **like** it?	[hæo•jə **lye** kit]
Could you **tell**?	[küjə **tell**]
Where did you send your **check**?	[wɛrjə senjer **check**]
What did your **fam**ily think?	[wəjer **fæm**lee think]
Did you find your **keys**?	[didjə fine jer **keez**]
We followed your in**struc**tions.	[we fällow jerin **strəc**tionz]
Congratu**la**tions!	[k'ngræj'**la**tionz]
edu**ca**tion	[edjə•**ca**tion]
indi**vid**ual	[ində**vij**ə(w)əl]
gradu**a**tion	[**græ**jə(w)**a**tion]
gradual	[**græ**jə(w)əl]

S + Y = SH

Yes, you are.	[**yesh**u are]
In**sur**ance	[in**shur**ance]
Bless you!	[**bless**hue]
Press your **hands** together.	[pressure **hanz** d'gethr]
Can you **dress** yourself?	[c'new **dresh**ier self]
You can pass your **exams** this year.	[yuk'n **pæsh**er eg**zæmz** thisheer]
I'll try to guess your **age**.	[æl trydə **gesh**ie**rage**]
Let him gas your **car** for you.	[leddim **gæsh**ier **cär** fr you]

Z + Y = ZH

How's your family?	[hæo**zh**ier **fæm**lee]
How was your **trip**?	[hæo•wə**zh**ier **trip**]
Who's your **friend**?	[hoo**zh**ier **frend**]
Where's your **mom**?	[wɛr**zh**'r **mäm**]
When's your **birth**day?	[wɛn**zh**'r **brth**day]
She says you're O**K**.	[she sɛ**zh**ierou **kay**]
Who does your **hair**?	[hoo də**zh**ier **hɛr**]
casual	[**kæ**•zhyə(w)əl]
visual	[**vi**•zhyə(w)əl]

Exercise 2-10: T, D, S, or Z + Y Liaisons *continued*   CD 2 Track 45

usual   [**yu**•zhyə⁽ʷ⁾əl]
version   [**vr**zh'n]
vision   [**vi**zh'n]

Exercise 2-11: T, D, S, or Z + Y Liaison Practice   CD 2 Track 46

Reconnect or rewrite the following words. Remember that there may be a [y] sound that is not written. Check Answer Key, beginning on page 193. Repeat.

    put your   [pücher]
    gradual   [gradjyə⁽ʷ⁾l]

1. did you   _____
2. who's your   _____
3. just your   _____
4. gesture   _____
5. miss you   _____
6. tissue   _____
7. got your   _____
8. where's your   _____
9. congratulations   _____
10. had your   _____

This word exchange really happened.

Now that you have the idea of how to link words, let's do some liaison work.

Exercise 2-12: Finding Liaisons and Glides   CD 2 Track 47

In the following paragraph connect as many of the words as possible. Mark your liaisons as we have done in the first two sentences. Add the (y) and (w) glides between vowels.

Hello, **my** name is _____. I'm taking American **Accent** Training. There's a **lot** to learn, but I **hope** to make it as **enjoyable** as possible. I should pick **up** on the American **intonation** pattern pretty **easily**, although the[(y)]**only** way to **get** it is to **practice** all of the time. I use the **up** and down, or **peaks** and valleys, **intonation** more than I **used** to. I've been paying attention to **pitch, too**. It's like **walking** down a **stair**case. I've been **talking** to[(w)]a lot of **Americans** lately, and they tell me that I'm **easier** to under**stand**. **Any**way, I could go **on** and on, but the **important** thing is to **listen** well and sound **good**. **Well**, what do you **think**? **Do** I?

▼ Practice reading the paragraph three times, focusing on running your words together.

✖ Turn the CD back on and repeat after me as I read. I'm going to exaggerate the linking of the words, drawing it out much longer than would be natural.

Exercise 2-13: Practicing Liaisons   CD 3 Track 1

Back up the CD to the last paragraph just read and repeat again. This time, however, read from the paragraph below. The intonation is marked for you in boldface. Use your rubber band on every stressed word.

Hello, **my** nay miz_____. I'm takingə merica **næccent**(t)raining. There zə **lättə** learn, bə däi **hope** t' ma ki desen **joy**ablez possible. I shüd pi **kə**pän the[(y)]əmerica nintənash'n pæddern pridy[(y)]**ezily**, although thee[(y)]**only** waydə **ge**ddidiz t' prækti sälləv th' time. I[(y)]use thee[(y)]**up**'n down, or **peak** s'n valley zintənashən more thə näi **used** to. Ivbn payingə tenshən t' **pitch, too**. Itsläi **kwäl**king dow nə **stair**case. Ivbn **tal**king to[(w)]ə läddəvə **mer**ican zla[(t)]ely, 'n they tell me the däi**mee**zier to[(w)]under**stænd**. **Any**way, I could go[(w)]ä nə nän, bu[(t)]thee[(y)]im**port**ant thingiz t' **lis**ənwellən soun[(d)] **good**. Well, whəddyü think? Do[(w)]I?

Exercise 2-14: Additional Liaison Practice CD 3 Track 2

▼ Use these techniques on texts of your own and in conversation.
  (1) Take some written material and mark the *intonation*, then the *word groups*, and finally the *liaisons*.
  (2) Practice saying it out loud.
  (3) Record yourself and listen back.

▼ In conversation, think which word you want to make stand out, and change your pitch on that word. Then, run the in-between words together in the valleys. Listen carefully to how Americans do it and copy the sound.

Exercise 2-15: Colloquial Reductions and Liaisons CD 3 Track 3

In order for you to recognize these sounds when used by native speakers, they are presented here, but I don't recommend that you go out of your way to use them yourself. If, at some point, they come quite naturally of their own accord in casual conversation, you don't need to resist, but please don't force yourself to talk this way. Repeat.

I have got to **go**.	I've gotta **go**.
I have got a **book**.	I've gotta **book**.
Do you want to **dance**?	Wanna **dance**?
Do you want a **banana**?	Wanna **banana**?
Let me **in**.	Lemme **in**.
Let me **go**.	Lemme **go**.
I'll let you **know**.	I'll letcha **know**.
Did you **do** it?	Dija **do** it?
Not **yet**.	Nä **chet**.
I'll meet you **later**.	I'll meechu **lay**der.
What do you **think**?	Whaddyu **think**?
What did you **do** with it?	Whajoo **do** with it?
How did you **like** it?	Howja **like** it?
When did you **get** it?	When ju **ge**ddit?
Why did you **take** it?	Whyju **tay** kit?
Why don't you **try** it?	Why don chu **try** it?
What are you **waiting** for?	Whaddya **wait**in' for?
What are you **doing**?	Whatcha **doin'**?
How is it **going**?	Howzit **go**ing?
Where's the **what**-you-may-call-it?	Where's the **what**chamacallit?
Where's **what**-is-his-name?	Where's **what**sizname?
How **about** it?	How '**bout** it?
He has got to **hurry** because he is **late**.	He's gotta **hurry** 'cuz he's **late**.
I could've been a **contender**.	I coulda bina con**ten**der.

Exercise 2-15: Colloquial Reductions and Liaisons *continued* CD 3 Track 3

Could you speed it **up**, please?	Couldjoo spee di **dup**, pleez?
Would you mind if I **tried** it?	Would joo mindifai **try** dit?
Aren't you Bob **Barker**?	Arnchoo Bab **Bar**ker?
Can't you see it **my** way for a change?	Kænchoo see it **my** way for a change?
Don't you **get** it?	Doancha **ge**ddit?
I should have **told** you.	I shoulda **tol**joo.
Tell her (that) I **miss** her.	Teller I **mi**sser.
Tell him (that) I **miss** him.	Tellim I **mi**ssim.

Extremely extreme reductions

Did you **eat**?	**Jeet**?
No, did **you**?	No, **joo**?
Why don't you get a **job**?	Whyncha getta **job**?
I don't know, it's too **hard**.	I dunno, stoo **härd**.
Could we **go**?	Kwee **gou**?
Let's **go**!	**Sko**!

Spoon or Sboon?

An interesting thing about liaisons is that so much of it has to do with whether a consonant is voiced or not. The key thing to remember is that the vocal cords don't like switching around at the midpoint. If the first consonant is voiced, the next one will be as well. If the first one is unvoiced, the second one will sound unvoiced, no matter what you do. For example, say the word *spoon*. Now, say the word *sboon*. Hear how they sound the same? This is why I'd like you to always convert the preposition *to* to *də* when you're speaking English, no matter what comes before it. In the beginning, to get you used to the concept, we made a distinction between *tə* and *də*, but now that your schwa is in place, use a single *d'* sound everywhere, except at the very beginning of a sentence.

After a voiced sound:	He had to **do** it.	[he hæ$^{(d)}$d' **du**$^{(w)}$'t]
After an unvoiced sound:	He got to **do** it.	[he gä$^{(t)}$d' **du**$^{(w)}$'t]
At the beginning of a sentence:	To **be** or **not** to be.	[t' **bee**$^{(y)}$r **nä**$^{(t)}$d'bee]

To have your liaisons tested, call (800) 457-4255.

Exercise 2-16: Liaison Staircases   CD 3 Track 4

*You are going to make staircases again from the paragraph below—pretty much as you did in Exercise 1-17 on page 16. This time, instead of putting a whole word on each stairstep, put a single sound on each step. This is also similar to the second part of the **Dogs Eat Bones** Exercise 1-38 on page 36. Use the liaison techniques you have just learned to connect the words; then regroup them and place one sound unit on a step. As before, start a new staircase every time you stress a word. Remember, new sentences don't have to start new staircases. A staircase can continue from one sentence to another until you come to a stressed word. Pause the CD.*

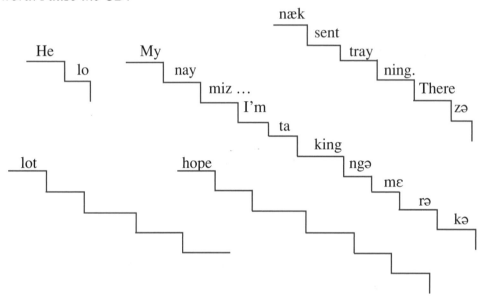

Note *The liaison practice presented in this chapter was the last of the basic principles you needed to know before tackling the finer points of pronunciation introduced in the next.*

Chapter 3

Cat? Caught? Cut?

CD 3 Track 5

After laying our foundation with intonation and liaisons, here we finally begin to refine your pronunciation! We are now going to work on the differences between [æ], [ä], and [ə], as well as [ō], [ā], and [ē]. Let's start out with the [æ] sound.

The [æ] Sound

Although not a common sound, [æ] is very distinctive to the ear and is typically American. In the practice paragraph in Exercise 3-2 this sound occurs five times. As its phonetic symbol indicates, [æ] is a combination of [ä] + [ε]. To pronounce it, drop your jaw down as if you were going to say [ä]; then from that position, try to say [ε]. The final sound is not two separate vowels, but rather the end result of the combination. It is very close to the sound that a goat makes: *ma-a-a-a*!

▼ Try it a few times now: [ä] ʃ [æ]

If you find yourself getting too nasal with [æ], pinch your nose as you say it. If [kæt] turns into [kεæt], you need to pull the sound out of your nose and down into your throat.

Note *As you look for the [æ] sound you might think that words like **down** or **sound** have an [æ] in them. For this diphthong, try [æ] + oh, or [æo]. This way, **down** would be written [dæon]. Because it is a combined sound, however, it's not included in the Cat? category. (See Pronunciation Point 4 on page ix).*

The [ä] Sound

The [ä] sound occurs a little more frequently; you will find ten such sounds in the exercise. To pronounce [ä], relax your tongue and drop your jaw as far down as it will go. As a matter of fact, put your hand under your chin and say [mä], [pä], [tä], [sä]. Your hand should be pushed down by your jaw as it opens. Remember, it's the sound that you make when the doctor wants to see your throat, so open it up and *dräp your jäw*.

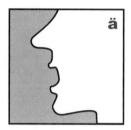

The Schwa [ə] Sound

Last is the schwa [ə], the *most common* sound in American English. When you work on Exercise 3-2, depending on how fast you speak, how smoothly you make liaisons, how strong your intonation is, and how much you relax your sounds, you will find from 50 to 75 schwas. Spelling doesn't help identify it, because it can appear as any one of the vowels, or a combination of them. It is a neutral vowel sound, *uh*. It is usually in an unstressed syllable, though it can be stressed as well. Whenever you find a vowel that can be crossed out and its absence wouldn't change the pronunciation of the word, you have probably found a schwa: *photography* [ph'togr'phy] (the two apostrophes show the location of the neutral vowel sounds).

Because it is so common, however, the wrong pronunciation of this one little sound can leave your speech strongly accented, even if you Americanized everything else.

Note *Some dictionaries use two different written characters, [ə] and [ʌ], but for simplicity, we are only going to use the first one.*

Silent or Neutral?

A schwa is neutral, but it is not silent. By comparison, the silent E at the end of a word is a signal for pronunciation, but it is not pronounced itself: *code* is [kod]. The E tells you to say an [o]. If you leave the E off, you have *cod*, [käd]. The schwa, on the other hand is neutral, but it is an actual sound—*uh*. For example, you could also write *photography* as *phuh•tah•gruh•fee*.

Because it's a neutral sound, the schwa doesn't have any distinctive characteristics, yet it is *the most common sound in the English language.*

To make the [ə] sound, put your hand on your diaphragm and push until a grunt escapes. Don't move your jaw, tongue, or lips; just allow the sound to flow past your vocal cords. It should sound like *uh*.

Once you master this sound, you will have an even easier time with pronouncing *can* and *can't*. In a sentence, *can't* sounds like [kæn(t)], but *can* becomes [kən], unless it is stressed, when it is [kæn], (as we saw in Exercise 1-43 on p. 41). Repeat.

I can **do** it.	[I kən **do** it]
I **can't do** it.	[I **kæn't do** it]

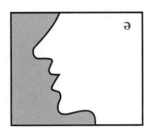

In the vowel chart that follows, the four corners represent the four most extreme positions of the mouth. The center box represents the least extreme position—the neutral schwa. For these four positions, only move your lips and jaw. Your tongue should stay in the same place—with the tip resting behind the bottom teeth.

Vowel Chart

lips back
jaw closed   *lips rounded*
                                                                                 jaw closed

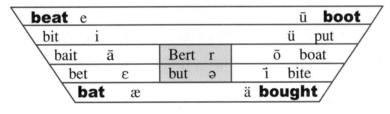

lips back   *lips rounded*
jaw open   *jaw open*

1. To pronounce *beat*, your lips should be drawn back, but your teeth should be close together. Your mouth should form the shape of a *banana*.
2. To pronounce *boot*, your lips should be fully rounded, and your teeth should be close together. Your mouth should form the shape of a *Cheerio*.
3. To pronounce *bought*, drop your jaw straight down from the *boot* position. Your mouth should form the shape of an *egg*.
4. To pronounce *bat*, keep your jaw down, pull your lips back, and try to simultaneously say [ä] and [ɛ]. Your mouth should form the shape of a *box*.

Note *Word-by-word pronunciation will be different than individual sounds within a sentence.* **That, than, as, at, and, have, had, can,** *and so on, are [æ] sounds when they stand alone, but they are weak words that reduce quickly in speech.*

Exercise 3-1: Word-by-Word and in a Sentence   CD 3 Track 6

Stressed		**Unstressed**		
that	thæt	th't	thət	He said th't it's OK.
than	thæn	th'n	thən	It's bigger th'n before
as	æz	'z	əz	'z soon 'z he gets here…
at	æt	't	ət	Look 't the time!
and	ænd	'n	ən	ham 'n eggs
have	hæv	h'v	həv	Where h'v you been?
had	hæd	h'd	həd	He h'd been at home.
can	cæn	c'n	cən	C'n you do it?

Exercise 3-2: Finding [æ], [ä], and [ə] Sounds   CD 3 Track 7

There are five [æ], ten [ä], and seventy-five [ə] sounds in the following paragraph. Underscore them in pen or pencil. (The first one of each sound is marked for you.)

Hello, my name is _____. I'm taking əmerəcən **æccent** Training. There's a **lät** to learn, but I **hope** to make it as **enjoyable** as possible. I should pick **up** on the American **intonation** pattern pretty **easily**, although the **only** way to **get** it is to **practice** all of the time. I use the **up** and down, or **peaks** and valleys **intonation** more than I **used** to. I've been paying attention to **pitch, too.** It's like **walking** down a **stair**case. I've been **talking** to a lot of **Americans** lately, and they tell me that I'm **easier** to under**stand. Any**way, I could go **on** and on, but the **important** thing is to **listen** well and sound **good. Well,** what do you **think? Do** I?

▼ Next, check your answers with the Answer Key, beginning on page 193. Finally, take your markers and give a color to each sound. For example, mark [æ] green, [ä] blue, and [ə] yellow.

✖ Turn your CD off and read the paragraph three times on your own.

Note *It sounds regional to end a sentence with [ustə]. In the middle of a sentence, however, it is more standard: [I ustə live there.]*

Exercise 3-3: Vowel-Sound Differentiation   CD 3 Track 8

Here we will read down from 1 to 24, then we will read each row across. Give the [ā] sound a clear double sound [ɛ + ee]. Also, the [o] is a longer sound than you might be expecting. Add the full ooh sound after each "o."

	æ	ä	ə	ou	a	ɛ
1.	Ann	on	un~	own	ain't	end
2.	ban	bond	bun	bone	bane	Ben
3.	can	con	come	cone	cane	Ken
4.	cat	caught/cot	cut	coat	Kate	ketch
5.	Dan	Don/dawn	done	don't	Dane	den
6.	fan	fawn	fun	phone	feign	fend
7.	gap	gone	gun	goat	gain	again
8.	hat	hot	hut	hotel	hate	het up
9.	Jan	John	jump	Joan	Jane	Jenny
10.	lamp	lawn	lump	loan	lane	Len
11.	man	monster	Monday	moan	main	men
12.	matter	motto	mutter	motor	made her	met her
13.	Nan	non~	none/nun	known	name	nemesis
14.	gnat	not/knot	nut	note	Nate	net
15.	pan	pawn	pun	pony	pain/pane	pen
16.	ran	Ron	run	roan	rain/reign	wren
17.	sand	sawn	sun	sewn/sown	sane	send
18.	shall	Sean	shut	show	Shane	Shen
19.	chance	chalk	chuck	choke	change	check
20.	tack	talk	tuck	token	take	tech
21.	van	Von	vug	vogue	vague	vent
22.	wax	want	won/one	won't	wane	when
23.	yam	yawn	young	yo!	yea!	yen
24.	zap	czar	result	zone	zany	zen

To have your pronunciation tested, call (800) 457-4255.

Exercise 3-4: Reading the [æ] Sound — CD 3 Track 9

The Tæn Mæn

A fashionably tan man sat casually at the bat stand, lashing a handful of practice bats. The manager, a crabby old bag of bones, passed by and laughed, "You're about average, Jack. Can't you lash faster than that?" Jack had had enough, so he clambered to his feet and lashed bats faster than any man had ever lashed bats. As a matter of fact, he lashed bats so fast that he seemed to dance. The manager was aghast. "Jack, you're a master bat lasher!" he gasped. Satisfied at last, Jack sat back and never lashed another bat.

✖ Pause the CD and read *The Tæn Mæn* aloud. Turn it back on to continue.

Exercise 3-5: Reading the [ä] Sound — CD 3 Track 10

A Lät of Läng, Hät Wälks in the Gärden

John was not sorry when the boss called off the walks in the garden. Obviously, to him, it was awfully hot, and the walks were far too long. He had not thought that walking would have caught on the way it did, and he fought the policy from the onset. At first, he thought he could talk it over at the law office and have it quashed, but a small obstacle* halted that thought. The top lawyers always bought coffee at the shop across the lawn and they didn't want to stop on John's account. John's problem was not office politics, but office policy. He resolved the problem by bombing the garden.

*lobster • a small lobster • lobstacle • a small obstacle

✖ Pause the CD and read *A Lät of Läng, Hät Wälks in the Gärden* aloud.

Exercise 3-6: Reading the [ə] Sound — CD 3 Track 11

When you read the following schwa paragraph, try clenching your teeth the first time. It won't sound completely natural, but it will get rid of all of the excess lip and jaw movement and force your tongue to work harder than usual. Remember that in speaking American English we don't move our lips much, and we talk though our teeth from far back in our throats. I'm going to read with my teeth clenched together and you follow along, holding your teeth together.

What Must the Sun Above Wonder About?

Some pundits proposed that the sun wonders unnecessarily about sundry and assorted conundrums. One cannot but speculate what can come of their proposal. It wasn't enough to trouble us,* but it was done so underhandedly that hundreds of sun lovers rushed to the defense of their beloved sun. None of this was relevant on Monday, however, when the sun burned up the entire country. *[ət wəzənənəf tə trəbələs]

✖ Pause the CD and read *What Must the Sun Above Wonder About?* twice. Try it once with your teeth clenched the first time and normally the second time.

Chapter 4

The American T

CD 3 Track 12

The American T is influenced very strongly by intonation and its position in a word or phrase. At the *top* of a staircase T is pronounced T as in *Ted* or *Italian*; a T in the *middle* of a staircase is pronounced as D [Beddy] [Idaly]; whereas a T at the *bottom* of a staircase isn't pronounced at all [ho(t)]. Look at *Italian* and *Italy* in the examples below. The [tæl] of *Italian* is at the top of the staircase and is strong: *Italian*. The [də] of *Italy* is in the middle and is weak: *Italy*.

Exercise 4-1: Stressed and Unstressed T	CD 3 Track 13

Repeat after me.

Italian	Italy
at**tack**	**att**ic
a**to**mic	**at**om
pho**to**graphy	**pho**tograph

tæl
I   y'n

I
d'
ly

Exercise 4-2: Betty Bought a Bit of Better Butter	CD 3 Track 14

*In the sentence **Betty bought a bit of better butter**, all of the Ts are in weak positions, so they all sound like soft Ds. Repeat the sentence slowly, word by word: [Beddy … badə … bidə… bedder … budder]. Feel the tip of your tongue flick across that area behind your top teeth. Think of the music of a cello again when you say, **Betty bought a bit of better butter**.*

Betty Bought a Bit of Better Butter

Betty bought a bit of better butter,	Beddy bä də bihda bedder budder,
But, said she,	Bu(t), said she,
This butter's bitter.	This budder'z bidder.
If I put it in my batter,	If I püdi din my bædder,
It'll make my batter bitter.	Id'll make my bædder bidder.

If you speak any language—such as Spanish, Japanese, Hindi, Italian, or Dutch, among others—where your R touches behind the teeth, you are in luck with the American T. Just fix the association in your mind so that when you see a middle position T, you automatically give it your native R sound. Say, *Beri bara bira …* with your native accent. (*Not* if you are

French, German, or Chinese!)

Along with liaisons, the American T contributes a great deal to the smooth, relaxed sound of English. When you say a word like *atom*, imagine that you've been to the dentist and you're a little numb, or that you've had a couple of drinks, or maybe that you're very sleepy. You won't be wanting to use a lot of energy saying [æ•tom], so just relax everything and say [adəm], like the masculine name, Adam. It's a very smooth, fluid sound. Rather than saying, *BeTTy boughT a biT of beTTer buTTer*, which is physically more demanding, try, *Beddy bada bidda bedder budder*. It's easy because you really don't need much muscle tension to say it this way.

The staircase concept will help clarify the various T sounds. The American T can be a little tricky if you base your pronunciation on spelling. Here are five rules to guide you.

1. **T is T** at the beginning of a word or in a stressed syllable.
2. **T is D** in the middle of a word.
3. **T is Held** at the end of a word.
4. **T is Held before N** in *-tain* and *-ten* endings.
5. **T is Silent after N** with lax vowels.

Exercise 4-3: Rule 1—Top of the Staircase   CD 3 Track 15

When a T is at the top of a staircase, in a stressed position, it should be a clear popped sound.

1. In the beginning of a word, T is [t].
   Ted took ten tomatoes.

2. With a stressed T and ST, TS, TR, CT, LT, and sometimes NT combinations, T is [t].
   He was content with the contract.

3. T replaces D in the past tense, after an unvoiced consonant sound — f, k, p, s, ch, sh, th — (except T).

   T: *laughed [læft], picked [pikt], hoped [houpt], raced [rast], watched [wächt], washed [wäsht], unearthed [uneartht]*
   D: *halved [hævd], rigged [rigd], nabbed [næbd], raised [razd], judged [j'jd], garaged [garazhd], smoothed [smoothd]*

Exceptions: wicked [wikəd], naked [nakəd], crooked [krükəd], etc.

Exercise 4-3: Rule 1—Top of the Staircase *continued*   CD 3 Track 15

Read the following sentences out loud. Make sure that the underlined (stressed) Ts are sharp and clear.

1. It took Tim ten times to try the telephone.
2. Stop touching Ted's toes.
3. Turn toward Stella and study her contract together.
4. Control your tears.
5. It's Tommy's turn to tell the teacher the truth.

Exercise 4-4: Rule 2—Middle of the Staircase   CD 3 Track 16

An unstressed T in the middle of a staircase between two vowel sounds should be pronounced as a soft D.

Betty bought a bit of better butter.   [Beddy bädə bida bedder budder]
Pat ought to sit on a lap.   [pædädə sidänə læp]

Read the following sentences out loud. Make sure that the underlined (unstressed) Ts sound like a soft D.

1. What a good **idea**.   [wədə gudai **dee**yə]
2. Put it in a **bottle**.   [püdidinə **bäddl**]
3. Write it in a **letter**.   [räididinə **leddr**]
4. Set it on the metal **gutter**.   [sedidän thə medl **gəddr**]
5. Put all the **data** in the **computer**.   [püdäl the **deidə** in the c'm**pyu**dr]
6. Insert a **quarter** in the **meter**.   [inserdə **kwor**der in the **mee**dr]
7. Get a better **water** heater.   [gedə beddr **wädr** heedr]
8. Let her put a **sweater** on.   [ledr püdə **swe**der än]
9. **Betty**'s at a **meeting**.   [**beddy**'s ædə **mee**ding]
10. It's getting hotter and **hotter**.   [its gedding häddr•rən **häddr**]
11. **Patty** ought to write a better **letter**.   [**pæddy**⁽ʸ⁾ädə ride a beddr **leddr**]
12. **Freida** had a **little** metal **bottle**.   [**free**də hædə **liddl** medl **bäddl**]

Exercise 4-5: Rule 3—Bottom of the Staircase   CD 3 Track 17

*T at the bottom of a staircase is in the **held** position. By held, I mean that the tongue is in the T position, but the air isn't released. To compare, when you say **T** as in **Tom**, there's a sharp burst of air over the tip of the tongue, and when you say **Betty**, there's a soft puff of air over the tip of the tongue. When you hold a T, as in **hot**, your tongue is in the position for **T**, but you keep the air in.*

1. She hit the hot **hut** with her **hat**.
2. We went to that 'Net site to get what we **needed**.
3. **Pat** was quite **right**, **wasn't** she?

Exercise 4-5: Rule 3—Bottom of the Staircase *continued*   CD 3 Track 17

4. **What**? Put my **hat** back!
5. hot, late, fat, goat, hit, put, not, hurt, what, set, paint, wait, sit, dirt, note, fit, lot, light, suit, point, incident, tight

---

Exercise 4-6: Rule 4—"Held T" Before N   CD 3 Track 18

*The "held T" is, strictly speaking, not really a T at all. Remember [t] and [n] are very close in the mouth (see Liaisons, Exercise 2-5). If you have an N immediately after a T, you don't pop the T—the tongue is in the T position—but you release the air with the N, **not** the T. There is no [t] and no [ə]. Make a special point of not letting your tongue release from the top of your mouth before you drop into the [n]; otherwise, **bu(tt)on** would sound like two words: **but-ton**. An unstressed T or TT followed by N is held. Read the following words and sentences out loud. Make sure that the underlined Ts are held. Remember, there is no "uh" sound before the [n].*

Note *Another point to remember is that you need a sharp upward sliding intonation up to the "held T," then a quick drop for the N.*

written		written	kitten
ri⁽ᵗ⁾n		sentence	patent
	t	forgotten	mutant
sentence		certain	latent
sen⁽ᵗ⁾ns		curtain	mountain
		mitten	recently
lately	**n**	Martin	lately
la⁽ᵗ⁾lee		bitten	partly
		button	frequently

1. He's **forgotten** the **carton** of satin **mittens**.
2. She's **certain** that he has **written** it.
3. The cotton **curtain** is not in the **fountain**.
4. The **hikers** went in the **mountains**.
5. **Martin** has gotten a **kitten**.
6. **Students** study **Latin** in **Britain**.
7. **Whitney** has a **patent** on those **sentences**.
8. He has not **forgotten** what was **written** about the **mutant** on the **mountain**.
9. It's not **certain** that it was gotten from the **fountain**.
10. You need to put an **orange** cotton **curtain** on that **window**.
11. We like that certain **satin** better than the **carton** of cotton **curtains**.
12. The intercontinental **hotel** is in **Seattle**.
13. The frightened **witness** had forgotten the **important** written **message**.
14. The child wasn't **beaten** because he had **bitten** the **button**.

Exercise 4-7: Rule 5—The Silent T

CD 3 Track 19

[t] and [n] are so close in the mouth that the [t] can simply disappear. Repeat.

1.	**in**terview	**inn**erview
2.	**in**terface	**inn**erface
3.	**In**ternet	**inn**ernet
4.	**inter**state	**inn**erstate
5.	inter**rupt**	inner**rupt**
6.	inter**fere**	inner**fere**
7.	inter**acti**ve	inner**acti**ve
8.	inter**na**tional	inner**na**tional
9.	ad**van**tage	əd**væn**'j
10.	per**cen**tage	per**cen**'j
11.	**twen**ty	**twen**ny
12.	**print**out	**prin**nout or **prin**ᵈout
13.	**print**er	**prin**ner or **prin**ᵈer
14.	**win**ter	**win**ner or **win**ᵈer
15.	**en**ter	**en**ner or **en**ᵈer

Exercise 4-8: Rule 5—The Silent T

CD 3 Track 20

Read the following sentences out loud. Make sure that the underlined Ts are silent.

1.	He had a great **in**terview.	[he hædə gray ᵈ**inn**erview]
2.	Try to en**t**er the infor**ma**tion.	[trydə enner the infr**ma**tion]
3.	Turn the **print**er on.	[trn thə **prin**nerän]
4.	Finish the **print**ing.	[f'n'sh thə **prin**ning]
5.	She's at the in**t**erna**t**ional cen**t**er.	[sheez'⁽ᵗ⁾the⁽ʸ⁾inner**na**tional senner]
6.	It's twen**t**y de**grees** in Toron**t**o.	['ts twenny d'**gree**zin **tra**nno]
7.	I don'**t** under**stand** i**t**.	[I doe nənder **stæn** d't]
8.	She inven**t**ed it in Santa **Mo**nica.	[she⁽ʸ⁾in**ven**əd'din sænə **mä**nəkə]
9.	He can'**t** even **do** it.	[he kæneevən **du**⁽ʷ⁾'t]
10.	They don'**t** even **want** it.	[they doe neevən **wän**'t]
11.	They won'**t** ever **try**.	[they woe never **try**]
12.	What's the **point** of it?	[w'ts the **poi** n'v't]
13.	She's the in**t**ercon**t**inen**t**al repre**sen**tative.	[shez thee⁽ʸ⁾inner**cän**⁽ᵗ⁾n•nenl repr'**zen**'d'v]
14.	**Has**n'**t** he?	[**hæz**ə nee]
15.	**Is**n'**t** he?	[**iz**ə nee]
16.	**Are**n'**t** I?	[**är** näi]
17.	**Won**'**t** he?	[**woe** nee]
18.	**Does**n'**t** he?	[**də**zənee]
19.	**Would**n'**t** it?	[**wü**dənit]
20.	**Did**n'**t** I?	[**did**n•näi]

Exercise 4-9: Karina's T Connections CD 3 Track 21

Here are some extremely common middle T combinations. Repeat after me:

	What	**But**	**That**
a	wədə	bədə	thədə
I	wədäi	bədäi	thədäi
I'm	wədäim	bədäim	thədäim
I've	wədäiv	bədäiv	thədäiv
if	wədif	bədif	thədif
it	wədit	bədit	thədit
it's	wədits	bədits	thədits
is	wədiz	bədiz	thədiz
isn't	wədiznᵗ	bədiznᵗ	thədiznᵗ
are	wədr	bədr	thədr
aren't	wədärnᵗ	bədärnᵗ	thədärnᵗ
he	wədee	bədee	thədee
he's	wədeez	bədeez	thədeez
her	wədr	bədr	thədr
you	wəchew	bəchew	thəchew
you'll	wəchül	bəchül	thəchül
you've	wəchoov	bəchoov	thəchoov
you're	wəchr	bəchr	thəchr

Exercise 4-10: Combinations in Context CD 3 Track 22

Repeat the following sentences.

1. I don't know what it **means**. I don⁽ᵗ⁾know wədit **meenz**
2. But it **looks** like what I **need**. bədi⁽ᵗ⁾**lük** sly kwədäi **need**
3. But you **said** that you **wouldn't**. bəchew **sed** thəchew **wüdnt**
4. I **know** what you **think**. I **know** wəchew **think**
5. But I don't **think** that he **will**. bədäi don⁽ᵗ⁾**think** thədee **will**
6. He said that if we can **do** it, he'll **help**. he sed the diff we k'n **do**⁽ʷ⁾it, hill **help**
7. But isn't it **easier** this way? bədizni **dee**zier thi sway?
8. We **want** something that isn't **here**. we **wänt** something thədiznᵗ **here**
9. You'll **like** it, but you'll **regret** it **later**. yül **lye** kit, bəchül r'**gre** dit **laydr**
10. But he's not **right** for what I **want**. bədeez nät **right** fr wədäi **wänt**
11. It's **amazing** what you've **accomplished**. its amazing wəchoovə**ccäm**plisht
12. What if he **forgets**? wədifee fr**gets**
13. OK, but aren't you **missing** something? OK, bədärnᵗ chew **miss**ing səmthing
14. I think that he's **OK** now. I think thədeez **OK** næo
15. She **wanted** to, but her **car** broke down. She **wän**əd to, bədr **cär** broke dæon
16. We **think** that you're taking a **chance**. We think thəchr taking a **chænce**
17. They don't know what it's **about**. They don't know wədit sə**bæot**

Exercise 4-11: Voiced and Unvoiced Sounds with T

This exercise is for the practice of the difference between words that end in either a vowel or a voiced consonant, which means that the vowel is lengthened or doubled. Therefore, these words are on a much larger, longer stairstep. Words that end in an unvoiced consonant are on a smaller, shorter stairstep. This occurs whether the vowel in question is tense or lax.

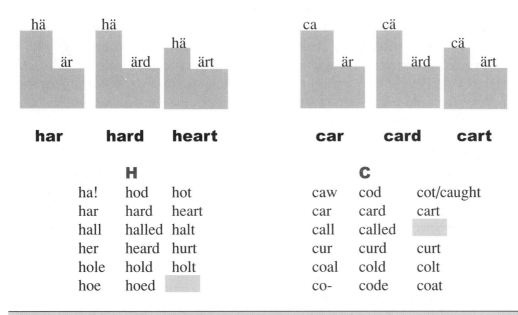

	H			**C**	
ha!	hod	hot	caw	cod	cot/caught
har	hard	heart	car	card	cart
hall	halled	halt	call	called	
her	heard	hurt	cur	curd	curt
hole	hold	holt	coal	cold	colt
hoe	hoed		co-	code	coat

Exercise 4-12: Finding American T Sounds

Once again, go over the following familiar paragraph. First, find all the T's that are pronounced D (there are nine to thirteen here). Second, find all the held Ts (there are seven). The first one of each is marked for you. Pause the CD to do this and don't forget to check your answers with the Answer Key, beginning on page 193, when you finish.

Hello, **my** name is _____. I'm taking American **Accen(t)** Training. There's a

lo(t) to learn, but[d] I **hope** to make it as **enjoyable** as possible. I should pick **up** on the

American **intonation** pattern pretty **easily**, although the **only** way to **get** it is to **practice** all

of the time. I use the **up** and down, or **peaks** and valleys, **intonation** more than I **used** to.

I've been paying attention to **pitch, too**. It's like **walking** down a **stair**case. I've been **talk-**

ing to a lot of **Americans** lately, and they tell me that I'm **easier** to under**stand**. **Any**way, I

could go **on** and on, but the **important** thing is to **listen** well and sound **good**. **Well**, what do

you **think**? **Do** I?

Voiced Consonants and Reduced Vowels

The strong intonation in American English creates certain tendencies in your spoken language. Here are four consistent conditions that are a result of intonation's tense peaks and relaxed valleys:

1. **Reduced vowels**

   You were introduced to reduced vowels in Chapter 1. They appear in the valleys that are formed by the strong peaks of intonation. The more you reduce the words in the valleys, the smoother and more natural your speech will sound. A characteristic of reduced vowels is that your throat muscles should be very relaxed. This will allow the unstressed vowels to reduce toward the schwa. Neutral vowels take less energy and muscularity to produce than tense vowels. For example, the word *unbelievable* should only have one hard vowel: [ənbəlēvəbəl].

2. **Voiced consonants**

   The mouth muscles are relaxed to create a voiced sound like [z] or [d]. For unvoiced consonants, such as [s] or [t], they are sharp and tense. Relaxing your muscles will simultaneously reduce your vowels and voice your consonants. Think of *voiced consonants* as *reduced consonants*. Both reduced consonants and reduced vowels are unconsciously preferred by a native speaker of American English. This explains why T so frequently becomes D and S becomes Z: *Get it is to* ... [gedidizdə].

3. **Like sound with like sound**

   It's not easy to change horses midstream, so when you have a voiced consonant; let the consonant that follows it be voiced as well. In the verb *used* [yuzd], for example, the S is really a Z, so it is followed by D. The phrase *used to* [yus tu], on the other hand, has a real S, so it is followed by T. Vowels are, by definition, voiced. So when one is followed by a common, reducible word, it will change that word's first sound—like the preposition *to*, which will change to [də].

   > The only way to get it is to practice all of the time.
   > [They only wei•də•geddidiz•də•practice all of the time.]

   Again, this will take time. In the beginning, work on recognizing these patterns when you hear them. When you are confident that you understand the structure beneath these sounds and you can intuit where they belong, you can start to try them out. It's not advisable to memorize one reduced word and stick it into an otherwise overpronounced sentence. It would sound strange.

4. **R'lææææææææææx**

   You've probably noticed that the preceding three conditions, as well as other areas that we've covered, such as liaisons and the schwa, have one thing in common—the idea that *it's physically easier this way*. This is one of the most remarkable characteristics of American English. You need to relax your mouth and throat muscles (except for [æ], [ä], and other tense vowels), and let the sounds flow smoothly out. If you find yourself tensing up, pursing your lips, or tightening your throat, you are going to strangle and lose the sound you are pursuing. Relax, relax, relax.

Chapter 5

The El

CD 3 Track 25

This chapter discusses the sound of L (not to be confused with that of the American R, which is covered in the next chapter). We'll approach this sound first, by touching on the difficulties it presents to foreign speakers of English, and next by comparing L to the related sounds of T, D, and N.

L and Foreign Speakers of English

The English L is usually no problem at the beginning or in the middle of a word. The native language of some people, however, causes them to make their English L much too short. At the end of a word, the L is especially noticeable if it is either missing (Chinese) or too short (Spanish). In addition, most people consider the L as a simple consonant. This can also cause a lot of trouble. Thus, two things are at work here: location of language sounds in the mouth, and the complexity of the L sound.

Location of Language in the Mouth

The sounds of many Romance languages are generally located far forward in the mouth. My French teacher told me that if I couldn't see my lips when I spoke French—it wasn't French! Spanish is sometimes even called the smiling language. Chinese, on the other hand, is similar to American English in that it is mostly produced far back in the mouth. The principal difference is that English also requires clear use of the tongue's tip, a large component of the sound of L.

The Compound Sound of L

The L is not a simple consonant; it is a compound made up of a vowel and a consonant. Like the [æ] sound discussed in Chapter 3, the sound of L is a combination of [ə] and [l]. The [ə], being a reduced vowel sound, is created in the throat, but the [l] part requires a clear movement of the tongue. First, the tip must touch behind the teeth. (This part is simple enough.) But then, the back of the tongue must then drop down and back for the continuing schwa sound. Especially at the end of a word, Spanish-speaking people tend to leave out the schwa and shorten the L, and Chinese speakers usually leave it off entirely.

One way to avoid the pronunciation difficulty of a final L, as in *call*, is to make a liaison when the next word begins with a vowel. For example, if you want to say *I have to call on my friend*, let the liaison do your work for you; say [I have to kälän my friend].

L Compared with T, D, and N

When you learn to pronounce the L correctly, you will feel its similarity with T, D, and N. Actually, the tongue is positioned in the same place in the mouth for all four sounds—behind the teeth. The difference is in how and where the air comes out. (See the drawings in Exercise 5-1.)

T and D

The sound of both T and D is produced by allowing a puff of air to come out over the tip of the tongue.

N

The sound of N is nasal. The tongue completely blocks all air from leaving through the mouth, allowing it to come out only through the nose. You should be able to feel the edges of your tongue touching your teeth when you say *nnn*.

L

With L, the tip of the tongue is securely touching the roof of the mouth behind the teeth, but the sides of the tongue are dropped down and tensed. This is where L is different from N. With N, the tongue is relaxed and covers the entire area around the back of the teeth so that no air can come out. With L, the tongue is very tense, and the air comes out around its sides.

At the beginning it's helpful to exaggerate the position of the tongue. Look at yourself in the mirror as you stick out the tip of your tongue between your front teeth. With your tongue in this position say *el* several times. Then, try saying it with your tongue behind your teeth. This sounds complicated, but it is easier to do than to describe. You can practice this again later with Exercise 5-3. Our first exercise, however, must focus on differentiating the sounds.

Exercise 5-1: Sounds Comparing L with T, D, and N   CD 3 Track 26

For this exercise, concentrate on the different ways in which the air comes out of the mouth when producing each sound of L, T, D, and N. Look at the drawings included here, to see the correct position of the tongue. Instructions for reading the groups of words listed next are given after the words.

T/D
Plosive

A puff of air comes out over the tip of the tongue. The tongue is somewhat tense.

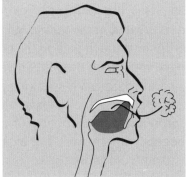

Exercise 5-1: Sounds Comparing L with T, D, and N *continued*   CD 3 Track 26

N
Nasal

Air comes out through the nose. The tongue is completely relaxed.

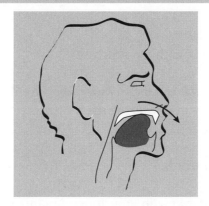

L
Lateral

Air flows around the sides of the tongue. The tongue is very tense. The lips are *not* rounded!

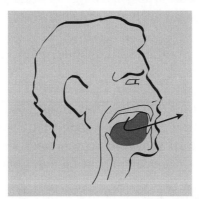

Exercise 5-2: Sounds Comparing L with T, D, and N   CD 3 Track 27

Repeat after me, first down and then across.

I. At the beginning of a word

law	gnaw	taw	daw
low	know	toe	dough
lee	knee	tea	D

2. In the middle of a word

belly	Benny	Betty
caller	Conner	cotter
alley	Annie's	at ease

3. At the end of a word

A

hole	hold	hone	hoed
call	called	con	cod

B

fill	full	fool	fail
fell	feel	fuel	furl

▼ Look at group 3, B. This exercise has three functions:

1. Practice final *els*.
2. Review vowels sounds.
3. Review the same words with the staircase.

Note *Notice that each word has a tiny schwa after the el. This is to encourage your tongue to be in the right position to give your words a "finished" sound. Exaggerate the final el and its otherwise inaudible schwa.*

▼ Repeat the last group of words.

Once you are comfortable with your tongue in this position, let it just languish there while you continue vocalizing, which is what a native speaker does.

▼ Repeat again: fillll, fullll, foollll, faillll, feellll, fuellll, furllll.

What Are All Those Extra Sounds I'm Hearing?

I hope that you're asking a question like this about now. Putting all of those short little words on a staircase will reveal exactly how many extra sounds you have to put in to make it "sound right." For example, if you were to pronounce *fail* as [fal], the sound is too abbreviated for the American ear—we need to hear the full [fayəlᵊ].

| **Exercise 5-3: Final El with Schwa** | **CD 3 Track 28** |

Repeat after me.

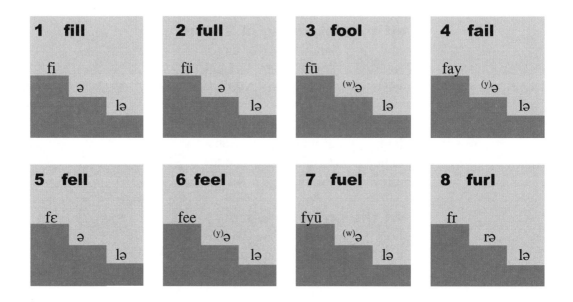

Exercise 5-4: Many Final Els   CD 3 Track 29

This time, simply hold the L sound extra long. Repeat after me.

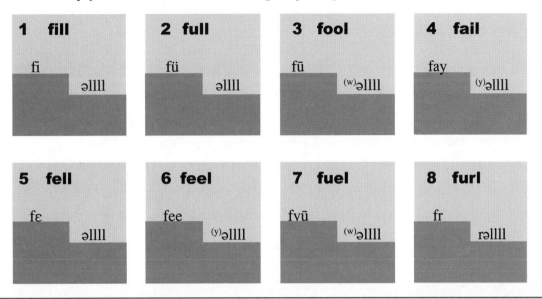

| 1 fill | 2 full | 3 fool | 4 fail |
| fi əllll | fü əllll | fū (w)əllll | fay (y)əllll |

| 5 fell | 6 feel | 7 fuel | 8 furl |
| fɛ əllll | fee (y)əllll | fvū (w)əllll | fr rəllll |

Exercise 5-5: Liaise the Ls   CD 3 Track 30

As you work with the following exercise, here are two points you should keep in mind. When a word ends with an L sound, either (a) connect it to the next word if you can, or (b) add a slight schwa for an exaggerated [lə] sound. For example:

(a) enjoyable as   [enjoyəbələz]
(b) possible   [pasəbələ]

Note *Although (a) is really the way you want to say it, (b) is an interim measure to help you put your tongue in the right place. It would sound strange if you were to always add the slight schwa. Once you can feel where you want your tongue to be, hold it there while you continue to make the L sound. Here are three examples:*

Call

caw	[kä]	(incorrect)
call	[cälə]	(understandable)
call	[källl]	(correct)

You can do the same thing to stop an N from becoming an NG.

Con

cong	[käng]	(incorrect)
con	[känə]	(understandable)
con	[kännn]	(correct)

Exercise 5-6: Finding L Sounds
CD 3 Track 31

Pause the CD, and find and mark all the L sounds in the familiar paragraph below; the first one is marked for you. There are seventeen of them; five are silent. Afterwards, check Answer Key, beginning on page 193.

He<u>ll</u>o, my name is_____. I'm taking American Accent Training. There's a lot to learn, but I hope to make it as enjoyable as possible. I should pick up on the American intonation pattern pretty easily, although the only way to get it is to practice all of the time. I use the up and down, or peaks and valleys, intonation more than I used to. I've been paying attention to pitch, too. It's like walking down a staircase. I've been talking to a lot of Americans lately, and they tell me that I'm easier to understand. Anyway, I could go on and on, but the important thing is to listen well and sound good. Well, what do you think? Do I?

Exercise 5-7: Silent Ls
CD 3 Track 32

Once you've found all the L sounds, the good news is that very often you don't even have to pronounce them. Read the following list of words after me.

1. would   could   should
2. chalk   talk   walk
3. calm   palm   psalm
4. already   alright   almond
5. although   almost   always
6. salmon   alms   Albany
7. folk   caulk   polka

Before reading about **Little Lola** in the next exercise, I'm going to get off the specific subject of L for the moment to talk about learning in general. Frequently, when you have some difficult task to do, you either avoid it or do it with dread. I'd like you to take the opposite point of view. For this exercise, you're going to completely focus on the thing that's most difficult: leaving your tongue attached to the top of your mouth. And rather than saying, "Oh, here comes an L, I'd better do something with my tongue," just leave your tongue attached *all through the entire paragraph!*

Remember our clenched-teeth reading of **What Must the Sun Above Wonder About?**, in Chapter 3? Well, it's time for us to make weird sounds again.

Exercise 5-8: Hold Your Tongue!   CD 3 Track 33

You and I are going to read with our tongues firmly held at the roofs of our mouths. If you want, hold a clean dime there with the tongue's tip; the dime will let you know when you have dropped your tongue because it will fall out. (Do not use candy; it will hold itself there since wet candy is sticky.) If you prefer, you can read with your tongue between your teeth instead of the standard behind-the-teeth position, and use a small mirror. Remember that with this technique you can actually see your tongue disappear as you hear your L sounds drop off.

It's going to sound ridiculous, of course, and nobody would ever intentionally sound like this, but no one will hear you practice. You don't want to sound like this: llllllllll. Force your tongue to make all the various vowels in spite of its position. Let's go.

Leave a little for Lola!

Exercise 5-9: Little Lola   CD 3 Track 34

Now that we've done this, instead of L being a hard letter to pronounce, it's the easiest one because the tongue is stuck in that position. Pause the CD to practice the reading on your own, again, with your tongue stuck to the top of your mouth. Read the following paragraph after me with your tongue in the normal position. Use good, strong intonation. Follow my lead as I start dropping h's here.

Little Lola felt left out in life. She told herself that luck controlled her and she truly believed that only by loyally following an exalted leader could she be delivered from her solitude. Unfortunately, she learned a little late that her life was her own to deal with. When she realized it, she was already eligible for Social Security and she had lent her lifelong earnings to a lowlife in Long Beach. She lay on her linoleum and slid along the floor in anguish. A little later, she leapt up and laughed. She no longer longed for a leader to tell her how to live her life. Little Lola was finally all well.

In our next paragraph about **Thirty Little Turtles**, we deal with another aspect of L, namely consonant clusters. When you have a *dl* combination, you need to apply what you learned about liaisons and the American T as well as the L.

Since the two sounds are located in a similar position in the mouth, you know that they are going to be connected, right? You also know that all of these middle Ts are going to be pronounced D, and that you're going to leave the tongue stuck to the top of your mouth. That may leave you wondering: Where is the air to escape? The L sound is what determines that. For the D, you hold the air in, the same as for a final D, then for the L, you release it around the sides of the tongue. Let's go through the steps before proceeding to our next exercise.

Exercise 5-10: Dull versus ~dle   CD 3 Track 35

Repeat after me.

laid   Don't pop the final D sound.

ladle   Segue gently from the D to the L, with a "small" schwa in-between. Leave your tongue touching behind the teeth and just drop the sides to let the air pass out.

lay dull   Here, your tongue can drop between the D and the L.

To hear the difference between [dᵊl] and [dəᵊl], contrast the sentences, *Don't lay dull tiles* and *Don't **ladle** tiles*.

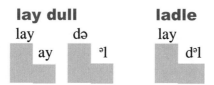

Exercise 5-11: Final L Practice   CD 3 Track 36

Repeat the following lists.

	üll	äll	æwl	ell	ale	oll	eel	dl
1.	bull	ball	bowel	bell	bale	bowl	Beal	bottle
2.		hall	howl	hell	hail	hole	heel	huddle
3.		hauled	howled	held	hailed	hold	healed	hurtle
4.	pull	pall	Powell	pell	pail	pole	peel	poodle
5.	wool	wall		well	whale	whole	wheel	wheedle
6.	full	fall	foul	fell	fail	foal	feel	fetal
7.	Schultz	shawl		shell	shale	shoal	she'll	shuttle
8.	tulle	tall	towel	tell	tale	toll	teal	turtle
9.		vault	vowel	veldt	veil	vole	veal	vital
10.	you'll	yawl	yowl	yell	Yale		yield	yodel
11.		call	cowl	Kelly	kale	cold	keel	coddle

Exercise 5-12: Thirty Little Turtles in a Bottle of Bottled Water   CD 3 Track 37

Repeat the following paragraph, focusing on the consonant + ²l combinations.

Thrdee Lidd²l Terdəl Zinə Bäddələ Bädd²l Dwäder

A bottle of bottled water held 30 little turtles. It didn't matter that each turtle had to rattle a metal ladle in order to get a little bit of noodles, a total turtle delicacy. The problem was that there were many turtle battles for the less than oodles of noodles. The littlest turtles always lost, because every time they thought about grappling with the haggler turtles, their little turtle minds boggled and they only caught a little bit of noodles.

🐢 🐢 🐢 🐢 🐢 🐢 🐢 🐢 🐢 🐢
🐢 🐢 🐢 🐢 🐢 🐢 🐢 🐢 🐢 🐢
🐢 🐢 🐢 🐢 🐢 🐢 🐢 🐢 🐢 🐢

Exercise 5-13: Speed-reading   CD 3 Track 38

We've already practiced strong intonation, so now we'll just pick up the speed. First I'm going to read our familiar paragraph, as fast as I can. Subsequently, you'll practice on your own, and then we'll go over it together, sentence by sentence, to let you practice reading very fast, right after me. By then you will have more or less mastered the idea, so record yourself reading really fast and with very strong intonation. Listen back to see if you sound more fluent. Listen as I read.

Hello, **my** name is _____. I'm taking American **Accent** Training. There's a **lot** to learn, but I **hope** to make it as **enjoyable** as possible. I should pick **up** on the American **intonation** pattern pretty **easily**, although the **only** way to **get** it is to **practice** all of the time. I use the **up** and down, or **peaks** and valleys, **intonation** more than I **used** to. I've been paying attention to **pitch, too**. It's like **walking** down a **stair**case. I've been **talking** to a lot of **Americans** lately, and they tell me that I'm **easier** to under**stand**. **Any**way, I could go **on** and on, but the **important** thing is to **listen** well and sound **good**. **Well**, what do you **think**? **Do** I?

✖ Pause the CD and practice speed-reading on your own five times.
▼ Repeat each sentence after me.
▼ Record yourself speed-reading with strong intonation.

Exercise 5-14: Tandem Reading   CD 3 Track 39

The last reading that I'd like you to do is one along with me. Up to now, I have read first and you have repeated in the pause that followed. Now, however, I would like you to read along at exactly the same time that I read, so that we sound like one person reading. Read along with me.

Voice Quality

In the next chapter, we'll be working on a sound that is produced deep in the throat—the American R. In Chapter 3, we studied two tense vowels, **æ** and **ä**, and the completely neutral schwa, **ə**. The **æ** sound has a tendency to sound a little nasal all on its own, and when other vowels are nasalized as well, it puts your whole voice in the wrong place. This is an opportune moment, then, to go into the quality of your voice. In my observation, when people speak a foreign language, they tense up their throat, so their whole communication style sounds forced, pinched, strained, artificial, or nasal. The foreign speaker's voice is also generally higher pitched than would be considered desirable. To practice the difference between high pitch and lower pitch, work on **uh-oh**. In addition to pitch, this exercise will let you discover the difference between a tinny, nasal tone and a deep, rich, mellifluous, basso profundo tone. The tilda (˜) is used to indicate a nasal sound.

Exercise 5-15: Shifting Your Voice Position

*Pinch your nose closed and say **æ**. You should feel a high vibration in your nasal passages, as well as in your fingers. Now, continue holding your nose, and completely relax your throat—allow an **ah** sound to flow from deep in your chest. There should be no vibration in your nose at all. Go back and forth several times. Next, we practice flowing from one position to the other, so you can feel exactly when it changes from a nasal sound to a deep, rich schwa. Remember how it was imitating a man's voice when you were little? Do that, pinch your nose, and repeat after me.*

Nose				Throat				Chest
ãæ	↔	ãæ	↔	ãä	↔	ä	↔	ə ↔ ə

Here, we will practice the same progression, but we will stick with the same sound, æ.

Nose				Throat				Chest
ãæ	↔	ãæ	↔	æ	↔	æ	↔	æ ↔ æ

*As you will see in Chapter 12, there are three nasal consonants, **m**, **n**, and **ng**. These have non-nasal counterparts, **m/b**, **n/d**, **ng/g**. We're going to practice totally denasalizing your voice for a moment, which means turning the nasals into the other consonants. We'll read the same sentence three times. The first will be quite nasal. The second will sound like you have a cold. The third will have appropriate nasal consonants, but denasalized vowels. Repeat after me.*

Nasal	**Clogged**	**Normal**
Mãry might need mõney.	Berry bite deed buddy.	Mary might need money.

Now that you have moved your voice out of your nose and down into your diaphragm, let's apply it.

A Lät of Läng, Hät Wälks in the Gärden. John was not sorry when the boss called off the walks in the garden. Obviously, to him, it was awfully hot, and the walks were far too long. He had not thought that walking would have caught on the way it did, and he fought the policy from the onset.

Chapter 6

The American R

CD 3 Track 42

American English, today—although continually changing—is made up of the sounds of the various people who have come to settle here from many countries. All of them have put in their linguistic two cents, the end result being that the easiest way to pronounce things has almost always been adopted as the most American. R is an exception, along with L and the sounds of [æ] and [th], and is one of the most troublesome sounds for people to acquire. Not only is it difficult for adults learning the language, but also for American children, who pronounce it like a W or skip over it altogether and only pick it up after they've learned all the other sounds.

The Invisible R

The trouble is that you can't see an R from the outside. With a P, for instance, you can see when people put their lips together and pop out a little puff. With R, however, everything takes place behind almost closed lips—back down in the throat—and who can tell what the tongue is doing? It is really hard to tell what's going on if, when someone speaks, you can only hear the *err* sound, especially if you're used to making an R by touching your tongue to the ridge behind your teeth. So, what should your tongue be doing?

This technique can help you visualize the correct tongue movements in pronouncing the R. (1) Hold your hand out flat, with the palm up, slightly dropping the back end of it. That's basically the position your tongue is in when you say *ah* [ä], so your flat hand will represent this sound. (2) Now, to go from *ah* to the *er*, take your fingers and curl them up slightly. Again, your tongue should follow that action. The sides of your tongue should come up a bit, too. When the air passes over that hollow in the middle of your tongue (look at the palm of your hand), that's what creates the *er* sound.

Try it using both your hand and tongue simultaneously. Say *ah*, with your throat open (and your hand flat), then curl your tongue up (and your fingers) and say *errr*. The tip of the tongue should be aimed at a middle position in the mouth, but never touching, and your throat should relax and expand. R, like L, has a slight schwa in it. This is what pulls the *er* down so far back in your throat.

Another way to get to *er* is to go from the *ee* sound and slide your tongue straight back like a collapsing accordion, letting the two sides of your tongue touch the insides of your molars; the tip of the tongue, however, again, should not touch anything. Now from *ee*, pull your tongue back toward the center of your throat, and pull the sound down into your throat:

ee ☞ ee ☞ eeeer

Since the R is produced in the throat, let's link it with other throat sounds.

Exercise 6-1: R Location Practice CD 3 Track 43

Repeat after me.

[g], [gr], greek, green, grass, grow, crow, core, cork, coral, cur, curl, girl, gorilla, her, erg, error, mirror, were, war, gore, wrong, wringer, church, pearl

While you're perfecting your R, you might want to rush to it, and in doing so, neglect the preceding vowel. There are certain vowels that you can neglect, but there are others that demand their full sound. We're going to practice the ones that require you to keep that clear sound before you add an R.

Exercise 6-2: Double Vowel Sounds with R CD 3 Track 44

Refer to the subsequent lists of sounds and words as you work through each of the directions that follow them. Repeat each sound, first the vowel and then the [ər], and each word in columns 1 to 3. We will read all the way across.

1	2	3	
[ä] + [er]	[hä•ərd]	hard	hä
[e] + [ər]	[he•ər]	here	ərd
[ɛ] + [ər]	[shɛ•ər]	share	
[o] + [ər]	[mo•ər]	more	
[ər] +[ər]	[wər•ər]	were	

We will next read column 3 only; try to keep that doubled sound, but let the vowel flow smoothly into the [ər]; imagine a double stairstep that cannot be avoided. Don't make them two staccato sounds, though, like [ha•rd]. Instead, flow them smoothly over the double stairstep: *Hääärrrrd.*

Of course, they're not *that* long; this is an exaggeration and you're going to shorten them up once you get better at the sound. When you say the first one, *hard*, to get your jaw open for the [hä], imagine that you are getting ready to bite into an apple: [hä]. Then for the *er* sound, you would bite into it: [hä•erd], *hard.*

✖ Pause the CD to practice five times on your own.

From a spelling standpoint, the American R can be a little difficult to figure out. With words like *where* [wɛər] and *were* [wər], it's confusing to know which one has two different vowel sounds (*where*) and which one has just the [ər] (*were*). When there is a full vowel, you must make sure to give it its complete sound, and not chop it short. [wɛ + ər].

For words with only the schwa + R [ər], don't try to introduce another vowel sound before the [ər], *regardless of spelling.* The following words, for example, do not have any other vowel sounds in them.

Looks like	Sounds like
word	[wərd]
hurt	[hərt]
girl	[gərl]
pearl	[pərl]

The following exercise will further clarify this for you.

Exercise 6-3: How to Pronounce Troublesome Rs   CD 3 Track 45

The following seven R sounds, which are represented by the ten words, give people a lot of trouble, so we're going to work with them and make them easy for you. Repeat.

1. were   [wər•ər]   wər
2. word   [wər•ərd]   ər
3. whirl   [wərrul]
4. world/whirled   [were rolled]
5. wore/war   [woər]
6. whorl   [worul]
7. where/wear   [wɛər]

1. *Were* is pronounced with a doubled [ər]: [wərər]
2. *Word* is also doubled, but after the second [ər], you're going to put your tongue in place for the D and hold it there, keeping all the air in your mouth, opening your throat to give it that full-voiced quality (imagine yourself puffing your throat out like a bullfrog): [wərərd], *word*. Not [wərd], which is too short. Not [wordə], which is too strong at the end. But [wər•ər^d] *word*.
3. In *whirl* the R is followed by L. The R is in the throat and the back of the tongue stays down because, as we've practiced, L starts with the schwa, but the tip of the tongue comes up for the L: [wər•rə•lə], *whirl*.
4. *World/whirled*, like 5 and 7, has two spellings (and two different meanings, of course). You're going to do the same thing as for *whirl*, but you're going to add that voiced D at the end, holding the air in: [wər•rəl^(d)], *world/whirled*. It should sound almost like two words: *wére rolled*.
5. Here, you have an [o] sound in either spelling before the [ər]: [wo•ər], *wore/war*.
6. For *whorl*, you're going to do the same thing as in 5, but you're going to add a schwa + L at the end: [wo•ərəl], *whorl*.
7. This sound is similar to 5, but you have [ɛ] before the [ər]: [wɛ•ər], *where/wear*.

The following words are typical in that they are spelled one way and pronounced in another way. The *ar* combination frequently sounds like [ɛr], as in *embarrass* [embɛrəs]. This sound is particularly clear on the West Coast. On the East Coast, you may hear [embærəs].

Exercise 6-4: Zbigniew's Epsilon List · CD 3 Track 46

Repeat after me.

			Common Combinations
embarrass	stationary	Larry	ar
vocabulary	care	Sarah	par
parent	carry	narrate	bar
parallel	carriage	guarantee	mar
paragraph	marriage	larynx	lar
para~	maritime	laryngitis	kar
parrot	barrier	necessary	war
apparent	baritone	itinerary	har
parish	Barron's	said	sar
Paris	library	says	nar
area	character	transparency	gar
aware	Karen	dictionary	rar
compare	Harry	many	
imaginary	Mary	any	

Exercise 6-5: R Combinations · CD 3 Track 47

Don't think about spelling here. Just pronounce each column of words as the heading indicates.

	ər	är	ɛr	or	eer	æwr
1.	earn	art	air	or	ear	hour
2.	hurt	heart	hair	horse	here	how're
3.	heard	hard	haired	horde	here's	
4.	pert	part	pair	pour	peer	power
5.	word		where	war	we're	
6.	a word		aware	award	a weird	
7.	work		wear	warm	weird	
8.	first	far	fair	four	fear	flower
9.	firm	farm	fairy	form	fierce	
10.	rather	cathartic	there	Thor	theory	11th hour
11.	murky	mar	mare	more	mere	
12.	spur	spar	spare	sport	spear	
13.	sure	sharp	share	shore	shear	shower
14.	churn	char	chair	chore	cheer	chowder

15. gird	guard	scared	gored	geared	Gower
16. cur	car	care	core	kir	cower
17. turtle	tar	tear	tore	tear	tower
18. dirt	dark	dare	door	dear	dour
19. stir	star	stair	store	steer	▓
20. sir	sorry	Sarah	sore	seer	sour
21. burn	barn	bear	born	beer	bower

Exercise 6-6: The Mirror Store   CD 3 Track 48

Repeat after me.

The Hurly Burly Mirror Store at Vermont and Beverly featured hundreds of first-rate mirrors. There were several mirrors on the chest of drawers, and the largest one was turned toward the door in order to make the room look bigger. One of the girls who worked there was concerned that a bird might get hurt by hurtling into its own reflection. She learned by trial and error how to preserve both the mirrors and the birds. Her earnings were proportionately increased at the mirror store to reflect her contribution to the greater good.

✖ Pause the CD to practice reading out loud three times on your own.

Exercise 6-7: Finding the R Sound   CD 3_ Track 49

Pause the CD and go through our familiar paragraph and find all the R sounds. The first one is marked for you.

Hello, my name is _____. I'm taking American **Accent** Training. There's a **lot** to learn, but I **hope** to make it as **enjoyable** as possible. I should pick **up** on the American **intonation** pattern pretty **easily**, although the **only** way to **get** it is to **practice** all of the time. I use the **up** and down, or **peaks** and valleys, **intonation** more than I **used** to. I've been paying attention to **pitch**, **too**. It's like **walking** down a **stair**case. I've been **talking** to a lot of **Americans** lately, and they tell me that I'm **easier** to under**stand**. **Any**way, I could go **on** and on, but the **important** thing is to **listen** well and sound **good**. **Well**, what do you **think**? **Do** I?

▼ Check your answers with the Answer Key, beginning on page 193.

Telephone Tutoring

Follow-up Diagnostic Analysis

CD 3 Track 50

After three to six months, you're ready for the follow-up analysis. If you're studying on your own, please contact toll-free **(800) 457-4255** or **www.americanaccent.com** for a referral to a qualified telephone analyst. The diagnostic analysis is designed to evaluate your current speech patterns to let you know where your accent is standard and nonstandard.

Think the United Auto Workers can beat Caterpillar Inc. in their bitter contract battle? Before placing your bets, talk to Paul Branan, who can't wait to cross the picket line at Caterpillar's factory in East Peoria. Branan, recently laid off by a rubber-parts plant where he earned base pay of $6.30 an hour, lives one block from a heavily picketed gate at the Cat complex. Now he's applying to replace one of 12,600 workers who have been on strike for the past five months. "Seventeen dollars an hour and they don't want to work?" asks Branan. "I don't want to take another guy's job, but I'm hurting, too."

1. saw, lost, cough
2. can, Dan, last
3. same, say, rail
4. yet, says, Paris
5. shine, time, my
6. sit, silk, been
7. seat, see, bean
8. word, girl, first
9. some, dull, possible
10. tooth, two, blue
11. look, bull, should
12. don't, so, whole
13. how, down, around
14. appoint, avoid, boil

A
1. parry
2. ferry
3. stew
4. sheet
5. two
6. choke
7. think
8. come
9. yes
10. wool
11. his
12. late
13. glow

B
1. bury
2. very
3. zoo
4. girl
5. do
6. joke
7. that
8. gum
9. rate
10. grow
11. me
12. next

C
1. apple
2. afraid
3. races
4. pressure
5. petal
6. gaucho
7. ether
8. bicker
9. accent
10. player
11. shower
12. ahead
13. collect
14. Kelly

D
1. able
2. avoid
3. raises
4. pleasure
5. pedal
6. gouger
7. either
8. bigger
9. exit
10. correct
11. carry
12. swimmer
13. connect
14. finger

E
1. mop
2. off
3. face
4. crush
5. not
6. rich
7. tooth
8. pick
9. tax
10. day
11. now
12. towel
13. needle

F
1. mob
2. of
3. phase
4. garage
5. nod
6. ridge
7. smooth
8. pig
9. tags
10. tower
11. neater
12. same
13. man
14. ring

1. Who opened it?
2. We opened it.
3. Put it away.
4. Bob ate an orange.
5. Can it be done?

1. Who(w)oup'n dit?
2. We(y)oup'n dit.
3. Pü di də way.
4. Bä bei d' nornj.
5. C'n't be dən?

1. Write a letter to Betty.

2. Ride a ledder d' Beddy.

3. tatter — tattoo
4. platter — platoon
5. pattern — perturb
6. critic — critique

7. bet — bed

Chapters 1-6

Review and Expansion

In the first six chapters of the American Accent Training program, we covered the concepts that form the basis of American speech—intonation, word groups, the staircase, and liaisons, or word connections. We also discussed some key sounds, such as [æ], [ä], and [ə] (Cat? Caught? Cut?), the El, the American T, and the American R. Let's briefly review each item.

Intonation

You've learned some of the reasons for changing the pitch (or saying a word louder or even streeetching it out) of some words in a sentence.

1. To introduce new information (nouns)
2. To offer an opinion
3. To contrast two or more elements
4. To indicate the use of the negative contraction *can't*

For example:

New information
He bought a **car**.

Opinion
It **feels** like mink, but I think it's **rabbit**.

Contrast
Timing is more important than **technique**.

Can't
He **can't do** it.

You've also learned how to change meaning by shifting intonation, without changing any of the actual words in a sentence.

I applied for the job (not **you**!).
I **applied** for the job (but I don't think I'll **get** it).
I applied **for** the job (not I applied myself **to** the job).
I applied for **the** job (the **one** I've been dreaming about for **years**!)
I applied for the **job** (not the **life**style!).

Miscellaneous Reminders of Intonation

When you have a verb/preposition combination, the stress usually goes on the preposition: *pick **up**, put **down**, fall **in***, and so on. Otherwise, prepositions are placed in the valleys of your intonation. *It's f'r **you**., They're fr'm **LA***.

When you have initials, the stress goes on the last letter: IB**M**, PO **Box**, ASA**P**, IO**U**, and so on.

Liaisons and Glides

Through liaisons, you learned about *voiced* and *unvoiced consonants*—where they are located in the mouth and which sounds are likely to attach to a following one. You were also introduced to glides.

1.	**Consonant and Vowel**	*Put it on.*	[Pu•di•dan.]
2.	**Consonant and Consonant**	*race track*	[ray•stræk]
3.	**Vowel and Vowel**	*No other*	[No⁽ʷ⁾other]
4.	**T and Y**	*Put you on*	[Puchü⁽ʷ⁾än]
	D and Y	***Had** you?*	[Hæjoo?]
	S and Y	***Yes**, you do.*	[Yeshu do.]
	Z and Y	*Is your **cat**?*	[Izher cat?]

Cat? Caught? Cut?

This lesson was an introduction to pronunciation, especially those highly characteristic sounds, [æ], [ä] and [ə].

[æ] The jaw moves down and back while the back of the tongue pushes forward and the tip touches the back of the bottom teeth. Sometimes it almost sounds like there's a Y in there: *cat* [kyæt]

[a] Relax the tongue, open the throat like you're letting the doctor see all the way to your toes: *aah.*

[ə] This sound is the sound that would come out if you were pushed (lightly) in the stomach: *uh.* You don't need to put your mouth in any particular position at all. The sound is created when the air is forced out of the diaphragm and past the vocal cords.

The American T

T is T, a clear popped sound, when it is at the **top** of the staircase.
- at the the beginning of a word, *table*
- in a stressed syllable, *intend*
- in ST, TS, TR, CT clusters, *instruct*
- replaces D after unvoiced consonants, *hoped* [hopt]

T is D, a softer sound, when it is in the **middle** of the staircase
- in an unstressed position between vowels, *cattle* [caddle]

T or TT, and D or DD are held, (*not* pronounced with a sharp burst of air) when they are at the **bottom** of the staircase.
- at the end of a word, *bought* [bä⁽ᵗ⁾]

T is held before N.
* unstressed and followed by *-ten* or *-tain, written* [wri(tt)en]

T is held before N.
* swallowed by N, *interview* [innerview]

The El

The El is closely connected with the schwa. Your tongue drops down in back as if it were going to say *uh*, but the tip curls up and attaches to the top of the mouth, which requires a strong movement of the tip of the tongue. The air comes out around the sides of the tongue and the sound is held for slightly longer than you'd think.

The American R

The main difference between a consonant and a vowel is that with a consonant there is contact at some point in your mouth. It might be the lips, P; the tongue tip, N; or the throat, G. Like a vowel, however, the R doesn't touch anywhere. It is similar to a schwa, but your tongue curls back in a retroflex movement and produces a sound deep in the throat. *The tongue doesn't touch the top of the mouth.* Another way to approach it is to put your tongue in position for *ee*, and then slide straight back to *eeer*. Some people are more comfortable collapsing their tongue back, like an accordion instead of curling it. It doesn't make any difference in the sound, so do whichever you prefer.

Application Exercises

Now you need to use the techniques you've learned so far and to make the transference to your everyday speech. In the beginning, the process is very slow and analytical, but as you do it over and over again, it becomes natural and unconscious. The exercises presented here will show you how. For example, take any phrase that may catch your ear during a conversation—because it is unfamiliar, or for whatever other reason—and work it though the practice sequence used in Review Exercise 1.

Review Exercise 1: To have a friend, be a friend.   CD 3 Track 51

Take the repeated phrase in the following application steps. Apply each concept indicated there, one at a time and in the sequence given. Read the sentence out loud two or three times, concentrating only on the one concept. This means that when you are working on liaisons, for instance, you don't have to pay much attention to intonation, just for that short time. First, read the phrase with no preparation and record yourself doing it.

To have a friend, be a friend.

Review Exercise 2: To have a friend, be a friend.   CD 3 Track 52

Pause the CD and go through each step using the following explanation as a guide.

1. Intonation

You want to figure out where the intonation belongs when you first encounter a phrase. In this example friend is repeated, so a good reason for intonation would be the contrast that lies in the verbs *have* and *be*:

To **have** a friend, **be** a friend.

2. Word groups

The pause in this case is easy because it's a short sentence with a comma, so we put one there. With your own phrases, look for a logical break, or other hints, as when you have the verb *to be*, you usually pause very slightly just before it, because it means that you're introducing a definition:

A ^(pause) is **B**.
Cows ^(pause) are **ruminants**.
To **have** a friend, ^(pause) be a **friend**.

3. Liaisons

Figure out which words you want to run together. Look for words that start with vowels and connect them to the previous word:

To hava friend, be⁽ʸ⁾a friend.

4. æ, ä, ə

Label these common sounds in the sentence:

Tə hævə friend, be ə friend.

5. The American T

Work with it, making it into a D or CH, holding it back or getting rid of it altogether, as appropriate. In this phrase, there are no Ts, but the D is held:

To have a frien⁽ᵈ⁾, be a frien⁽ᵈ⁾.

6. The American R

Mark all the Rs.

To have a f<u>r</u>iend, be a f<u>r</u>iend.

7. Combination of concepts 1-6

Tə **hæ**və frɛn⁽ᵈ⁾, ^(pause) **be**⁽ʸ⁾ə frɛnd⁽ᵈ⁾.

▼ Practice the sequence of steps a couple of times and then record yourself again; place your second recording right after the first one on your tape. Play them both back and see if you hear a strong difference.

Review Exercise 3: Get a Better Water Heater! CD 3 Track 53

Pause the CD and go through the same steps with "Get a better water heater!"

1. Intonation   **Get** a better **water** heater!
2. Word groups   Get a better water heater! (pause)
3. Liaisons   Geta better water heater!
4. [æ], [a], [ə]   Getə better wäter heater!
5. The American T   Ged a bedder wadder heeder!
6. The American R   Get a bette_r_ wate_r_ heate_r_!
7. Combination of Concepts 1-6   **G**ɛdə bɛddr **w**ädr heedr!

Review Exercise 4: Your Own Sentence CD 3 Track 54

Pause the CD and apply the steps to your own sentences.

1. Intonation _____
2. Word groups _____
3. Liaisons _____
4. [æ], [a], [ə] _____
5. The American T _____
6. The American R _____
7. Combination of Concepts 1-6 _____

Are you shy? Does doing this embarrass you? Are you thinking that people will notice your new accent and criticize you for it? In the beginning, you may feel a little strange with these new sounds that you are using, but don't worry, it's like a new pair of shoes—they take a while to break in and make comfortable. Nevertheless, I hope that you are enjoying this program. Adopting a new accent can become too personal and too emotional an issue, so don't take it too seriously. Relax. Have a good time. Play with the sounds that you are making. Whenever a word or phrase strikes your fancy, go somewhere private and comfortable and try out a couple of different approaches, styles, and attitudes with it—as you are going to do in the next exercise. If possible, record yourself on tape so you can decide which one suits you best.

Review Exercise 5: Varying Emotions CD 3 Track 55

Repeat the following statement and response expressing the various feelings or tone indicated in parentheses.

anger	I told you it wouldn't work!!	I thought it would!
excitement	I told you it wouldn't work!!	I thought it would!
disbelief	I told you it wouldn't work?	And I thought it would?
smugness	I told you it wouldn't work.	I thought it would. *(I-told-you-so attitude)*

Review Exercise 5: Varying Emotions *continued*   CD 3 Track 55

humor   I told you it wouldn't work.   I thought it would
sadness   I told you it wouldn't work.   I thought it would.
relief   I told you it wouldn't work.   Whew! I thought it would.
resignation I told you it wouldn't work.   I thought it would.

✖ Pause the CD and repeat the statement using three other tones that you'd like to try.

your choice I told you it wouldn't work!!   I thought it would!
your choice I told you it wouldn't work!!   I thought it would!
your choice I told you it wouldn't work!!   I thought it would!

Now that you've run through a couple of emotions and practiced speaking with both meaning and feeling, try having some two-word conversations. These are pretty common in day-to-day situations.

Review Exercise 6: Really? Maybe!   CD 3 Track 56

Repeat the following statements and responses expressing the various feelings.

1. Really? (general curiosity)   Maybe. (general potential)
2. Really? (avid curiosity)   Maybe. (suggestive possibility)
3. Really? (boredom)   Maybe (equal boredom)
4. Really? (laughing with disbelief)   Maybe. (slight possibility)
5. Really? (sarcasm)   Maybe. (self justification)
6. Really? (sadness)   Maybe. (equal sadness)
7. Really? (relief)   Maybe. (hope)
8. Really? (coy interrogation)   Maybe. (coy confirmation)
9. Really? (seeking confirmation)   Rilly!   (confirmation)

✖ Pause the CD and try three on your own.

10. Really? (your choice)   Maybe. (your choice)
11. Really? (your choice)   Maybe. (your choice)
12. Really? (your choice)   Maybe. (your choice)

Review Exercise 7: Who Did It? I Don't Know!   CD 3 Track 57

Repeat the following statements and responses expressing the various feelings.

1. Who did it? (curiosity)   I don't know. (ignorance)
2. Who did it? (interrogation)   I don't know. (self-protection)
3. Who did it? (anger)   I don't know. (insistence)

Review Exercise 7: Who Did It? I Don't Know! *continued* — CD 3 Track 57

4.	Who did it? (repeating)	I don't know. (strong denial)
5.	Who did it? (sarcasm)	I don't know. (self-justification)
6.	Who did it? (sadness)	I don't know. (despair)
7.	Who did it? (relief)	I sure don't know. (blithe ignorance)
8.	Whooo did it? (coy interrogation)	I don't know. (sing-song)
9.	Who did it? (annoyance)	I don't know. (equal annoyance)
10.	Who did it? (laughing with disbelief)	I don't know. (laughing ignorance)
11.	Who did it? (surprise)	I dunno. (sullenness)
12.	Who did it? (your choice)	I don't know. (your choice)

Review Exercise 8: Russian Rebellion — CD 3 Track 58

Rəshəz əfensəv əgenst rebəlz in thə breikəway reejənəv Chechnyə iz entering ə nyu feiz. än thə wən hænd, Rəshən forsəzr teiking fül kəntrol əv thə Rəshən kæpədəl Gräzny, ənd Mäskæo sez thə wor seemz tə be trning in its feivr. än thee əthr hænd, thə rebəlz küd be reetreeding Gräzny jəst tə fight ənəthr day—enshring ə läng grrilə wor. Thə for-mənth känflikt täpt thee əjendə tədəy during Sekrətery əv State Mædəlin älbräit's täks with ækting Rəshən prezəd'nt Vlædəmir Putin. älbräit then left fr Kro⁽ʷ⁾eishə, əbæot which will hear more shortly. Bət frst, we trn tə thə Wrldz Nenet Shevek in Mäskæo.

olbräit en Pu-tin met feu lɔnger thən plennd tədəy—feu nillee three äwez. äftə theə tɔks, olbrait kɔld the meeting intens, bət pleznt, en ɔfeud this esesmɛnt ef Rəshəz ekting prezidɛnt.

I fæond him ə very well informd persən. Heez äveeəslee ə Rəshən paytreeət ən älso səmwən who seeks a norməl pəzishən fr Rəshə within thə West—ən he strɔck me əzə präbləm sälvr

~ ❖ ~

Russia's offensive against rebels in the breakaway region of Chechnya is entering a new phase. On the one hand, Russian forces are taking full control of the Russian capital Grozny, and Moscow says the war seems to be turning in its favor. On the other hand the rebels could be retreating Grozny just to fight another day—ensuring a long guerilla war. The four-month conflict topped the agenda today during Secretary of State Madeline Albright's talks with acting Russian president Vladimir Putin. Albright then left for Croatia, about which we'll hear more shortly. But first, we turn to the World's Nennet Shevek in Moscow.

"Albright and Putin met for longer than planned today—for nearly three hours. After the talks, Albright called the meeting intense, but pleasant, and offered this assessment of Russia's acting president."

"I found him a very well informed person. He's obviously a Russian patriot and also someone who seeks a normal position for Russia within the West—and he struck me as a problem solver."

Two-Word Phrases

Review Exercise A: Contrasting Descriptive and Set Phrases CD 3 Track 59

*Here we are reprising the exercise from Exercises 1-24 to 1-37. To review, an adjective and a noun make a **descriptive phrase**, and the second word is stressed. Two nouns make a compound noun, or **set phrase**, and the first word is stressed. Repeat the following sentences. Copy your descriptive phrases and set phrases (Ex. 1-31). You will continue using these word combinations throughout this series of exercises.*

	Descriptive Phrase	Set Phrase
1.	It's a short **nail**.	It's a **finger**nail.
2.	It's a chocolate **cake**.	It's a **pan**cake.
3.	It's a hot **bath**.	It's a **hot** tub.
4.	It's a long **drive**. 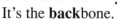	It's a **hard** drive.
5.	It's the back **door**.	It's the **back**bone.
6.	There are four **cards**.	It's a **card** trick.
7.	It's a small **spot**.	It's a **spot**light.
8.	It's a good **book**.	It's a **phone** book.
9.	It's a _____	It's a _____
10.	It's a _____	It's a _____
11.	It's a _____	It's a _____

Review Exercise B: Intonation Review Test CD 3 Track 60

Pause the CD and put an accent mark over the word that should be stressed. Check the Answer Key, beginning on page 193.

1. They live in <u>Los Angeles</u>.
2. Give me a <u>paper bag</u>.
3. Is that your <u>lunch bag</u>?
4. 7-11 is a <u>convenience store</u>.
5. Lucky's is a <u>convenient store</u>.
6. Do your <u>homework</u>!
7. He's a <u>good writer</u>.
8. It's an <u>apple pie</u>.
9. It's a <u>pineapple</u>.
10. We like <u>all things</u>.
11. We like <u>everything</u>.
12. It's a <u>moving van</u>.
13. It's a <u>new paper</u>.
14. It's the <u>newspaper</u>.
15. The doll has <u>glass eyes</u>.
16. The doll has <u>eyeglasses</u>.
17. It's a <u>high chair</u>.
18. It's a <u>highchair</u>. *(for babies)*
19. It's a <u>baseball</u>.
20. It's a <u>blue ball</u>.

Three-Word Phrases

Review Exercise C: Modifying Descriptive Phrases   CD 3 Track 61

*When you modify a **descriptive phrase** by adding an adjective or adverb, you maintain the original intonation pattern and simply add an additional stress point.*

Descriptive Phrase	**Modified Descriptive Phrase**
1. It's a short **nail**.	It's a **really** short **nail**.
2. It's a chocolate **cake**.	It's a **tasty** chocolate **cake**.
3. I took a hot **bath**.	I took a **long**, hot **bath**.
4. It's a hard **drive**.	It's a **long**, hard **drive**.
5. It's the back **door**.	It's the **only** back **door**.
6. There are four **cards**.	There are **four** slick **cards**.
7. It's a little **spot**.	It's a **little** black **spot**.
8. It's a good **book**.	It's a **really** good **book**.
9. It's a _____	It's a _____
10. It's a _____	It's a _____
11. It's a _____	It's a _____

Review Exercise D: Modifying Set Phrases   CD 3 Track 62

*When you modify a **set phrase**, you maintain the same pattern, leaving the new adjective unstressed.*

Set Phrase	**Modified Set Phrase**
1. It's a **finger**nail.	It's a short **finger**nail.
2. It's a **pan**cake.	It's a delicious **pan**cake.
3. It's a **hot** tub.	It's a leaky **hot** tub.
4. It's a **hard** drive.	It's an expensive **hard** drive.
5. It's the **back**bone.	It's a long **back**bone.
6. It's a **card** trick.	It's a clever **card** trick.
7. It's a **spot**light.	It's a bright **spot**light.
8. It's a **phone** book.	It's the new **phone** book.
9. It's a _____	It's a _____
10. It's a _____	It's a _____
11. It's a _____	It's a _____

Review Exercise E: Two- and Three-Word Set Phrases CD 3 Track 63

*You should be pretty familiar with the idea of a set phrase by now. The next step is when you have more components that link together to form a new thing—a three-word set phrase. Combine **three things**: finger + nail + clipper. Leave the stress on the first word:* **finger**nail clipper. *Although you are now using three words, they still mean **one new thing**. Write your own sentences, using the word combinations from the previous exercises.*

Two-Word Set Phrase	Three-Word Set Phrase
1. It's a **finger**nail.	It's a **finger**nail clipper.
2. It's a **pan**cake.	It's a **pan**cake shop.
3. It's a **hot** tub.	It's a **hot** tub maker.
4. It's a **hard** drive.	It's a **hard** drive holder.
5. It's the **back**bone.	It's a **back**bone massage.
6. It's a **playing** card.	It's a **playing** card rack.
7. It's a **spot**light.	It's a **spot**light stand.
8. It's a **phone** book.	It's a **phone** book listing.
9. It's a _____	It's a _____
10. It's a _____	It's a _____
11. It's a _____	It's a _____

Review Exercise F: Three-Word Phrase Summary CD 3 Track 64

Repeat the following sentences. Write your own sentences at the bottom, carrying over the same examples you used in the previous exercise.

Modified Description	Modified Set Phrase	3-Word Set Phrase
1. a **really** short **nail**	a long **finger**nail	a **finger**nail clipper
2. a **big** chocolate **cake**	a thin **pan**cake	a **pan**cake shop
3. a **long**, hot **bath**	a leaky **hot** tub	a **hot** tub maker
4. a **long**, boring **drive**	a new **hard** drive	a **hard** drive holder
5. a **broken** back **door**	a long **back**bone	a **back**bone massage
6. **four** slick **cards**	a new **playing** card	a **playing** card rack
7. a **small** black **spot**	a bright **spot**light	a **spot**light stand
8. a **well**-written **book**	an open **phone** book	a **phone** book listing
9.	a blind **sales**man	a **blind** salesman
	(He can't see.)	*(He sells blinds.)*
10.	a light **house**keeper	a **light**house keeper
	(She cleans the house.)	*(She lives in a lighthouse.)*
11.	a green **house**plant	a **green**house plant
	(It's a healthy houseplant.)	*(It's from a greenhouse.)*

12. It's a _____ . It's a _____ . It's a _____ .
13. It's a _____ . It's a _____ . It's a _____ .
14. It's a _____ . It's a _____ . It's a _____ .

Review Exercise G: Three-Word Phrase Story—Three Little Pigs   CD 4 Track 1

*Notice where there are patterns, where the words change, but the rhythm stays the same (**straw**-cutting tools, **wood**cutting tools, **brick**laying tools). Read the story aloud.*

Once upon a time, there were ***three little pigs***. They lived with their ***kind** old **mother*** near a ***large**, dark **forest***. One day, they decided to build ***their** own **houses***. The ***first** little pig* used straw. He took his ***straw**-cutting tools* and his *new **lawnmower***, and built a ***little** straw **house***. The ***second** little pig* used sticks. He took his ***wood**cutting tools* and some *old **paintbrushes*** and built a *small **wooden** house*. The ***third** little pig*, who was a ***very hard** worker*, used bricks. He took his ***brick**laying tools*, an *expensive **mortarboard***, and built a *large **brick** house*. In the forest, lived a ***big bad wolf***. He wanted to eat the ***three little pigs***, so he went to the ***flimsy** straw **abode*** and tried to blow it down. "Not by the hair of my ***chinny** chin **chin***!" cried the ***three little porkers***. But the house was ***not very strong***, and the ***big bad beast*** blew it down. The ***three little pigs*** ran to the *rickety **wooden** structure*, but the ***big bad wolf*** blew **it** down, **too**. Quickly, the ***three little piggies*** ran to the *sturdy **brick** dwelling* and hid inside. The ***big bad wolf*** huffed and he puffed, but he couldn't blow the *strong **brick** house* down. The ***three little pigs*** laughed and danced and sang.

Review Exercise H: Sentence Balance—Goldilocks   CD 4 Track 2

*One of the most fascinating things about spoken English is how the intonation prepares the listener for what is coming. As you know, the main job of intonation is to announce new information. However, there is a secondary function, and that is to alert the listener of changes down the road. Certain shifts will be dictated for the sake of **sentence balance**. Set phrases and contrast don't change, but the intonation of a **descriptive phras**e will move from the second word to the first, **without changing the meaning**. The stress change indicates that it's not the end of the sentence, but rather, there is more to come. This is why it is particularly important to speak in phrases, instead of word by word.*

*When we practiced **Gold**ilocks and the Three **Bears** the first time, on page 34, we had very short sentences so we didn't need sentence balance. All of the underlined descriptive phrases would otherwise be stressed on the second word, if the shift weren't needed.*

There is a <u>***little girl***</u> called ***Gold**ilocks*. She is <u>***walking** through*</u> a *sunny **forest*** and sees a *small **house***. She ***knocks*** on the door, but ***no** one* answers. She <u>***goes** inside*</u> to see what's **there**. There are <u>***three** chairs*</u> in the *large **room***. ***Gold**ilocks* sits on the ***biggest** chair*. It's <u>***too** high*</u> for her to ***sit** on*. She sits on the ***middle**-sized* one, but it's is *too **low***. She sits on the *small **chair*** and it is *just **right***. On the table, there are <u>***three** bowls*</u> of **porridge**. She tries the ***first** one*, but it is <u>***too hot***</u> to **swallow**. The ***second** one* is *too **cold***, and the ***third** one* is *just **right***, so she eats it all. ***After** that*, she <u>***goes** upstairs*</u> to *look **around***. There are <u>***three** beds*</u> in

111

the **bed**room. She _sits down_ on the **biggest** one. It's _too hard_ to **sleep** on. The **middle**-sized bed is _too soft_. The **little** one is _just right_, so she _lies down_ and _falls_ **asleep**.

In the **mean**time, the family of _three bears_ comes home — the **Papa** bear, the **Mama** bear, and the **Baby** bear. They **look** around and **say**, "Who's been sitting in our chairs and eating our porridge?" Then they **run** upstairs and **say**, "Who's been sleeping in our beds?" _Goldilocks_ __wakes up__ when she hears all the noise and is __so scared__ that she __runs out__ of the house and never _comes_ **back**.

Four-Word Phrases

When you continue to modify a set phrase, you maintain the original intonation pattern and simply add an additional stress point.

	Modified Set Phrase	**Remodified Set Phrase**
1.	It's a short **finger**nail.	It's a **really** short **finger**nail.
2.	It's a banana **pan**cake.	It's a **tasty** banana **pan**cake.
3.	It's a leaky **hot** tub.	It's a **leaky** old **hot** tub.
4.	It's a new **hard** drive.	It's a **brand** new **hard** drive.
5.	It's a long **back**bone.	It's a **long**, hard **back**bone.
6.	It's a wrinkled **playing** card.	It's a **wrinkled**, old **playing** card.
7.	It's a bright **spot**light.	It's a **bright** white **spot**light.
8.	It's the new **phone** book.	It's a **new** age **phone** book.
9.	It's a _____	It's a _____
10.	It's a _____	It's a _____
11.	It's a _____	It's a _____

In short phrases (#1 and #2), ~teen can be thought of as a separate word in terms of intonation. In longer phrases, the number + ~teen becomes one word. Repeat after me.

1. How **old** is he?
   He's four**teen**. [for**téen**]
   He's **for**ty. [fórdy]

2. How long has it **been**?
   Fourteen **years**.
   Forty **years**.

3. How **old** is he?
   He's **four**teen years **old**.
   He's **for**ty years **old**.

Review Exercise K: Modifying Three-Word Set Phrases   CD 4 Track 5

When you continue to modify a set phrase, you maintain the original intonation pattern and simply add an unstressed modifier.

Three-Word Set Phrase	**Modified Three-Word Set Phrase**
1. It's a **finger**nail clipper.	It's a new **finger**nail clipper.
2. It's a **pan**cake shop.	It's a good **pan**cake shop.
3. He's a **hot** tub maker.	He's the best **hot** tub maker.
4. It's a **hard** drive holder.	It's a plastic **hard** drive holder.
5. It's a **back**bone massage.	It's a painful **back**bone massage.
6. It's a **playing** card rack.	It's my best **playing** card rack.
7. It's a **spot**light bulb.	It's a fragile **spot**light bulb.
8. It's a **phone** book listing.	It's an unusual **phone** book listing.
9. It's a _____.	It's a _____.
10. It's a _____.	It's a _____.
11. It's a _____.	It's a _____.

Review Exercise L: Four-Word Phrase Story—Little Red Riding Hood

CD 4 Track 6

Repeat after me.

Once upon a time, there was a ***cute* *little* *redhead*** named ***Little* Red *Riding* Hood**. One day, she told her mother that she wanted to take a ***well-*stocked *picnic* basket** to her ***dear* old grandmother** on the other side of the ***dark, scary* Black *Forest***. Her mother warned her not to talk to strangers — especially the *dangerous **big** bad **wolf***. *Little* Red **Riding** Hood said she would be careful, and left. Halfway there, she saw a ***mild*-mannered *hitch*hiker**. She pulled over in her ***bright* red *sports* car** and offered him a ride. Just before they got to the ***freeway* turn*off*** for her *old **grandmother**'s house*, the ***heavily* bearded *young* man** jumped out and ran away. (Was he the wolf?) He hurried ahead to the *waiting **grandmother**'s house*, let himself in, ate her, and jumped into her bed to wait for ***Little* Red *Riding* Hood**. When ***Little* Red *Riding* Hood** got to the house, she was surprised, "Grandmother, what big *eyes* you have!" The wolf replied, "The better to *see* you with, my dear…" "But Grandmother, what big *ears* you have!" "The better to *hear* you with, my dear…" "Oh, Grandmother, what big *teeth* you have!" "The better to *eat* you with!" And the wolf jumped out of the bed to eat ***Little* Red *Riding* Hood**. Fortunately for her, she was a ***recently* paid-up *member*** of the ***infamous* National *Rifle* Association** so she pulled out her ***brand* new *shot*gun** and shot the wolf dead.

Review Exercise M: Building Up to Five-Word Phrases
CD 4 Track 7

Repeat after me, then pause the CD and write your own phrases, using the same order and form.

1. It's a **pot**. — *noun*
2. It's **new**. — *adjective*
3. It's a new **pot**. — *descriptive phrase (noun)*
4. It's brand **new**. — *descriptive phrase (adjective)*
5. It's a **brand** new **pot**. — *modified descriptive phrase*
6. It's a **tea**pot. — *two-word set phrase*
7. It's a new **tea**pot. — *modified set phrase*
8. It's a **brand** new **tea**pot. — *modified set phrase*
9. It's a **tea**pot lid. — *three-word set phrase*
10. It's a new **tea**pot lid. — *modified three-word set phrase*
11. It's a **brand** new **tea**pot lid. — *modified three-word set phrase*

1. _____ — *noun*
2. _____ — *adjective*
3. _____ — *descriptive phrase (noun)*
4. _____ — *descriptive phrase (adjective)*
5. _____ — *modified descriptive phrase*
6. _____ — *two-word set phrase*
7. _____ — *modified set phrase*
8. _____ — *modified set phrase*
9. _____ — *three-word set phrase*
10. _____ — *modified three-word set phrase*
11. _____ — *modified three-word set phrase*

1. _____
2. _____
3. _____
4. _____
5. _____
6. _____
7. _____
8. _____
9. _____
10. _____
11. _____

1. _____
2. _____
3. _____
4. _____
5. _____
6. _____
7. _____
8. _____
9. _____
10. _____
11. _____

Review Exercise 9: Ignorance on Parade CD 4 Track 8

*Now, let's dissect a standard paragraph, including its title, as we did in Review Exercise 1. **First**—in the boxes in the first paragraph, decide which is a descriptive phrase, which is a set phrase, and where any additional stress might fall. Remember, descriptive phrases are stressed on the second word and set phrases on the first. Use one of your colored markers to indicate the stressed words. **Second**—go through the paragraph and mark the remaining stressed words. **Third**—put slash marks where you think a short pause is appropriate. Listen as I read the paragraph.*

✖ Pause the CD and do the written exercises including intonation, word groups, liaisons, [æ], [ä], [ə], and the American T.

1. Two-word phrases, intonation and phrasing
Ignorance on Parade

You say you don't know a proton from a crouton? Well, you're not the only one. A recent nationwide survey funded by the National Science Foundation shows that fewer than 6 percent of American adults can be called scientifically literate. The rest think that DNA is a food additive, Chernobyl is a ski resort, and radioactive milk can be made safe by boiling.* *Judith Stone / 1989 Discover Publications*

2. Word Connections
Ignoran sän Parade

You say you don't know a proton from a crouton? Well, you're not the only one. A recent nationwide survey funded by the National Science Foundation shows that fewer than 6 percent of American adults can be called scientifically literate. The rest think that DNA is a food additive, Chernobyl is a ski resort, and radioactive milk can be made safe by boiling.

3. [æ], [ä], [ə]
Ignərənce än Pərade

You say you don't know a proton from a crouton? Well, you're not the only one. A recent nationwide survey funded by the National Science Foundation shows that fewer than 6 percent of American adults can be called scientifically literate. The rest think that DNA is a food additive, Chernobyl is a ski resort, and radioactive milk can be made safe by boiling.

4. The American T
Ignoran͟ts on Para͟de

You say you don't know a proton from a crouton? Well, you're not the only one. A recent nationwide survey funded by the National Science Foundation shows that fewer than 6 percent of American adults can be called scientifically literate. The rest think that DNA is a food additive, Chernobyl is a ski resort, and radioactive milk can be made safe by boiling.

Review Exercise 10: Ignorance on Parade Explanations   CD 4 Track 9

Here, go over each topic, point by point.

1. Two-word phrases, intonation and phrasing

a **proton** from a **crouton**? (*contrast*)

Well, **you're** not the **only** one. (*contrast*)

A **recent** nationwide **survey** (*modified descriptive phrase*)

National **Science** Foundation (*modified set phrase*)

6 percent of American **adults** (*descriptive phrase with sentence balance*)

scientifically **literate** (*descriptive phrase*)

The **rest** think (*contrast*)

DNA (*acronym*)

food additive (*set phrase*)

ski resort (*set phrase*)

radioactive **milk** (*descriptive phrase*)

Ignorance on Par**a**de (stop)

You say you don't know a **pro**ton from a **crou**ton? (pause) Well, (pause) **you're** not the **only** one. (pause) A **recent** nationwide **survey** (pause) funded by the National **Science** Foundation (pause) shows that fewer than **6** percent of American **adults** (pause) can be called scientifically **literate**.(stop) The **rest** think (pause) that DNA is a **food** additive, (pause) Chernobyl is a **ski** resort, (pause) and radioactive **milk** (pause) can be made **safe** by boil-ing.

2. Word Connections

Ignoran sän Parade

You sa(y)you don(t)knowa **pro**ton froma **crou**ton? **Well**, you're no(t)the(y)**only** one. A **recen**(t)nationwide**sur**vey funded by the National**Sci**(y)ence Foundation showzthat fewer than**six** percen'v'merica na**dults** can be called**sci**entifically **lit**erate. The **res**sthink that Dee(y)εNA(y)iza **foo** daddditive, Chern**o**byliza **ski** resort, and radi(y)o(w)active **milk** can be made**safe** by **boi**ling.

3. [æ], [ä], [ə]

Ignərəncə än Pərade

You say you dont know ə **pro**tän frəm ə **croo**tän? Well, yer nät thee(y)**only** wən. ə **res**ənt nashənwide **srv**ey fəndəd by thə **Næ**shənəl **Sci**(y)əns **Fæ**ondashən showz thət fewər thən **6** prcen əv əmerəcən ə**dəlts** cən be cälld sci(y)əntifəklee **lid**erət. Thə **rest** think thət Dee Yeh **Nay**(y)izə **food** æddətv, **Chr**nobl izə **skee** rəzort, ən radee(y)o(w)æctəv **milk** cən be made **safe** by **boi**ling.

Review Exercise 10: Ignorance on Parade Explanations *continued*   **CD 4 Track 9**

4. The American T

Ignorants on Parade

You say you don[(t)] know a **pro**Ton from a **crou**Ton? Well, you're nä[(t)] the **only** one. A **recen**[(t)] nationwide **sur**vey funded by the National **Sci**ence Foundation shows tha[(t)] fewer than **6** percen of American a**dulT**s can be called scienTifically **lid**erə[(t)]. The **ress** think tha[(t)] DNA is a **food** addidive, Chernobyl is a **ski** resor[(t)], and radioakdiv **milk** can be made **safe** by **boi**ling.

5. Combined

Ignərən sän P**ə**rade

You sa[(y)]you don[(t)]no wə **prot**än frəmə **croo**tän?[(stop)]Well,[(pause)]yer nät thee[(y)]**only** wən.[(pause)]ə **ree**sən[(t)] nashənwide **srvey**[(pause)]fəndəd by thə Næshənəl **Sci**[(y)]əns Fæondashən[(pause)]shoz thə[(t)] fewər thən **6** prcenə vəmerəcə nə**dəlts**[(pause)]cən be cälld sci[(y)]əntifəklee **lid**erət.[(stop)]Thə **ress** think[(pause)]thə[(t)] Dee Yeh **Nay**[(y)]izə **foo** dæddətv,[(pause)]Chrnobə lizə **skee** rəzort,[(pause)]ən raydee[(y)]o[(w)]æctəv **milk**[(pause)]cən be made **safe** by **boi**ling.

Chapter 7

Tee Aitch

CD 4 Track 10

I'd like you to consider words as rocks for a moment. When a rock first rolls into the ocean, it is sharp and well defined. After tumbling about for a few millennia, it becomes round and smooth. A word goes through a similar process. When it first rolls into English, it may have a lot of sharp, well-defined vowels or consonants in it, but after rolling off of a few million tongues, it becomes round and smooth. This smoothing process occurs when a tense vowel becomes reduced and when an unvoiced consonant becomes voiced. The most common words are the smoothest, the most reduced, the most often voiced. There are several very common words that are all voiced: *this, that, the, those, them, they, their, there, then, than, though.* The strong words such as *thank, think,* or *thing,* as well as long or unusual words such as *thermometer* or *theologian,* stay unvoiced.

The sound of the TH combination seems to exist only in English, Greek, and Castillian Spanish. Just as with most of the other consonants, there are two types—*voiced* and *unvoiced.* The voiced TH is like a D, but instead of being in *back* of the teeth, it's $\frac{1}{4}$ inch lower and forward, *between* the teeth. The unvoiced TH is like an S between the teeth. Most people tend to replace the unvoiced TH with S or T and the voiced one with Z or D, so instead of *thing,* they say *sing,* or *ting,* and instead of *that,* they say *zat* or *dat.*

To pronounce TH correctly, think of a snake's tongue. You don't want to take a big relaxed tongue, throw it out of your mouth for a long distance and leave it out there for a long time. Make only a very quick, sharp little movement. Keep your tongue's tip very tense. It darts out between your teeth and snaps back very quickly—*thing, that, this.* The tongue's position for the unvoiced TH is similar to that of S, but for TH the tongue is extended through the teeth, instead of hissing behind the back of the teeth. The voiced TH is like a D except that the tongue is placed between the teeth, or even pressed behind the teeth. Now we're ready for some practice.

Exercise 7-1: The Throng of Thermometers   CD 4 Track 11

I'm going to read the following paragraph once straight through, so you can hear that no matter how fast I read it, all the THs are still there. It is a distinctive sound, but, when you repeat it, don't put too much effort into it. Listen to my reading.

<u>Th</u>e throng of <u>th</u>ermometers from **th**e Thuringian Thermometer Folks arrived on <u>Th</u>ursday. <u>Th</u>ere were a <u>th</u>ousand <u>th</u>irty-<u>th</u>ree <u>th</u>ick <u>th</u>ermometers, **th**ough, instead of a <u>th</u>ousand <u>th</u>irty-six <u>th</u>in <u>th</u>ermometers, which was <u>th</u>ree <u>th</u>ermometers fewer **th**an **th**e <u>th</u>ousand <u>th</u>irty-six we were expecting, not to mention **th**at **th**ey were <u>th</u>ick ones ra**th**er **th**an <u>th</u>in ones. We <u>th</u>oroughly <u>th</u>ought **th**at we had ordered a <u>th</u>ousand <u>th</u>irty-six, not a <u>th</u>ousand <u>th</u>irty-<u>th</u>ree, <u>th</u>ermometers, and asked **th**e Thuringian Thermometer Folks to reship **th**e <u>th</u>ermometers; <u>th</u>in, not <u>th</u>ick. **Th**ey apologized for sending only a <u>th</u>ousand <u>th</u>irty-<u>th</u>ree <u>th</u>ermometers ra**th**er **th**an a <u>th</u>ousand <u>th</u>irty-six and promised to replace **th**e <u>th</u>ick <u>th</u>ermometers wi**th** <u>th</u>in <u>th</u>ermometers.

th = voiced (17)   <u>th</u> = unvoiced (44)

Run Them All Together [runnemälld'gether]

As I was reading, I hope you heard that in a lot of places, the words ran together, such as in *rather than.* You don't have to go way out of your way to make a huge new sound, but rather create a smooth flowing from one TH to the next by leaving your tongue in an anticipatory position.

As mentioned before (see Liaisons, page 63), when a word ends in TH and the next word starts with a sound from behind the teeth, a combination or composite sound is formed, because you are anticipating the combination. For example: *with-lemon*; not *with lemon.*

Anticipating the Next Word

The anticipation of each following sound brings me to the subject that most students raise at some point—one that explains their resistance to wholly embracing liaisons and general fluency. People feel that because English is not their native tongue, they can't anticipate the next sound because they never know what the next word is going to be.

Accurate or not, for the sake of argument, let's say that you do construct sentences entirely word by word. This is where those pauses that we studied come in handy. During your pause, line up in your head all the words you want to use in order to communicate your thought, and then push them out in groups. If you find yourself slowing down and talking…word…by…word, back up and take a running leap at a whole string of words.

Now, take out your little mirror again. You need it for the last exercise in this chapter, which follows.

Exercise 7-2: Targeting The TH Sound — CD 4 Track 12

*In order to target the TH sound, **first**, hold a mirror in front of you and read our familiar paragraph silently, moving only your tongue. It should be visible in the mirror each time you come to a TH. **Second**, find all of the THs, both voiced and unvoiced. Remember, a voiced sound makes your throat vibrate, and you can feel that vibration by placing your fingers on your throat. There are ten voiced and two unvoiced THs here. You can mark them by underscoring the former and drawing a circle around the latter. Or, if you prefer, use two of your color markers. Pause the CD to mark the TH sounds. Don't forget to check your answers against the Answer Key, beginning on page 193.*

Hello, **my** name is _____. I'm taking American **Accent** Training. There's a **lot** to learn, but I **hope** to make it as **enjoyable** as possible. I should pick **up** on the American **intonation** pattern pretty **easily**, although the **only** way to **get** it is to **practice** all of the time. I use the **up** and down, or **peaks** and valleys, **intonation** more than I **used** to. I've been paying attention to **pitch, too**. It's like **walking** down a **stair**case. I've been **talking** to a lot of **Americans** lately, and they tell me that I'm **easier** to under**stand. Any**way, I could go **on** and on, but the **important** thing is to **listen** well and sound **good. Well**, what do you **think**? **Do** I?

Exercise 7-3: Tongue Twisters — CD 4 Track 13

Feeling confident? Good! Try the following tongue twisters and have some fun.

1. The sixth sick Sheik's sixth thick sheep.

2. This is a zither. Is this a zither?

3. I thought a **thought**. But the thought I **thought** wasn't the thought I **thought** I thought. If the thought I **thought** I thought had been the thought I **thought**, I wouldn't have **thought** so much.

Chapter 8

More Reduced Sounds

CD 4 Track 14

There are two sounds that look similar, but sound quite different. One is the tense vowel [u], pronounced *ooh*, and the other is the soft vowel [ü], whose pronunciation is a combination of *ih* and *uh*. The [u] sound is located far forward in the mouth and requires you to round your lips. The [ü] is one of the four reduced vowel sounds that are made in the throat: The most tense, and highest in the throat is [ɛ], next, slightly more relaxed is [i], then [ü], and deepest and most relaxed is the neutral schwa [ə]. For the reduced semivowel *schwa + R*, the throat is relaxed, but the tongue is tense.

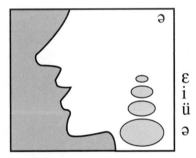

Exercise 8-1: Comparing [u] and [ü]

CD 4 Track 15

*Look at the chart that follows and repeat each word. We are contrasting the sound [u] (first column)—a strong, nonreducible sound, **ooh**, that is made far forward in the mouth, with the lips fully rounded—with the reduced [ü] sound in the second and fourth columns.*

	u	ü		u	ü
1.	booed	book	11.	Luke	look
2.	boo	bushel	12.	nuke	nook
3.	cooed	could	13.	pool	pull
4.	cool	cushion	14.	pooch	put
5.	food	foot	15.	shoe	sugar
6.	fool	full	16.	suit	soot
7.	gooed	good	17.	shoot	should
8.	who'd	hood	18.	stewed	stood
9.	kook	cook	19.	toucan	took
10.	crew	crook	20.	wooed	would

Exercise 8-2: Lax Vowels CD 4 Track 16

The lax vowels are produced in the throat and are actually quite similar to each other. Let's practice some lax vowels. See also Chapter 11 to contrast with tense vowels. Remember to double the vowel when the word ends in a voiced consonant.

	e	i	ü	ə	ər
1.	end	it		un~	earn
2.	bet	bit	book	but	burn
3.	kept	kid	could	cut	curt
4.	check	chick		chuck	church
5.	debt	did		does	dirt
6.	fence	fit	foot	fun	first
7.	fell	fill	full		furl
8.	get	guilt	good	gut	girl
9.	help	hit	hook	hut	hurt
10.	held	hill	hood	hull	hurl
11.	gel	Jill		jump	jerk
12.	ked	kill	cook	cud	curd
13.	crest	crypt	crook	crumb	
14.	let	little	look	lump	lurk
15.	men	milk		muck	murmur
16.	net	knit	nook	nut	nerd
17.	pet	pit	put	putt	pert
18.	pell	pill	pull		pearl
19.	red	rid	root	rut	rural
20.	said	sit	soot	such	search
21.	shed	shin	should	shut	sure
22.	sled	slim		slug	slur
23.	stead	still	stood	stuff	stir
24.	It's stewed.	It'd stick.	It stood.	It's done.	It's dirt.
25.	stretch	string		struck	
26.	tell	tip	took	ton	turn
27.	then	this		thus	
28.		thing		thug	third
29.	vex	vim		vug	verb
30.	wet	wind	would	was	word
31.	yet	yin		young	yearn
32.	zen	Zinfandel		result	deserve

Tense Vowels

Sound	Symbol	Spelling
ɛi	[bāt]	bait
ee	[bēt]	beat
äi	[bīt]	bite
ou	[bōᵘt]	boat
ooh	[būt]	boot
ah	[bät]	bought
ä+e	[bæt]	bat
æ+o	[bæot]	bout

Lax Vowels

Sound	Symbol	Spelling
eh	[bɛt]	bet
ih	[bit]	bit
ih+uh	[püt]	put
uh	[bət]	but
er	[bərt]	Bert

Exercise 8-3: Bit or Beat?   CD 4 Track 17

*We've discussed intonation in terms of new information, contrast, opinion, and negatives. As you heard on p. 3, Americans tend to stretch out certain one-syllable words ... but which ones? The answer is simple—when a single syllable word ends in an unvoiced consonant, the vowel is on a **single** stairstep—short and sharp. When the word ends in a voiced consonant, or a vowel, the vowel is on a **double** stairstep. (For an explanation of voiced and unvoiced consonants, see page 62.) You can also think of this in terms of musical notes.*

*Here you are going to compare the four words **bit**, **bid**, **beat**, and **bead**. Once you can distinguish these four, all of the rest are easy. Repeat.*

	single	double
tense	beat	bead
lax	bit	bid

Note *You may hear **tense vowels** called **long vowels**, but this can cause confusion when you are talking about the long, or doubled vowel before a voiced consonant. Use the rubber band to distinguish: Make a short, sharp snap for the single note words (beat, bit) and a longer, stretched out loop for the double note words (bead, bid).*

Exercise 8-4: Bit or Beat? Bid or Bead?   CD 4 Track 18

Read each column down. Next, contrast the single and double tense vowels with each other; and the single and double lax vowels with each other. Finally read all four across.

	Tense Vowels			Lax Vowels	
1.	beat	bead	•	bit	bid
2.	seat	seed		sit	Sid
3.	heat	he'd		hit	hid
4.	Pete	impede	•	pit	rapid
5.	feet	feed	•	fit	fin
6.	niece	knees		miss	Ms.
7.	geese	he's		hiss	his
8.	deep	deed	•	disk	did
9.	neat	need		knit	(nid)
10.	leaf	leave		lift	live

Note *Bear in mind that the single/double intonation pattern is the same for all final voiced and unvoiced consonants, not just T and D.*

Exercise 8-5: Tense and Lax Vowel Exercise   CD 4 Track 19

*Let's practice tense and lax vowels in context. The intonation is marked for you. When in doubt, try to leave out the lax vowel rather than run the risk of overpronouncing it: **l'p** in place of **lip**, so it doesn't sound like **leap**. Repeat:*

	Tense	Lax	
1.	eat	it	I **eat** it.
2.	beat	bit	The **beat** is a bit strong.
3.	keys	kiss	Give me a **kiss** for the **keys**.
4.	cheek	chick	The chick's **cheek** is soft.
5.	deed	did	He **did** the **deed**.
6.	feet	fit	These **shoes** fit my **feet**.
7.	feel	fill	Do you feel that we should **fill** it?
8.	green	grin	The Martian's **grin** was **green**.
9.	heat	hit	Last **summer**, the **heat** hit **hard**.
10.	heel	hill	Put your **heel** on the **hill**.
11.	jeep	Jill	Jill's **jeep** is here.
12.	creep	crypt	Let's **creep** near the **crypt**.
13.	leap	lip	He bumped his **lip** when he **leaped**.
14.	meal	mill	She had a **meal** at the **mill**.
15.	neat	knit	He can **knit neatly**.
16.	peel	pill	Don't **peel** that **pill**!
17.	reed	rid	Get rid of the **reed**.
18.	seek	sick	We seek the **sixth** sick sheik's **sheep**.
19.	sheep	ship	There are **sheep** on the **ship**.
20.	sleep	slip	The girl **sleeps** in a **slip**.
21.	steal	still	He still **steals**.
22.	Streep	strip	Meryl **Streep** is in a **comic** strip.
23.	team	Tim	**Tim** is on the **team**.
24.	these	this	**These** are better than **this** one.
25.	thief	thing	The **thief** took my **thing**.
26.	weep	whip	Who **weeps** from the **whips**?

In the time you have taken to reach this point in the program, you will have made a lot of decisions about your own individual speech style. Pronunciation of reduced sounds is more subjective and depends on how quickly you speak, how you prefer to express yourself, the range of your intonation, how much you want to reduce certain vowels, and so on.

Exercise 8-6: The Middle "I" List

CD 4 Track 20

The letter I in the unstressed position devolves consistently into a schwa. Repeat.

~ity	[ədee]
~ify	[əfäi]
~ited	[əd'd]
~ible	[əbªl]
~ical	[əcªl]
~imal	[əmªl]
~ization	[əzāsh'n]
~ication	[əcāsh'n]
~ination	[ənāsh'n]
~ifaction	[əfəcāsh'n]
~itation	[ətāsh'n]

ability
accident
accountability
activity
adversity
America
analytical
animal
applicant
application
article
astronomical
audible
auditor
authority
availability
beautiful
brutality
calamity
California
candidate
capacity
celebrity
charity
Christianity
clinical
clerical
chemical

chemistry
chronological
clarity
commodity
community
communication
complexity
confident
confidentiality
contribution
creativity
credit
critical
cubicle
curiosity
difficult
dignity
disparity
diversity
Edison
editor
electricity
eligibility
eliminated
engineer
episode
equality
evidence
experiment
facility
familiarity
feasibility
flexibility
Florida
foreigner
formality
fraternity
gravity
heredity
hospitality

hostility
humanity
humidity
humility
identity
imitation
immaturity
immigration
immunity
incident
individuality
infinity
insecurity
instability
institute
investigation
invisible
invitation
janitor
Jennifer
legalization
liability
Madison
maturity
medicine
mentality
majority
maximum
Michigan
minimum
minority
modify
Monica
monitor
municipality
nationality
naturalization
necessity
negative
nomination

opportunity
organization
partiality
physical
pitiful
politics
positive
possible
possibility
president
principle
priority
psychological
publicity
qualify
quality
quantity
radical
reality
rectify
resident
responsibility
sacrifice
sanity
security
seminar
seniority
severity
sensitivity
similar
skeptical
superiority
technical
testify
typical
uniform
unity
university
validity
visitor

Exercise 8-7: Reduction Options
CD 4 Track 21

*In the following example, you will see how you can fully sound out a word (such as **to**), reduce it slightly, or do away with it altogether.*

1. ... easier tū⁽ʷ⁾ənderstand.
2. ... easier tü⁽ʷ⁾ənderstand.
3. ... easier tə ənderstand.
4. ... easier tənderstand.
5. ... easier dənderstand.

Each of the preceding examples is correct and appropriate when said well. If you have a good understanding of intonation, you might be best understood if you used the last example.

How would this work with the rest of our familiar paragraph, you ask? Let's see.

Exercise 8-8: Finding Reduced Sounds
CD 4 Track 22

Go through the paragraph that follows and find the three [ü]'s and the five to seven [u]'s. Remember that your own speech style can increase the possibilities. With "to" before a vowel, you have a choice of a strong [u], a soft [ü], a schwa, or to telescope the two words and eliminate the vowel entirely. Pause the CD to mark the [ü] and [u] sounds. The first one is marked for you. Remember to check Answer Key, beginning on page 193.

Hello, my name is _____. I'm taking American **Accent** Training. There's a **lot** to learn, but I **hope** to make it as **enjoyable** as possible. I shüd pick **up** on the American **intonation** pattern pretty **easily**, although the **only** way to **get** it is to **practice** all of the time. I ūse the **up** and down, or **peaks** and valleys **intonation** more than I **used** to. I've been paying attention to **pitch, too.** It's like **walking** down a **stair**case. I've been **talking** to a lot of **Americans** lately, and they tell me that I'm **easier** to under**stand. Any**way, I could go **on** and on, but the **important** thing is to **listen** well and sound **good. Well,** what do you **think? Do** I?

Exercise 8-9: How Much Wood Would a Woodchuck Chuck?   CD 4 Track 23

How fast can you say:

How much wood	hæo məch wüd
would a wood chuck chuck,	wüdə wüdchək chək
if a woodchuck	ifə wüdchəck
could chuck	cüd chək
wood?	wüd
How many cookies	hæo meny cükeez
could a good cook cook,	cüdə güd cük cük
if a good cook	ifə güd cük
could cook	cüd cük
cookies?	cükeez

In the following two exercises, we will practice the two vowel sounds separately.

Exercise 8-10: Büker Wülsey's Cükbük   CD 4 Track 24

Repeat after me.

Booker Woolsey was a good cook. One day, he took a good look at his full schedule and decided that he could write a good cookbook. He knew that he could, and thought that he should, but he wasn't sure that he ever would. Once he had made up his mind, he stood up, pulled up a table, took a cushion, and put it on a bushel basket of sugar in the kitchen nook. He shook out his writing hand and put his mind to creating a good, good cookbook.

Exercise 8-11: A True Fool   CD 4 Track 25

Repeat after me.

A true fool will choose to drool in a pool to stay cool. Who knew that such fools were in the schools, used tools, and flew balloons? Lou knew and now you do, too.

Intonation and Attitude

There are certain sounds in any language that are considered nonsense syllables, yet impart a large amount of information to the informed listener. Each language has a different set of these sounds, such as **eto ne** in Japanese, **em** in Spanish, **eu** in French, and **um** in English. In this particular case, these are the sounds that a native speaker makes when he is thinking out loud—holding the floor, but not yet committing to actually speaking.

Exercise 8-12: Nonverbal Intonation   CD 4 Track 26

The top eight are the most common non-word communication sounds. They can all be na-salized or not, and said with the mouth open or closed. Intonation is the important factor here. Repeat after me.

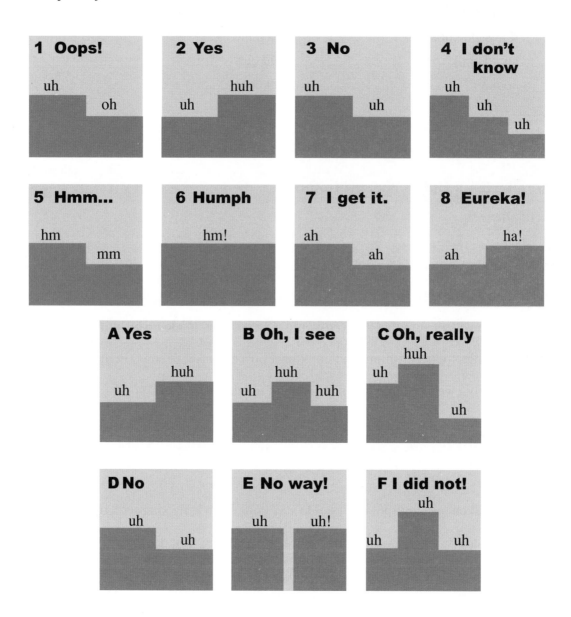

Chapter 9

"V" as in Victory

CD 4 Track 27

When pronounced correctly, V shouldn't stand out too much. Its sound, although notice-able, is small. As a result, people, depending on their native language, sometimes confuse V with B (Spanish, Japanese), with F (German), or with W (Chinese, Hindi). These four sounds are not at all interchangeable.

The W is a semivowel and there is no friction or contact. The B, like P, uses both lips and has a slight pop. American tend to have a strong, popping P. You can check your pro-nunciation by holding a match, a sheet of paper, or just your hand in front of your mouth. If the flame goes out, the paper wavers, or you feel a distinct puff of air on your hand, you've said P not B. B is the voiced pair of P.

Although F and V are in exactly the same position, F is a hiss and V is a buzz. The V is the voiced pair of F, as you saw in Chapter 2 (p. 62). When you say F, it is as if you are *whispering*. So, for V, say F and simply add some voice to it, which is the whole difference between *fairy* and *very*, as you will hear in our next exercise. (The F, too, presents problems to Japanese, who say H. To pronounce F, the lower lip raises up and the inside of the lip very lightly touches the outside of the upper teeth and you make a slight hissing sound. *Don't bite the outside of your lip at all.*)

Note In speaking, *of* is reduced to [əv].

Exercise 9-1: Mind Your Vees

CD 4 Track 28

Repeat the following words and sounds after me.

	P	B	F	V	W
1.	Perry	berry	fairy	very	wary
2.	pat	bat	fat	vat	wax
3.	Paul	ball	fall	vault	wall
4.	pig	big	fig	vim	wig
5.	prayed	braid	frayed		weighed
6.	poi	boy	foil	avoid	
7.	pull	bull	full		wool
8.	purr	burr	fur	verb	were

Exercise 9-2: The Vile VIP   CD 4 Track 29

Repeat after me, focusing on V and W.

When re**v**ising his **v**isitor's **v**ersion o**f** a plan for a **v**ery **w**ell-pa**v**ed a**v**enue, the **V**IP **w**as ad**v**ised to re**v**eal none o**f** his moti**v**es. E**v**entually, ho**w**e**v**er, the hapless **v**isitor disco**v**ered his kna**v**ish **vie**w**s and confided that it **w**as **v**ital to re**v**ie**w** the plans together to a**v**oid a conflict. The **V**IP **w**as not con**v**inced, and a**v**erred that he **w**ould ha**v**e it **v**etoed by the **v**ice president. This quite **v**exed the **v**isitor, who then **vo**w**ed to in**v**ent an indestructible pa**v**ing compound in order to a**v**enge his good name. The **V**IP found himself on the **v**erge o**f** a ci**v**il **w**ar **w**ith a **v**isitor **w**ith whom he had pre**v**iously con**v**ersed easily. It **w**as only due to his insufferable **v**anity that the ine**v**itable di**v**ision arri**v**ed as soon as it did. Ne**v**er again did the **v**isitor con**v**erse **w**ith the **v**ain **V**IP and they remained di**v**ided fore**v**er.

Exercise 9-3: Finding V Sounds   CD 4 Track 30

Underline the five V sounds in this paragraph. The first one is marked for you. Don't forget "of."

Hello, **my** name is _____. I'm taking American **Accent** Training. There's a **lot** to learn, but I **hope** to make it as **enjoyable** as possible. I should pick **up** on the American **intonation** pattern pretty **easily**, although the **only** way to **get** it is to **practice** all o**f** the time. I use the **up** and down, or **peaks** and valleys, **intonation** more than I **used** to. I've been paying attention to **pitch, too**. It's like **walking** down a **stair**case. I've been **talking** to a lot of **Americans** lately, and they tell me that I'm **easier** to unde**r**stand. **Any**way, I could go **on** and on, but the **important** thing is to **listen** well and sound **good. Well**, what do you **think**? **Do** I?

Chapter 10

S or Z?

The sound of the letter S is [s] only if it follows an unvoiced consonant. Otherwise, it becomes a Z in disguise. When an S follows a vowel, a voiced consonant, or another S, it turns into a [z]. The following exercise will let you hear and practice S with its dual sound. There are many more Z sounds in English than S sounds.

Exercise 10-1: When S Becomes Z　　　　　　　　　　　　　　CD 4 Track 31

Under Contrast, in the list that follows, notice how the voiced word is drawn out and then repeat the word after me. Both voiced and unvoiced diphthongs have the underlying structure of the tone shift, or the double stairstep, but the shift is much larger for the voiced ones.

prä
äis
price

prä
äiz
prize

Contrast

	S	Z
1.	price	prize
2.	peace	peas
3.	place	plays
4.	ice	eyes
5.	hiss	his
6.	close	to close
7.	use	to use
8.	rice	rise
9.	pace	pays
10.	lacey	lazy
11.	thirsty	Thursday
12.	bus	buzz
13.	dust	does
14.	face	phase
15.	Sue	zoo
16.	loose	lose

	S	Z
nouns	books	waxes
	maps	pencils
	months	dogs
	hats	trains
	pops	oranges
	bats	clothes
	bikes	windows
	laughs	washes
verbs	thanks	arrives
	eats	comes
	takes	goes
	speaks	lunches
contractions	it's	there's
	what's	he's
	that's	she's
possessives	a cat's eye	a dog's ear

Exercise 10-2: A Surly Sergeant Socked an Insolent Sailor   CD 4 Track 32

Repeat the S sounds in the paragraph below.

Sam, a surly sergeant from Cisco, Texas, saw a sailor sit silently on a small seat reserved for youngsters. He stayed for several minutes, while tots swarmed around. Sam asked the sailor to cease and desist but he sneered in his face. Sam was so incensed that he considered it sufficient incentive to sock the sailor. The sailor stood there for a second, astonished, and then strolled away. Sam was perplexed, but satisfied, and the tots scampered like ants over to the see-saw.

Exercise 10-3: Allz Well That Endz Well   CD 4 Track 33

Repeat the Z sounds in the paragraph below.

A lazy Thursday at the zoo found the zebras grazing on zinnias, posing for pictures, and teasing the zookeeper, whose nose was bronzed by the sun. The biggest zebra's name was Zachary, but his friends called him Zack. Zack was a confusing zebra whose zeal for reason caused his cousins, who were naturally unreasoning, to pause in their conversations. While they browsed, he philosophized. As they grazed, he practiced zen. Because they were Zack's cousins, the zebras said nothing, but they wished he would muzzle himself at times.

As mentioned on page 84, like sounds follow naturally. If one consonant is voiced, chances are, the following plural S will be voiced as well. If it's unvoiced, the following sound will be as well. In the past tense, S can be both voiced [z] and unvoiced [s] in some cases.

Exercise 10-4: Voiced and Unvoiced Endings in the Past Tense   CD 4 Track 34

The following will explain the differences between four expressions that are similar in appearance but different in both meaning and pronunciation.

	Meaning	Example	Pronunciation
S	Past action	I used to eat rice.	[yūst tu]
	To be accustomed to	I am used to eating rice.	[yūs tu]
Z	Present passive verb	Chopsticks are used to eat rice.	[yūzd tu]
	Simple past	I used chopsticks to eat rice.	[yūzd]

Used to, depending on its position in a sentence, will take either a tense [ū] or a schwa. At the end of a sentence, you need to say, … *more than I used tooo*; in the middle of a sentence you can say, *He usta live there.*

Exercise 10-5: Finding S and Z Sounds
CD 4 Track 35

Go through the paragraph and underline all of the [s] sounds. The first, [ækṣent] is marked for you. Next, circle all of the [z] sounds, no matter how the word is written (is = [iz], as = [æz], and so on.)

Hello, **my** name iz _____. I'm taking American **ækṣent** Training. There's a **lot** to learn, but I **hope** to make it as **enjoyable** as possible. I should pick **up** on the American **intonation** pattern pretty **easily**, although the **only** way to **get** it is to **practice** all of the time. I use the **up** and down, or **peaks** and valleys, **intonation** more than I **used** to. I've been paying attention to **pitch, too**. It's like **walking** down a **stair**case. I've been **talking** to a lot of **Americans** lately, and they tell me that I'm **easier** to under**stand**. **Any**way, I could go **on** and on, but the **important** thing is to **listen** well and sound **good**. **Well**, what do you **think**? **Do** I?

▼ Practice reading the paragraph three times on your own, concentrating on strong Zs.

Exercise 10-6: Application Steps with S and Z
CD 4 Track 36

Build up the following sentence, adding each aspect one at a time.

Always be a little kinder than necessary.

1. **Intonation**
   Always be a little **kinder** than **necessary**.
2. **Word Groups**
   Always be a little kinder (pause) than necessary.
3. **Liaisons**
   Always be(y)a little kinder tha(n)necessary.
4. **[æ] [ä] [ə]**
   äweez be ə littᵊl kinder thən necəssary.
5. **The American T**
   Always be a liddle kinder than necessary.
6. **The American R**
   Always be a little kindər than necessɛry.
7. **Combination of concepts 1 through 6**
   äweez be(y)ə liddᵊl kindər (pause) thə(n)necəssɛry.

Exercise 10-7: Your Own Application Steps with S and Z — CD 4 Track 37

Write your own sentence, and then build it up, adding each aspect one at a time.

_____

1. **Intonation**

_____

2. **Word Groups**

_____

3. **Liaisons**

_____

4. **[æ] [ä] [ə]**

_____

5. **The American T**

_____

6. **The American R**

_____

7. **Combination of concepts 1 through 6**

_____

Chapter 11

Tense and Lax Vowels

In this chapter, we tackle tense and lax vowels. This is the difference between [ā], *tense*, and [ɛ], *lax*, [ē], *tense*, and [i], *lax*. We will start with tense vowels.

*Don't pay attention to spelling or meaning. Just remember, if you are in the ä column, they all have the same **ah** sound. Repeat.*

	æ	æo	ä	ī	ā	ē	ū	ōu
1.	at	out	ought	I'd	ate	eat	ooze	own
2.	bat	about	bought	bite	bait	beat	boot	boat
3.	cat	couch	caught	kite	cane	keys	cool	coat
4.	chat	chowder	chalk	child	chair	cheer	choose	chose
5.	dad	doubt	dot	dial	date	deed	do	don't
6.	fat	found	fought	fight	fate	feet	food	phone
7.	fallow	fountain	fall	file	fail	feel	fool	foal
8.	gas	gown	got	kite	gate	gear	ghoul	go
9.	hat	how	hot	height	hate	heat	hoot	hope
10.	Hal	howl	hall	heil	hail	heel	who'll	hole
11.	Jack	jowl	jock	giant	jail	jeep	jewel	Joel
12.	crab	crowd	crawl	crime	crate	creep	cruel	crow
13.	last	loud	lost	line	late	Lee	Lou	low
14.	mat	mountain	mop	might	mate	mean	moon	moan
15.	gnat	now	not	night	Nate	neat	noon	note
16.	pal	pound	Paul	pile	pail	peel	pool	pole
17.	rat	round	rot	right	rate	real	rule	role
18.	sat	sound	soft	sight	sale	seal	Sue	soul
19.	shall	shower	shawl	shine	shade	she	shoe	show
20.	slap	slouch	slop	slide	slade	sleep	slew	slow
21.	stag	stout	stop	style	stale	steal	stool	stole
22.	strap	Stroud	straw	stride	straight	stream	strew	stroll
23.	tap	town	top	type	tape	team	tool	told
24.	that	thou	thar	thine	they	these	░░░	though
25.	thang	thousand	thought	thigh	thane	thief	░░░	throw
26.	van	vow	volume	viper	vain	veal	voodoo	vote
27.	wax	Wow!	wash	wipe	wane	wheel	woo	woe
28.	yank	Yow!	yawn	yikes	Yale	year	you	yo
29.	zap	Zowie!	zombie	xylophone	zany	zebra	zoo	Zoe

135

Exercise 11-2: Tense Vowels Practice Paragraph   CD 4 Track 39

*Go through the subsequent paragraph and mark all the tense vowels, starting with [ā]
(there are 12 here). The first one is n**ā**me [nɛim], not [nɛm]. The first [ē] sound (14) is th**e**
American. The same 5 [æ] sounds can be found as in Exercise 3-2 on page 74, plus the
[æo] of **sound**. Pause the CD to do the marking. Check your answer in the Answer Key,
beginning on page 193.*

Hello, **my** nāme is _____. I'm taking American **Accent** Training. There's a

lot to learn, but I **hope** to make it as **enjoyable** as possible. I should pick **up** on thē Ameri-

can **intonation** pattern pretty **easily**, although the **only** way to **get** it is to **practice** all of the

time. I use the **up** and down, or **peaks** and valleys, **intonation** more than I **used** to. I've

been paying attention to **pitch, too**. It's like **walking** down a **stair**case. I've been **talking** to

a lot of **Americans** lately, and they tell me that I'm **easier** to under**stand**. Any**way**, I could

go **on** and on, but the **important** thing is to **listen** well and sæond **good**. **Well**, what do you

think? Do I?

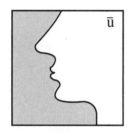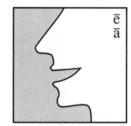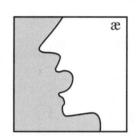

*Tense vowels
use the lips
and jaw
muscles.*

Exercise 11-3: Lax Vowels   CD 4 Track 40

As we saw in Chapter 8, these are the lax vowels.

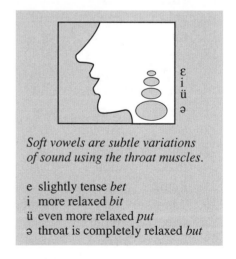

	e	i	ü	ə	ər
1.	end	it		un~	earn
2.	bet	bit	book	but	burn
3.	kept	kiss	could	cut	curt
4.	check	chick		chuck	church
5.	debt	did		does	dirt
6.	fence	fit	foot	fun	first
7.	fell	fill	full		furl
8.	get	gill	good	gut	girl
9.	help	hit	hook	hut	hurt
10.	held	hill	hood	hull	hurl

*Soft vowels are subtle variations
of sound using the throat muscles.*

e slightly tense *bet*
i more relaxed *bit*
ü even more relaxed *put*
ə throat is completely relaxed *but*

Exercise 11-4: Lax Vowels Practice Paragraph   CD 4 Track 41

*Again, go over this paragraph and mark the lax vowels, starting with [ɛ]. The first one (of about 12 possible) is in h**e**llo or Am**er**ican. The first [i] sound (of 9 to 22) may be found in **i**s. (The numbers are approximations because you may have already reduced the [ɛ] of **hello** and the [i] of **is** into schwas.) Pause the CD to do the marking. Check your answer in the Answer Key, beginning on page 193.*

Hello, my name is _____. I'm taking American **Accent** Training. There's a **lot** to learn, but I **hope** to make it as **enjoyable** as possible. I should pick **up** on the American **intonation** pattern pretty **easily**, although the **only** way to **get** it is to **practice** all of the time. I use the **up** and down, or **peaks** and valleys, **intonation** more than I **used** to. I've been paying attention to **pitch, too.** It's like **walking** down a **stair**case. I've been **talking** to a lot of **Americans** lately, and they tell me that I'm **easier** to unde**rs**tand. **Any**way, I could go **on** and on, but the **important** thing is to **listen** well and sound **good. Well**, what do you **think**? **Do** I?

Exercise 11-5: Take a High-Tech Tack   CD 4 Track 42

Repeat the following paragraph and words after me.

Sāy, Rāy, tāke a tack. A high-tack tack? No, Rāy, a high-tech tack, eight high-tech tacks, tāke them. Then find a wāy to māke a plāce for the tacks on the dāy bed. Hey, you lāy the tacks on the pāper plāce mat on the tāble, not on the dāy bed, Rāy. At your āge, why do you always māke the sāme mistākes?

| lāte | lack | let | | tāke | tack | tech | | mate | mat | met |
| hāil | Hal | hell | | fāte | fat | fetch | | cane | can | Ken |

Exercise 11-6: Pick a Peak   CD 4 Track 43

Repeat the following paragraph and words after me. Boldfaced elements represent the [ē] sound. The [i] is only marked with underscoring.

People who p**i**ck **peaks weekly seem** to **need** to appear **deep** **i**n order to be d**i**st**i**ngu**i**shed from **mere pea** p**i**ckers. **Peter,** a champ**i**on **peak** p**i**cker, thought he'd **be even neater i**f **he** were the **deepest peak** p**i**cker **i**n **Peoria, Phoenix,** and New Zealand. On h**i**s **peak peak** p**i**ck**i**ng **week,** though, **Peter,** a **peak** p**i**cker's **peak** p**i**cker, realized that he was not **deep.** Th**is** **i**s not **ea**sy for a **peak** p**i**cker to adm**i**t and **i**t p**i**tched **Peter i**nto a p**i**t of **peak** p**i**ck**i**ng d**e**spair. **He** was p**i**t**i**ful for s**i**x **weeks** and then l**i**fted h**i**mself to h**i**therto unrev**ea**led personal **peaks.**

| eat / it | sheep / ship | seat / sit | neat / nit | feet / fit | sleep / slip |

Grammar in a Bigger Nutshell

In Chapter 1 we studied compound nouns (Ex. 1-24 to 1-37) and complex verb tenses (Ex. 1-38). Now, we are going to put them together and practice the intonation of some complicated sentences.

Exercise 11-7: Compound Nouns and Complex Verbs   CD 4 Track 44

No matter how complex the verb gets, remember to follow the basic **Dogs** *eat* **bones** *intonation, where you stress the nouns. For the noun intonation, stick with the basic* **set phrase** *or* **description** *rule. Let's build up one complex noun for the subject, and another one for the object, starting with* **The millionaires were impressed by the equipment.**

Subject	Object
The **millionaires**	the **equipment**.
The elderly **millionaires**	**eaves**dropping equipment.
The **elderly** Texas **millionaires**	electronic **eaves**dropping equipment.
The two **elderly** Texas **millionaires**…**sophisticated** electronic **eaves**dropping equipment.	
The two **elderly** Texas **millionaires** were impressed by the **sophisticated** electronic **eaves**dropping equipment.	

The two elderly Teksəs millyənair zwerim presst by the
səfistəkaydədəlektränik ēvzdräppiŋə kwipmənt.

zərim prest

1. The two **elderly** Texas **millionaires**'re impressed by the **sophisticated** electronic **eaves**dropping equipment.

zwərim prest

2. The two **elderly** Texas **millionaires** were impressed by the **sophisticated** electronic **eaves**dropping equipment.

zər beeyingim prest

3. At the moment, the two **elderly** Texas **millionaires**'re being impressed by the **sophisticated** electronic **eaves**dropping equipment.

zəl beeyim prest

4. The two **elderly** Texas **millionaires**'ll be impressed by the **sophisticated** electronic **eaves**dropping equipment.

zəd beeyim prest

5. The two **elderly** Texas **millionaires**'d be impressed by the **sophisticated** electronic **eaves**dropping equipment if there were more practical applications for it.

zədəv binim prest

6. The two **elderly** Texas **millionaires**'d've been impressed by the **sophisticated** electronic **eaves**dropping equipment if there had been more practical applications for it.

zədəv bin so im prest

7. The two **elderly** Texas **millionaires** that've been so impressed by the **sophisticated** electronic **eaves**dropping equipment are now researching a new program.

Exercise 11-7: Compound Nouns and Complex Verbs *continued*   **CD 4 Track 44**

zəv binim prest
8. The two **elderly** Texas **millionaires**'ve been impressed by the **sophisticated** electronic **eaves**dropping equipment for a long time now.

zəd binim prest
9. The two **elderly** Texas **millionaires**'d been impressed by the **sophisticated** electronic **eaves**dropping equipment long before the burglary was thwarted. [thwordəd]

zələv bin thərə lee(y)im prest
10. The two **elderly** Texas **millionaires**'ll've been thoroughly impressed by the **sophisticated** electronic **eaves**dropping equipment by the time I've done my presentation.

zädə bee(y)im prest
11. The two **elderly** Texas **millionaires** ought to be impressed by the **sophisticated** electronic **eaves**dropping equipment.

shüd bee(y)im prest
12. The two **elderly** Texas **millionaires** should be impressed by the **sophisticated** electronic **eaves**dropping equipment.

shüd•n beetoo(w)im prest
13. The two **elderly** Texas **millionaires** shouldn't be too impressed by the **sophisticated** electronic **eaves**dropping equipment.

shüdəv binim prest
14. The two **elderly** Texas **millionaires** should've been impressed by the **sophisticated** electronic **eaves**dropping equipment.

shüdn•nəv bin thæ dim prest
15. Given the circumstances, the two **elderly** Texas **millionaires** shouldn't've been that impressed by the **sophisticated** electronic **eaves**dropping equipment.

cüdee zəlee bee(y)im prest
16. We think that the two **elderly** Texas **millionaires** could easily be impressed by the **sophisticated** electronic **eaves**dropping equipment.

cüd•n bee(y)im prest
17. No matter what we did, the two **elderly** Texas **millionaires** couldn't be impressed by even the most **sophisticated** electronic **eaves**dropping equipment.

cüdəv binim prest
18. The two **elderly** Texas **millionaires** could've been impressed by the **sophisticated** electronic **eaves**dropping equipment, but we're not sure.

cüdn•nəv binim prest
19. The two **elderly** Texas **millionaires** couldn't've been impressed by the **sophisticated** electronic **eaves**dropping equipment, because they left after 5 minutes.

myt bee(y)im prest
20. The two **elderly** Texas **millionaires** might be impressed by the **sophisticated** electronic **eaves**dropping equipment this time around.

mydəv binim prest
21. The two **elderly** Texas **millionaires** might've been impressed by the **sophisticated** electronic **eaves**dropping equipment, but they gave no indication one way or the other.

Exercise 11-7: Compound Nouns and Complex Verbs *continued*   CD 4 Track 44

məss bee(y)im prest
22. The two **elderly** Texas **millionaires** must be impressed by the **sophisticated** electronic **eaves**dropping equipment because they are considering a huge order.

məsdəv binim prest
23. The two **elderly** Texas **millionaires** must have been impressed by the **sophisticated** electronic **eaves**dropping equipment because they ordered so much of it.

cən bee(y)im prest
24. The two **elderly** Texas **millionaires** can be impressed by the **sophisticated** electronic **eaves**dropping equipment because they don't know much about surveillance.

cæn(t) bee(y)im prest
25. The two **elderly** Texas **millionaires** can't be impressed by the **sophisticated** electronic **eaves**dropping equipment because they invented most of the state of the art technology currently available.

Exercise 11-8: Your Own Compound Nouns   CD 4 Track 45

Pause the CD and build up your own compound nouns, both subject and object.

Subject	Object
_____	_____
_____	_____
_____	_____
_____	_____
_____	_____
_____	_____
_____	_____
_____	_____

Exercise 11-9: Your Compound Nouns and Complex Verbs   CD 4 Track 46

Using your compound nouns from Ex. 11-8, choose a verb and put it through all the changes. Remember that it helps to have a verb that starts with a vowel. Add explanatory words to round out the sentence, complete the thought, and support the verb.

eat	1.	_____
ate	2.	_____
are eating	3.	_____
will eat	4.	_____
would eat	5.	_____
would have eaten	6.	_____
that have eaten	7.	_____
have eaten	8.	_____
had eaten	9.	_____
will have eaten	10.	_____
ought to eat	11.	_____
should eat	12.	_____
should not eat	13.	_____
should have eaten	14.	_____
should not have	15.	_____
could eat	16.	_____
could not eat	17.	_____
could have eaten	18.	_____
could not have	19.	_____
might eat	20.	_____
might have eaten	21.	_____
must eat	22.	_____
must have eaten	23.	_____
can eat	24.	_____
can't eat	25.	_____

Exercise 11-10: Practical Application—U.S./Japan Trade Friction CD 4 Track 47

Listen to the following excerpt, and compare the two versions.

Forty years after the end of World War II, Japan and the U.S. are again engaged in conflict. Trade frictions, which began as minor irritants in an otherwise smooth relationship in the 1960s, have gradually escalated over the years.

The conflict is more dangerous than it appears because its real nature is partially hidden. It masquerades as a banal and sometimes grubby dispute over widgets with the stakes being whether American or Japanese big business makes more money.

In truth, the issue is strategic and geopolitical in nature. Japan is once again challenging the U.S., only this time the issue is not China or the Pacific, but world industrial and technological leadership and the military and economic powers which have always been its corollaries. *By permission of *U.S. News and World Report*

Fordee yir zæftr(pause)thee(y)end'v wrl dwor too,(pause)J'pæn'n thə US(pause)ärə genin geij din(pause)cänfl'ct.(pause)Trəid fr'ksh'nz,(pause)w'ch b'gæn'z mynr rirrət'nts(pause)in'n ətherwise (pause) smooth r'leish'nship in the näinteen siksdeez(pause)h'v græjəlee(y)escəladəd(pause)dover thə yirz.

Thə **kän**fl'k d'z mor **dein**jer's thəni dəpirz b'kəzəts **ree**(y)əl neichyr'z pärshəlee **h'dd**'n. It mæske**reid** zəzə bənälən səmtäimz **grə**bee d'spyu dover **wij**'ts withthə **steiks** be(y)ing wetherə **mer**əkəner Jæpəneez big **bizn**'s meiks mor **mə**nee.

In **truth,** thee(y)**ishu**(w)iz strəteejəkən jee(y)opəlidəkələn neichyer. Jəpænəz wən səgen **chæl**ənjing thə you(w)**ess,** only **this** täim, thee(y)**ishu**(w)iz nät **Chäi**nə or thə Pəs'fək, bət wr rolld'in **dəs**stree(y)l'n tɛknəläjəkəl **leed**ershipən the **mil**ətɛree(y)ənɛkənämək pæwrz w'ch h'**vä**weez bi n'ts **korəl**ereez.

The Letter A

You've seen many examples of illogical spelling by now, and the letter A is a major contributor. A can be:

[æ] c<u>a</u>t   [ä] p<u>a</u>rt   [ā] m<u>a</u>ke   [ə] fin<u>a</u>l   [ɛ] p<u>a</u>rallel   [o] w<u>a</u>r

Note People who speak Chinese frequently pronounce [a], [æ] and [ɛ] the same. The common denominator of the three sounds is [ɛ]. When a Chinese speaker says *mate, mat, met,* it can sound like *met, met, met.* If this happens to be your case, in order to say common words like *make* and *man* correctly, first practice putting them on the stairsteps and drawing them out. Don't be afraid to exaggerate. You can even draw them out with a final unvoiced consonant.

may
        eek

make

mæ
        æan

man

#	æ	æo	u	i	ee	ü	ɛ	a	ə	ä	r	är	o	i	oi
1	back	bow	booed	Bic	beak	book	beck	bake	buck	Bach	Burke	bark	boat	bite	point
2	black	blouse	blued	bliss	bleed	books	bled	blade	blood	block	blurred	blarney	bloat	blight	boy
3	brad	browse	brood	brick	breed	brook	bread	break	brother	brought	fir	far	broke	bright	broil
4	pat	about	boot	pit	peak	put	pet	paid	putt	pot	pert	part	post	pike	boil
5	cat	couch	coot	kit	parakeet	cookie	kept	Kate	cut	caught	curt	cart	coat	kite	coin
6	cad	cowed	cooed	kid	keyed	could	Keds	okayed	cud	cod	curd	card	code	cried	coil
7	fat	found	food	fit	feet	foot	fed	fade	fun	fog	first	farm	phone	fight	Foyt
8	flack	flower	fluke	flick	fleet	put	fleck	flake	flood	father	flurry	tar	flow	flight	Floyd
9	fragile	frown	fruit	frill	free	fructose	French	afraid	from	frog	further	farther	fro	fright	Freud
10	fallow	foul	fool	fill	feel	full	fell	fail	fuss	fall	furl	Carl	photo	file	foil
11	gas	gout	gooed	give	geek	good	get	gate	gun	gone	gird	guard	goad	guide	goiter
12	catch	couch	cool	kick	key	cook	ketch	cake	come	calm	Kirk	carp	coal	kind	coy
13	lack	loud	Luke	lick	leak	look	lecture	lake	luck	lock	lurk	lark	local	like	lawyer
14	mallet	mound	mood	mill	meal	wooden	men	main	mother	mom	murmur	march	mobile	mile	Des Moines
15	pal	Powell	pool	pill	peel	pull	pell	pail	puck	pock	pearl	park	pole	pile	poison
16	sand	sound	soon	sin	seen	soot	send	same	some	sawn	sir	sorry	sewn	sign	soil
17	satin	mountain	gluten	mitten	eaten	wouldn't	retina	latent	button	gotten	certain	carton	potent	tighten	ointment
18	shad	shout	shoed	Schick	sheet	should	shed	shade	shun	shop	insured	sharp	show	shy	
19	shack	shower	shooed	shiver	chic	shook	chef	shake	shuck	shock	shirt	shark	shows	shyster	
20	shallow	shower	shoot	shift	sheep	sugar	shell	shale	shut	shot	sure	shard	shown	shine	
21	chance	chowder	choose	chin	cheek		chest	change	chuck	chalk	churn	charge	chose	child	choice
22	tack	towel	two	tick	teak	took	tech	take	tuck	talk	turkey	tarp	toke	tyke	toy
23	that	thousand	through	this	these		then	they	the	thought	third	cathartic	though	thigh	thyroid
24	had	how'd	who'd	hid	he'd	hood	hen	hate	hud	hod	heard	hard	hoed	hide	hoi polloi
25	hat	about	hoot	hit	heat	foot	heck	Hague	hut	hot	hurt	heart	hotel	height	Hoyle
26	value	vow	review	villain	reveal		vegetable	vague	vug	von	verve	varnish	vote	vile	avoid
27	whack	wow	wooed	wick	weak	would	wed	weighed	what	walk	word	harm	woke	white	woi

Exercise 11-11: Presidential Candidates' Debate

CD 4 Track 48

Thə prezədənt təmärrou näidiz əxpectədiniz steidəv thə yoonyən mesəj tə prəpouz fedrəl səbzədeez tə help lou⁽ʷ⁾inkəm fæmleez ouvrkəm thə sou-käld dijədəl dəväid. Izidə nəpropree⁽ʸ⁾ət yusəv gəvrmnt fənz tə hændæot kəmpyudrz ən prəväid innernet æksɛs tə thouz hu cæn⁽ᵈ⁾əford it; ənd if nät, why nät. Will bəgin with Mr. Keez.

I think this iz ənəthər keis wheer pälətishənz try də jəmpän thə bændwægən əv səmthing thæt's going än in thee⁽ʸ⁾əcänəmee, sou evreebədeez gənnə think thət they ækchəlee hæv səmthing tə do with thə rəzəlt when they dont. Thɛrz nou need fr this. Wiräl reddy seeing æot ther prəpouzəlz fr thə distrəbyushən əv free PeeCees, nät beis dän səm pälətishən meiking ə judgment ən spending tæxpeiyer mənee, bət beis dän thə self-intrst əv thouz hu⁽ʷ⁾är involvd inə nyu world, ə nyu world ən which p'rtisəpeishən iz thə kee də präfit— ənd in which ther iz ækchəlee ə sträng insentiv əmäng thouz hu prtisəpeidin thə präivət sektər tə giv æksɛss tə indəvijəls sou thət they c'n impruv their äpərtyunədeez fr präfit, fr infərmeishn shering. Thæts whəts älredee bin going än—it will kəntinyu. Ther iz nou need fr thə gəvərmənt tə prətend thæt it needs tə teik leedership hir. I think thæts jəst pəlidəkəl päsjuring.

Senədər Mə⁽ᵏ⁾kein.

I bəleev th't wee du hæv ə präbləm. æn thædiz thət therizə growing gæp bətween thə hævz ənd hæv-näts in əmɛrəkə, thouz thədr ɛibl də tɛik pärdin this infərmeishn teknäləjee ən thouz th't hævnt. Wee took ə meijər step forwərd when wee dəsaidəd də wäi⁽ʸ⁾r evree skool ən lybreree in əmerikə tə thee⁽ʸ⁾innərnet. Thætsə güd prougrəm. Wee hæv tə hæv step tu, three, ən four, which meenz güd əkwipmənt, güd teechərz ənd güd clæssroomz. No, I wüdn du⁽ʷ⁾it d'rektlee. Bət thɛrz läts əv weiz th'chyu kən inkerəj korpəreishnz, who in their own self-intrest, wüd wänt tə prəvaid… wüd rəseev tæks benəfits, wüd rəseev kredit, ənd mɛny əthər weiz fr beeing invəlvd in thə skoolz, in əpgreiding thə kwälədee əv əkwipmənt th't thei hæv, thə kwälədee əv thə styudənts ənd therby prəvaiding ə məch-needed well-treind wərkfors.

Thæng kyu. Mr. Forbz.

The president tomorrow night is expected in his State of the Union message to propose federal subsidies to help low-income families overcome the so-called digital divide. Is it an appropriate use of government funds to hand out computers and provide Internet access to those who can't afford it, and if not, why not? We'll begin with Mr. Keyes.

"I think this is another case where politicians try to jump on the bandwagon of something that's going on in the economy, so everybody's gonna think that they actually have something to do with the result when they don't. There's no need for this. We're already seeing out there proposals for the distribution of free PCs, not based on some politician making a judgment and spending taxpayer money, but based on the self-interest of those who are involved in a new world, a new world in which participation is the key to profit—and in which there is actually a strong incentive among those who participate on the private sector to give access to individuals so that they can improve their opportunities for profit, for information sharing. That's what's already been going on—it will continue. There is no need for the government to pretend that it needs to take leadership here. I think that's just political posturing."

Senator McCain.

"I believe that we do have a problem. And that is that there is a growing gap between the *haves* and *have-nots* in America, those that are able to take part in this information technology and those that haven't. We took a major step forward when we decided to wire every school and library in America to the Internet. That's a good program. We have to have step two, three, and four, which means good equipment, good teachers, and good classrooms. No, I wouldn't do it directly. But there's lots of ways that you can encourage corporations, who in their own self-interest, would want to provide … would receive tax benefits, would receive credit, and many other ways for being involved in the schools, in upgrading the quality of equipment that they have, the quality of the students, and thereby providing a much-needed well-trained workforce."

Thank you. Mr. Forbes.

Chapter 12

Nasal Consonants

CD 4 Track 49

We now turn to the three consonants whose sound comes out through the nose—M, N, and the NG combination. They each have one thing in common, their sound is blocked in the mouth in one of three locations. Two of them, N and NG, you can't even see, as with R, so they're hard to pick up on.

[m] is the easiest and most obvious. Like [b], the lips come together, the air can't get out, so it has to come out through the nose.

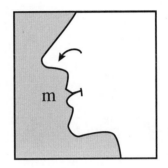

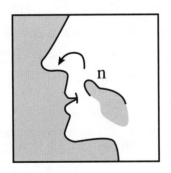

[n] is in a position similar to [t], but it can't be at all tense. It has to be completely relaxed, filling the whole mouth, touching the insides of all the teeth, leaving no room for the air to escape, except by the nose.

[ng] is back in the throat with [g]. The back of the tongue presses back, and again, the air comes out through the nose.

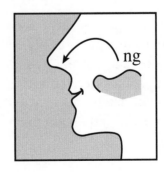

Exercise 12-1: Nasal Consonants CD 4 Track 50

We are going to contrast nasals with regular consonant sounds. Repeat after me.

	Initial		Middle		Final	
m/b	me	bee	llama	lobber	ROM	rob
n/d	kneels	deals	Lana	lauder	Ron	rod
ng/g	long eels	geese	longer	logger	wrong	log

Exercise 12-2: Ending Nasal Consonants CD 4 Track 51

Here we will focus on the final sounds. Repeat after me.

M	N	NG
rum^ə	run^ə	rung^ə
sum/some	sun/son	sung
bum	bun	bung
tum	ton	tongue
dumb	done	dung
psalm	sawn	song

Exercise 12-3: Reading Nasal Consonant Sounds CD 4 Track 52

We will read the following paragraph. Repeat after me.

The young King Kong can sing along on anything in the kingdom, as long as he can bring a strong ringing to the changing songs. He can only train on June mornings when there is a full moon, but June lends itself to singing like nothing else. Ding Dong, on the other hand, is not a singer; he cannot sing for anything. He is a man often seen on the green lawn on the Boston Open, where no one ever, ever sings.

Exercise 12-4: Finding [n] and [ng] Sounds CD 4 Track 53

Find and mark the final [n] and [ng] sounds.

Hello, **my** name is _____. I'm taking American **Accent** Training. There's a **lot** to learn, but I **hope** to make it as **enjoyable** as possible. I should pick **up** on the American **intonation** pattern pretty **easily**, although the **only** way to **get** it is to **practice** all of the time. I use the **up** and down, or **peaks** and valleys, **intonation** more than I **used** to. I've been paying attention to **pitch, too**. It's like **walking** down a **stair**case. I've been **talking** to a lot of **Americans** lately, and they tell me that I'm **easier** to under**stand**. **Any**way, I could go **on** and on, but the **important** thing is to **listen** well and sound **good**. **Well**, what do you **think**? **Do** I?

Chapter 13

Throaty Consonants

There are five consonant sounds that are produced in the throat: [h] [k] [g] [ng] [er]. Because R can be considered a consonant, its sound is included here. For pronunciation purposes, however, elsewhere this book treats it as a semivowel.

Exercise 13-1: Throaty Consonants   CD 4 Track 54

Here we will read across the lists of initial, middle, and final consonants.

	Initial	**Middle**	**Final**
[h]	haw	reheat	
	hood	in half	
	he'll	unhinge	
	hat	unheard of	
[k]	caw	accident	rink
	could	accent	rack
	keel	include	cork
	cat	actor	block
[g]	gaw	regale	rug
	good	ingrate	hog
	geese	agree	big
	gat	organ	log
[ng]	Long Island	Bronx	wrong
	a long wait	inky	daring
	Dang you!	larynx	averaging
	being honest	English	clung
[r]	raw	error	rare
	roof	arrow	air
	real	mirror	injure
	rat	carbon	prefer

Exercise 13-2: The Letter X   CD 4 Track 55

The letter X can sound like either KS or GZ, depending on the letter that follows the X and where the stress falls.

[ks]	excite	[ɛksäit]
Followed by the	extra	[ɛkstrə]
letter C or other	exercise	[ɛksersiz]
unvoiced	experience	[ɛks**piree**(ʸ)əns]
consonants	except	[əks**ɛpt**]
	execute	[ɛksekyut]
	excellent	[ɛksələnt]

[gz]	example	[əg**zæmp**əl]
Followed by a	exist	[əg**zist**]
vowel and usually	exam	[əg**zæm**]
stressed on the	exert	[əg**zrt**]
second syllable	examine	[əg**zæm**ən]
	executive	[əg**zɛk**yudəv]
	exit	[**ɛg**zit]
	exactly	[əg**zæk**lee]

Exercise 13-3: Reading the H, K, G, NG, and R sounds   CD 4 Track 56

Repeat after me.

H

"<u>H</u>elp!" <u>h</u>issed t<u>h</u>e <u>h</u>arried intern. "We <u>h</u>ave to <u>h</u>urry! The <u>h</u>alfwit w<u>h</u>o was <u>h</u>ired to <u>h</u>elp <u>h</u>er <u>h</u>ome <u>h</u>it <u>h</u>er <u>h</u>ard with t<u>h</u>e <u>H</u>onda. S<u>h</u>e didn't <u>h</u>ave a <u>h</u>elmet on <u>h</u>er <u>h</u>ead to protect <u>h</u>er, so s<u>h</u>e <u>h</u>as to <u>h</u>ave a checkup a<u>h</u>ead of t<u>h</u>e ot<u>h</u>ers."

K

The <u>c</u>omputer <u>c</u>ursor <u>c</u>areened a<u>c</u>ross the s<u>c</u>reen, erasing <u>k</u>ey <u>c</u>hara<u>c</u>ters as it s<u>c</u>rolled past. The te<u>c</u>hnician was e<u>q</u>ually <u>c</u>onfused by the <u>c</u>omputer te<u>c</u>hnology and the <u>c</u>ompli<u>c</u>ated <u>k</u>eyboard, so he <u>c</u>licked off the <u>c</u>omputer, <u>c</u>leaned off his des<u>k</u>, a<u>c</u>cepted his payche<u>c</u>k, and <u>c</u>aught a ta<u>x</u>i<u>c</u>ab for the airport, destination <u>C</u>ara<u>c</u>as.

G

The Wizard of Og

There was a man named…	Og
Who was his best friend?	Dog
Where did he live?	Bog
What was his house made of?	Log
Who was his neighbor?	Frog

What did he drink?	Eggnog
What did he do for fun?	Jog
What is the weather in his swamp?	Fog

NG

The stunning woman would not have a fling with the strong young flamingo trainer until she had a ring on her finger. He was angry because he longed for her. She inquired if he were hungry, but he hung his head in a funk. The flamingo trainer banged his fist on the fish tank and sang out, "Dang it, I'm sunk without you, Punkin!" She took in a long, slow lungful of air and sighed.

R

War is horrible. During any war, terrible things occur. The result is painful memories and disfiguring scars for the very people needed to rebuild a war-torn country. The leaders of every country must learn that wars are never won, lives are always lost, and history is doomed to repeat itself unless we all decide to live in harmony with our brothers and sisters.

Exercise 13-4: Glottal Consonant Practice Paragraph CD 4 Track 57

Pause the CD and go through the paragraph and mark the [h], [k], [g], [ng], and [r] sounds.

Hello, **my** name is _____. I'm taking American **Accent** Training. There's a **lot** to learn, but I **hope** to make it as **enjoyable** as possible. I should pick **up** on the American **intonation** pattern pretty **easily**, although the **only** way to **get** it is to **practice** all of the time. I use the **up** and down, or **peaks** and valleys, **intonation** more than I **used** to. I've been paying attention to **pitch, too**. It's like **walking** down a **stair**case. I've been **talking** to a lot of **Americans** lately, and they tell me that I'm **easier** to under**stand**. **Any**way, I could go **on** and on, but the **important** thing is to **listen** well and sound **good**. **Well**, what do you **think**? **Do** I?

Telephone Tutoring

Final Diagnostic Analysis

CD 4 Track 58

After a year, you're ready for the final analysis. If you're studying on your own, please contact toll-free **(800) 457-4255** or **www.americanaccent.com** for a referral to a qualified telephone analyst. The diagnostic analysis is designed to evaluate your current speech patterns to let you know where your accent is standard and nonstandard.

> The Nasdaq composite index on Monday suffered its biggest loss in three weeks after a wave of selling slammed Internet and other tech shares in Asia and Europe overnight—suggesting many investors are increasingly nervous about tech shares' current heights. The Nasdaq index ended down 141.38 points, or 2.8%, at 4,907.24, though it recovered from a morning sell-off that took it down as much as 209 points from Friday's record high. Biotechnology stocks were particularly hard hit. The broader market was also lower, though the Dow Jones industrial average managed to inch up 18.31 points to 9,947.13.

1. law, job, collar
2. class, chance, last
3. name, date, way
4. ten, many, says
5. China, dime, fly
6. if, is, been
7. eve, ease, bean
8. worm, third, hard
9. won, color, Florida
10. new, blue, through
11. good, put, could
12. won't, know, go
13. about, now, down
14. joy, royal, deploy

A	B	C	D	E	F
1. pat	1. bat	1. apparition	1. abolition	1. lap	1. lab
2. fat	2. vat	2. a rifle	2. arrival	2. life	2. live
3. stink	3. zinc	3. graces	3. grazes	3. dice	3. dies
4. sheer	4. girl	4. mesher	4. measure	4. dish	4. deluge
5. ten	5. den	5. latter	5. ladder	5. ought	5. odd
6. cheer	6. jeer	6. nature	6. major	6. etch	6. edge
7. thing	7. the	7. author	7. other	7. breath	7. breathe
8. core	8. gore	8. lacking	8. lagging	8. snack	8. snag
9. yet	9. rice	9. access	9. example	9. box	9. bogs
10. wolf	10. prance	10. association	10. refract	10. way	10. bar
11. her	11. my	11. actual	11. arrive	11. down	11. mutter
12. lice	12. not	12. behind	12. climber	12. ball	12. name
13. plants		13. reflect	13. innate	13. muddle	13. ran
		14. alive	14. singer		14. wrong

1. Sue arranged it.
2. She organized her office.
3. Get your report done.
4. Where did you put it?
5. She's your usual television star.

1. soo⁽ʷ⁾ərɛinj dit
2. shee⁽ʸ⁾orgənizdr räfəs
3. gɛcher r'port dən
4. wɛrjə püd't
5. shezhier yuzhəwᵊl tɛləvizhən stär

1. Get a better water heater.

2. Gedda bedder wädr heedr.

3.	alter	later
4.	intern	enter
5.	data	deter
6.	metal	metallic

| 7. | let | led |

Chapters 1-13

Review and Expansion

CD 5

We will be reviewing the concepts that form the basis of American speech—intonation, word groups, the staircase, and liaisons, as well as pronunciation. Let's briefly review each item in order. This time around, there will be no explanation.

Review Exercise 1-1: Rubber Band Practice with Nonsense Syllables

1. **blah** blah **blah**	1. blah blah **blah**	1. blah **blah** blah	1. **blah** blah blah
2. **ding** ding **ding**	2. ding ding **ding**	2. ding **ding** ding	2. **ding** ding ding
A	**B**	**C**	**D**
1. **duh** duh **duh**	1. duh duh **duh**	1. duh **duh** duh	1. **duh** duh duh
2. **X Y Z**	2. uncon**cerned**	2. in**cluding**	2. educate
3. **8 9 10**	3. He sells **fish.**	3. He's **selfish.**	3. **soft**ball game
4. Cows give **milk.**	4. We like **Bob.**	4. I **think** so.	4. **Bring** me some.

Review Exercise 1-2: Noun Intonation

1. **Cats** eat **fish.**	6. **Ed** found a **job.**
2. **Boys** like **toys.**	7. **Max** cut his **finger.**
3. **Lou** lost his **mind.**	8. **Mary** flew a **kite.**
4. **Gail** earned a **fortune.**	9. **Rick** passed the **test.**
5. **Betty** grows **tomatoes.**	10. Our **car** lost a **wheel.**

Review Exercise 1-3: Noun and Pronoun Intonation

1. **Patrick** speaks **French.**	1. He **speaks** it.
2. The **neighbors** sold their **car.**	2. They **sold** it.
3. The **police** chased the **felon.**	3. They **chased** him.
4. The **house**keeper did some **laundry.**	4. She **did** some.
5. The **architect** and I designed a **house.**	5. We **designed** one.

Review Exercise 1-4: Sentence Intonation Test

1. They took it.	6. Sam called him.
2. Mary had a baby.	7. The dogs howled at the moon.
3. Louis talked on the phone.	8. Did you order any?
4. We forgot about it.	9. We noticed her.
5. She had one.	10. The books fell on the floor.

Review Exercise 1-6: Pitch and Meaning Change

1. He looks like **Bob**.
2. He **looks** like Bob, but he's **not**.
3. He **knows** Bob, but he doesn't **trust** him.
4. He **can't trust** him. He **can't do** it.

Review Exercise 1-7: Individual Practice

1. Convey the information that it is Bob. ✤
2. Convey the opinion that he only resembles Bob. ✤
3. Convey the different feelings that someone has about Bob. ✤
4. Convey the fact that trust is a problem with Bob. ✤

Review Exercise 1-8: Meaning of "Pretty," "Sort of," "Kind of," and "Little"

Question: How was it?
Answer:
1. *It was pretty **expensive**. It was **pretty** expensive.*
2. *It was sort of **funny**. It was **sort** of funny.*
3. *It was kind of **rude**. It was **kind** of rude.*
4. *It was a little **late**. It was a **little** late.*

Review Exercise 1-9: Inflection

1. **Her** boyfriend almost never sends her flowers, but **mine** does.
2. Her **boyfriend** almost never sends her flowers, but her **sisters** always do.
3. Her boyfriend **almost** never sends her flowers, but every **once** in a while he does.
4. Her boyfriend almost **never** sends her flowers, no matter **what**!
5. Her boyfriend almost never **sends** her flowers, but he **planted** a lot in her **garden**.
6. Her boyfriend almost never sends **her** flowers, but he **never** forgets **Mother's** Day!
7. Her boyfriend almost never sends her **flowers**, but he **showers** her with **other** gifts.

Review Exercise 1-10: Individual Practice

1. Indicate that her boyfriend prefers live plants to cut ones. (5) ✤
2. Indicate that her sisters are attentive to her horticultural needs. (2) ✤
3. Indicate that her boyfriend gives her non-floral presents. (7) ✤
4. Indicate that my boyfriend is good in the flower department. (1) ✤
5. Indicate that it is a true rarity for her boyfriend to send flowers. (4) ✤
6. Indicate that there is actually a slim chance that he might send flowers. (3) ✤
7. Indicate that her boyfriend remembers to send flowers to his mother. (6) ✤

Review Exercise 1-11: Translation

*Pause the CD and translate **Her boyfriend almost never sends her flowers** into your native language.*

_____

Review Exercise 1-12: Create Your Own Intonation Contrast

Normal intonation _____

Changed intonation _____

Review Exercise 1-13: Variable Stress

1. *How do you **know**?*
2. *How do **you** know?*
3. *How **do** you know?*
4. ***How** do you know?*

Review Exercise 1-14: Make a Variable Stress Sentence

1. _____
2. _____
3. _____

4. _____
5. _____
6. _____
7. _____

Review Exercise 1-15: Application of Stress

Think the United Auto Workers can beat Caterpillar Inc. in their bitter contract battle? Before placing your bets, talk to Paul Branan, who can't wait to cross the picket line at Caterpillar's factory in East Peoria. Branan, recently laid off by a rubber-parts plant where he earned base pay of $6.30 an hour, lives one block from a heavily picketed gate at the Cat complex. Now he's applying to replace one of 12,600 workers who have been on strike for the past five months. "Seventeen dollars an hour and they don't want to work?" asks Branan. "I don't want to take another guy's job, but I'm hurting, too."

Review Exercise 1-17: Staircase Intonation Practice

On a separate piece of paper, draw a staircase and put each word where it belongs.

Review Exercise 1-18: Reading with Staircase Intonation

Think the United **Auto** Workers can beat Caterpillar **Inc.** in their bitter **contract** battle? Before placing your **bets**, talk to Paul **Branan**, who **can't wait** to cross the **picket** line at Caterpillar's **factory** in East **Peoria**. **Branan**, **recently** laid **off** by a **rubber**-parts plant where he earned **base** pay of **$6.30** an **hour**, lives **one** block from a **heavily** picketed **gate** at the **Cat** complex. **Now** he's applying to replace one of **12,600 workers** who have been on **strike** for the **past** five **months**. "**Seven**teen dollars an **hour** and **they** don't want to **work?**" asks Branan. "**I** don't want to take **another** guy's **job**, but **I'm** hurting, **too**."

Review Exercise 1-19: Spelling and Numbers

CEO	See Eee **Oh**	Catch	See Ei Tee See **Aitch**
ATM	Ei Tee **Em**	Nate	En Ei Tee **Eee**
IRS	Ai Are **Ess**		
BMW	Bee Em **Dubba**you	Area Code	213
JFK	Jay Eff **Kay**	Zip Code	90291
M & M	ema**nem**	Date	9/15/**88**

Review Exercise 1-20: Sound/Meaning Shifts

icy	I see.	attic	a **tick**
achy	a **key**	comedy	committee
history	his **tree**	paradise	pair of **dice**
interest	in **trust**	selfish	sell **fish**
orange	ar**range**	underwear	under **where?**
eunuch	unique	ambulance	unbalanced

Review Exercise 1-21: Squeezed-Out Syllables

actually	[**æk**•chully]	finally	[**fine**•lee]
business	[**biz**•ness]	general	[**gen**•r'l]
comfortable	[**c'mf**•t'b'l]	interest	[**in**•tr'st]
different	[**dif**•r'nt]	natural	[**næch**•r'l]
every	[**ev**•ree]	orange	[**ornj**]
favorite	[**fa**•vr't]	probably	[**prä**•blee]
family	[**fæm**•lee]	separate	[**sep**•r't]
vegetable	[**vej**•t'b'l]	several	[**sev**•r'l]

Review Exercise 1-22: Syllable Patterns

1
la!   la-a…
cat   dog

. . . .

2
la-**la**   la-la
a **dog**   **hot** dog

. . . .

3

la-la-**la**	la-la-**la**	la-**la**-la	la-**la**-la
Bob's hot **dog**	a hot **dog**	a **hot** dog	**hot** dog stand

. . . .

4

la-la-la-**la**	la-la-la-**la**	la-la-**la**-la
Spot's a hot **dog**.	It's a hot **dog**.	**Bob** likes **hot** dogs.
la-la-**la**-la	la-**la**-la-la	**la**-la-la-la
It's my **hot** dog.	a **hot** dog stand	**light**house keeper

Review Exercise 1-23: Syllable Count Test

1.	confront ___	8.	He like red ones. ___	15.	European ___
2.	detail ___	9.	He bought me one. ___	16.	with dignity ___
3.	a blind date ___	10.	It's very nice. ___	17.	popcorn machine ___
4.	my date book ___	11.	Jim likes hot rods. ___	18.	a mortarboard ___
5.	consequence ___	12.	lake ___	19.	robin redbreast ___
6.	consequential ___	13.	days ___	20.	telescope ___
7.	Will needs a car. ___	14.	It's your birthday? ___	21.	telescopic ___

Review Exercise 1-24: Single-Word Phrases

	Noun	**Adjective**
1.	It's a **cat**.	It's **black**.
2.	It's an **egg**.	It's **scrambled**.
3.	It's a **car**.	It's **fast**.

Review Exercise 1-25: Sentence Stress with Descriptive Phrases

	Adjective	**Noun and Adjective**
1.	It's **black**.	It's a black **cat**.
2.	It's **scrambled**.	It's a scrambled **egg**.
3.	It's **fast**.	It's a fast **car**.

Review Exercise 1-26: Two Types of Descriptive Phrases

	Adjective Noun	**Adverb Adjective**
1.	It's a black **cat**.	It's dark **black**.
2.	It's a scrambled **egg**.	It's totally **scrambled**.
3.	It's a fast **car**.	It's too **fast**.

Review Exercise 1-27: Descriptive Phrase Story—Snow White and The Seven Dwarves

*Snow **White*** was a *beautiful **princess***. On the *castle **wall***, there was an *enchanted **mirror*** owned by an *old woman*—a *wicked **witch***! "Mirror, mirror, on the wall, who's the fairest of them all?" When the mirror answered, "*Snow **White***," the *young **girl*** was banished from her *glorious **castle*** to live in the *dark **woods***. She met *seven **dwarves***, and they lived in a *small **hut***. The *evil **witch*** tried to kill the *poor **girl*** with a *poisoned **apple***, but she was saved by a *handsome **prince***. They had a *beautiful **wedding*** and lived happily *ever **after***.

Review Exercise 1-28: Sentence Stress with Set Phrases

Noun	Noun/Adj.	Set Phrase
1. It's a **cat**.	It's **wild**.	It's a **wild**cat.
2. It's an **egg**.	It's a **timer**.	It's an **egg** timer.
3. It's a **car**.	It's a **crash**.	It's a **car** crash.

Review Exercise 1-29: Making Set Phrases

1. a box _____
2. a sitter _____
3. a palm _____
4. a cake _____
5. a tea _____
6. a opener _____

Review Exercise 1-30: Set Phrase Story—Our Mailman

Our *mailman* loves *junk food*. At *dinnertime*, he has *potato* chips and a *hot dog*. He puts some *soy sauce* on his *eggplant*, but it gives him a *stomachache*. For dessert, he has a *watermelon*, a *grapefruit*, and some *ice cream*. *Afterwards*, he leaves the *dinner* table and goes to the *bookshelf* in his *bedroom*. He takes down a *notebook* and does his *homework*. He puts a clean *pillowcase* on his pillow, covers up with the *bedspread*, and goes to *dreamland*.

Review Exercise 1-31: Contrasting Descriptive and Set Phrases

Descriptive Phrase	Set Phrase
1. It's a black **cat**.	It's a **wild**cat.
2. It's a scrambled **egg**.	It's an **egg** timer.
3. It's a fast **car**.	It's a **car** crash.

Review Exercise 1-32: Two-Word Stress

Descriptive Phrase	Set Phrase
1. a rocky **garden**	a **rock** garden
2. a gilded **cage**	a **bird** cage
3. melted **butter**	a **butter** knife
4. tomato **soup**	**tomato** sauce
5. a baby **goat**	a **scape**goat

Review Exercise 1-33: Nationality Intonation Quiz

1. a French guy	4. a french fry	7. French-Canadian
2. a French restaurant	5. french toast	8. a French teacher
3. French food	6. a french horn	9. a french door

Review Exercise 1-34: Contrasting Descriptive and Set Phrases

Set Phrase	Descriptive Phrase
A **French** teacher…	A French **teacher**…
…teaches French.	…is from France.
A **French** book…	A French **book** … is on any subject,
…teaches the French language.	but it came from France.
French food…	A French **restaurant**…
…is croissants for breakfast.	…serves croissants for breakfast.

Review Exercise 1-35: Contrast of Compound Nouns

1. a dark **room**
2. a **dark**room
3. an antique shop
4. an antique dealer
5. an antique chair
6. a new video
7. the video store
8. a coffee table
9. hot coffee
10. a coffeepot
11. a chemistry set
12. a chemical reaction
13. a sixth sense
14. six cents
15. a sixth grader
16. the sixth grade
17. long hair
18. a hairdresser
19. a haircut
20. the wrong station
21. a police station
22. a radio station
23. orange juice
24. a guitar case
25. an electric guitar
26. trick photography
27. a photo-op
28. a wedding ceremony
29. a beautiful ceremony
30. a wedding cake

Review Exercise 1-36: Description and Set Phrase Test

1. The **schoolkids** took the **subway downtown** for their **field trip** on **urban living**.
2. Our **local sheriff** had a **bumper sticker** on his **back bumper**.
3. The **homeowners** thought they had to pay **property taxes** to the **federal government**.
4. There were **small tremblors** after the **earthquake** in San Francisco.
5. The **Geology Club** went on a **camping trip** to Mount Hood.
6. The **award ceremony** at the **Hilton Hotel** lasted for **two hours**.
7. **Bob Smith** took his **surfboard** out on a **stormy day** near **Diamond Head**.
8. The **boy scouts** pitched their **pup tents** on the **mountaintop** in the **pouring rain**.
9. It's a **little late** to ask the **babysitter** to stay **over night**.
10. The **sixth graders** were reading **comic books** and drinking **chocolate milk**.

Review Exercise 1-38: Consistent Noun Stress in Changing Verb Tenses

erode	1. The **floods** erode the **mountains**.	th' **fl'dz**əroud th' **mæon**[(t)]**nz**
eroded	2. The **floods** eroded the **mountains**.	th' **fl'd** zəroudəd th' **mæon**[(t)]**nz**
are eroding	3. The **floods**'re eroding the **mountains**.	th' **fl'd** zr•rərouding th' **mæon**[(t)]**nz**
will erode	4. The **floods**'ll erode the **mountains**.	th' **fl'd** zələroud th' **mæon**[(t)]**nz**
would erode	5. The **floods**'d erode the **mountains**.	th' **fl'd** zədəroud th' **mæon**[(t)]**nz**
would have eroded	6. The **floods**'d've eroded the **mountains**.	th' **fl'd** zədəvəroudəd th' **mæon**[(t)]**nz**
that have eroded	7. The **floods** that've eroded the **mountains**.	th' **fl'd** zədəvəroudəd th' **mæon**[(t)]**nz**
have eroded	8. The **floods**'ve eroded the **mountains**.	th' **fl'd** zəvəroudəd th' **mæon**[(t)]**nz**
had eroded	9. The **floods**'d eroded the **mountains**.	th' **fl'd** zədəroudəd th' **mæon**[(t)]**nz**
will have eroded	10. The **floods**'ll've eroded the **mountains**.	th' **fl'd** zələvəroudəd th' **mæon**[(t)]**nz**
ought to erode	11. The **floods** ought to erode the **mountains**.	th' **fl'd** zädə eeroud th' **mæon**[(t)]**nz**
should erode	12. The **floods** should erode the **mountains**.	th' **fl'dz** shüdəroud th' **mæon**[(t)]**nz**
should not erode	13. The **floods** shouldn't erode the **mountains**.	th' **fl'dz** shüdn•nəroud th' **mæon**[(t)]**nz**
should've eroded	14. The **floods** should've eroded the **mountains**.	th' **fl'dz** shüdəvəroudəd th' **mæon**[(t)]**nz**
should not have	15. The **floods** shouldn't've eroded the **mountains**.	th' **fl'dz** shüdn•nəvəroudəd th' **mæon**[(t)]**nz**
could erode	16. The **floods** could erode the **mountains**.	th' **fl'dz** cüdəroud th' **mæon**[(t)]**nz**
could not erode	17. The **floods** couldn't erode the **mountains**.	th' **fl'dz** cüdn•nəroud th' **mæon**[(t)]**nz**
could have eroded	18. The **floods** could've eroded the **mountains**.	th' **fl'dz** cüdəvəroudəd th' **mæon**[(t)]**nz**
could not have	19. The **floods** couldn't've eroded the **mountains**.	th' **fl'dz** cüdn•nəvəroudəd th' **mæon**[(t)]**nz**
might erode	20. The **floods** might erode the **mountains**.	th' **fl'dz** mydəroud th' **mæon**[(t)]**nz**
might have	21. The **floods** might've eroded the **mountains**.	th' **fl'dz** mydəvəroudəd th' **mæon**[(t)]**nz**

must erode	22. The **floods** must erode the **mountains**.	th' **fl'dz** məsdəroud th' **mæon**⁽ᵗ⁾**nz**
must have	23. The **floods** must've eroded the **mountains**.	th' **fl'dz** məsdəvəroudəd th' **mæon**⁽ᵗ⁾**nz**
can erode	24. The **floods** can erode the **mountains**.	the **fl'dz** kənəroud th' **mæon**⁽ᵗ⁾**nz**
can't erode	25. The floods **can't erode** the mountains.	the fl'dz **kæn**⁽ᵈ⁾**əroud** th' mæon⁽ᵗ⁾nz

---

Review Exercise 1-39: Consistent Pronoun Stress in Changing Verb Tenses

present	1. It **erodes** them.	idə**roudz**'m
past	2. It **eroded** them.	idə**roud**'d'm
continuous	3. It's **eroding** them.	itsə**roud**ing'm
future	4. It'll **erode** them if it keeps up.	idələ**roud**'m
present conditional	5. It'd **erode** them if it kept up.	idə**roud**'m
past conditional	6. It'd've **eroded** them if it'd kept up.	idəvə**roud**'d'm
relative pronoun	7. The one that's **eroded** them is quite odd.	the wənthətsə**roud**'d'm *(is…)*
present perfect	8. It's **eroded** them for eons.	itsə**roud**'d'm
past perfect	9. It'd **eroded** them before the last ice age.	idə**roud**'d'm
future perfect	10. It'll've **eroded** them by the end of the millennium.	idələvə**roud**'d'm
obligation	11. It ought to **erode** them.	idädə ee**roud**'m
obligation	12. It should **erode** them.	it sh'də**roud**'m
obligation	13. It shouldn't **erode** them.	it sh'dn•nə**roud**'m
obligation	14. It should have **eroded** them.	it sh'dəvə**roud**'d'm
obligation	15. It shouldn't've **eroded** them.	it sh'dn•nəvə**roud**'d'm
possibility/ability	16. It could **erode** them.	it c'də**roud**'m
possibility/ability	17. It couldn't **erode** them.	it c'dn•nə**roud**'m
possibility/ability	18. It could have **eroded** them.	it c'dəvə**roud**'d'm
possibility/ability	19. It couldn't have **eroded** them.	it c'dn•nəvə**roud**'d'm
possibility	20. It might **erode** them.	it mydə**roud**'m
possibility	21. It might have **eroded** them.	it mydəvə**roud**'d'm
probability	22. It must **erode** them.	it məss də**roud**'m
probability	23. It must have **eroded** them.	it məsdəvə**roud**'d'm
ability	24. It can **erode** them.	it c'nə**roud**'m
ability	25. It **can't erode** them.	it **cæn**⁽ᵈ⁾**əroud**'m

---

Review Exercise 1-40: Intonation in Your Own Sentence

On a separate piece of paper, write the Review Exercise as on pages 38-40.

Review Exercise 1-41: Supporting Words

1. The **floods** erode the **mountains** every **day**.
   th' **fləd** zəroud th' **mæon**⁽ᵗ⁾**n** zɛvree **day**

2. The **floods** eroded th' **mountains** for **centuries**.
   th' **fləd** zəroudəd th' **mæon**⁽ᵗ⁾**nz** fr **sen** chr•reez

3. The **floods**'re eroding the **mountains** right now.
   th' **fləd** zr•r'rouding th' **mæon**⁽ᵗ⁾**nz** räit næo

4. The **floods**'ll erode th' **mountains** if this keeps **up**.
   th' **fləd** zələroud th' **mæon**⁽ᵗ⁾**nz** if this keep **səp**

5. The **floods**'d erode the **mountains** if this kept **up**.
   th' **fləd** zədəroud th' **mæon**⁽ᵗ⁾**nz** if this kepdəp

6. The **floods**'d've eroded th' **mountains** if it'd kept **up**.
   th' **fləd** zədəvəroud'd th' **mæon**⁽ᵗ⁾**nz** if id kepdəp

7. The **floods** that've eroded the **mountains** are over.
th' **fləd** zədəvəroud'd th' **mæon**⁽ᵗ⁾n zr•rovr

8. The **floods**'ve eroded the **mountains** over the **years**.
th' **fləd** zəvəroud'd th' **mæon**⁽ᵗ⁾n zovr th' **yirz**

9. The **floods**'d already eroded the **mountains** before the last **ice** age.
th' **fləd** zədäreddy əroud'd th' **mæon**⁽ᵗ⁾nz b'for th' **læss**dice age

10. The **floods**'ll've totally eroded th' **mountains** by the next **ice** age.
th' **fləd** zələv toudəlee⁽ʸ⁾əroud'd th' **mæon**⁽ᵗ⁾nz by th' nex **dy**sage

---

Review Exercise 1-42: Contrast Practice

would erode	5. The **floods**'d erode the **mountains**.	th' **fləd** zədəroud th' **mæon**⁽ᵗ⁾nz
had eroded	9. The **floods**'d eroded the **mountains**.	th' **fləd** zədəroud'd th' **mæon**⁽ᵗ⁾nz
would have eroded	6. The **floods**'d've eroded the **mountains**.	th' **fləd** zədəvəroud'd th' **mæon**⁽ᵗ⁾nz
that have eroded	7. The **floods** that've eroded the **mountains**.	th' **fləd** zədəvəroud'd th' **mæon**⁽ᵗ⁾nz
will erode	4. The **floods**'ll erode the **mountains**.	th' **fləd** zələroud th' **mæon**⁽ᵗ⁾nz
would erode	5. The **floods**'d erode the **mountains**.	th' **fləd** zədəroud th' **mæon**⁽ᵗ⁾nz
would have eroded	6. The **floods**'d've eroded the **mountains**.	th' **fləd** zədəvəroud'd th' **mæon**⁽ᵗ⁾nz
have eroded	8. The **floods**'ve eroded the **mountains**.	th' **fləd** zəvəroud'd th' **mæon**⁽ᵗ⁾nz
had eroded	9. The **floods**'d eroded the **mountains**.	th' **fləd** zədəroud'd th' **mæon**⁽ᵗ⁾nz
will have eroded	10. The **floods**'ll've eroded the **mountains**.	th' **fləd** zələvəroud'd th' **mæon**⁽ᵗ⁾nz
would erode	5. The **floods**'d erode the **mountains**.	th' **fləd** zədəroud th' **mæon**⁽ᵗ⁾nz
ought to erode	11. The **floods** ought to erode the **mountains**.	th' **fləd** zädə eeroud th' **mæon**⁽ᵗ⁾nz
can erode	24. The **floods** can erode the **mountains**.	the **flədz** c'nəroud th' **mæon**⁽ᵗ⁾nz
can't erode	25. The **floods** can't erode the **mountains**.	the flədz **cæn**⁽ᵈ⁾əroud th' mæon⁽ᵗ⁾nz

---

Review Exercise 1-43: Yes, You *Can* or No, You *Can't*?

I can **tell** you.	[I k'n **tell** you]	*positive*
I **can't tell** you.	[I **kæn**⁽ᵗ⁾tell you]	*negative*
I **can** tell you.	[I **kææn** tell you]	*extra positive*
I **can't** tell you.	[I **kæn**⁽ᵗ⁾tell you]	*extra negative*

Review Exercise 1-44: Building an Intonation Sentence

I **saw** him. ❖ I **saw** him **again**. ❖ I **saw** him at **work** again. ❖ I think I **saw** him at **work** again. ❖ I really think I **saw** him at **work** again. ❖ I **really** think I saw him at **work** again in the **yard**. ❖ I **really** think I saw him at **work** again in the **yard** behind the **house**.

Review Exercise 1-45: Building Your Own Intonation Sentences

On a separate piece of paper, build up your own sentences.

Review Exercise 1-46: Regular Transitions of Nouns and Verbs

Nouns		Verbs	
an accent	[**æks**'nt]	to accent	[**æks**ent]
a contract	[**kän**træct]	to contract	[k'n**trækt**]
an insert	[**in**sert]	to insert	[in**sert**]
an object	[**äb**jekt]	to object	[əb**ject**]
progress	[**prägr**'s]	to progress	[pr'**gress**]

Review Exercise 1-47: Regular Transitions of Adjectives and Verbs

Nouns/Adjectives		Verbs	
alternate	[**äl**tern't]	to alternate	[**äl**ternɛit]
estimate	[**est**'m't]	to estimate	[**est**'mɛit]
separate	[**sepr**'t]	to separate	[**sep**erɛit]

Review Exercise 1-48: Regular Transitions of Adjectives and Verbs

1. Would you please *alternate* seats with the other *alternate*?
2. They signed a *contract* in order to *contract* their services.
3. Who could *object* to *progress*?
4. The unidentified flying *object progressed* slowly across the night sky.
5. We need a written *estimate* in order to *estimate* the payment.

Review Exercise 1-51: Extended Listening Practice

1. ____ ____ ____ ____ ____ ____ ____ ____ ____.
2. ____ ____ ____ ____ ____ ____ ____ ____ ____ ____.
3. ____ ____ ____ ____ ____ ____ ____ ____ ____ ____ ____.

Review Exercise 1-53: Reduced Sounds

To	Looks Like...	Sounds Like...
unvoiced	The president hoped to veto the bill.	[th' **prez**ədnt houptə veetou th' **bill**]
	Deposit it to my account, please.	[d'**päz**'di⁽ᵗ⁾t' myə kæon⁽ᵗ⁾, pleez]
voiced	Their boss told them to wait.	[thɛr **bäss** toldəmdə **weit**]
	The coach showed us how to pitch.	[the **coch** showdəs hæodə **pitch**]
At	Everyone stared at the mess.	[everyone stɛrdə⁽ᵗ⁾th' **mess**]
unvoiced	Stay at my house for a while.	[stayə⁽ᵗ⁾ **my** hæos frə while]
voiced	Jim looked at his watch impatiently.	[**jim** lük d'diz **watch**im pɛish'ntlee]
	He's at his brother's.	[heez'diz **brə**thrz]
It	They said it took too long.	[they sedi⁽ᵗ⁾**tük** too läng]
unvoiced	Do you think it turned out?	[dyu thing kit turn **dæot**]
voiced	Let's keep it in perspective.	[lets keepidin pers**pek**d'v]
	Can we keep it for another day?	[kwee keepi⁽ᵗ⁾ frə n'ther day]
For	This'll do for now.	[thissəl **du** fr **næo**]
	The students all worked for hours.	[th' **studn** tsäll wrkt fr**hæ**wrz]
From	We learned it from the coach.	[we **lrn** di⁽ᵗ⁾ frm th' **coch**]
	The tourists came from all over.	[the **tr•**rists came frə**mäl**lovr]
In	We made it just in time.	[we **mei**dit jəsdin **time**]
	The place was in an uproar.	[th' **pleis**wəzinənəp roar]
An	It was an odd remark.	[it wəzənäd rə**märk**]
	He's an open book to me.	[heezə noupən **bük** tə me]
And	Everyone sat and chatted for a while.	[evreewən sæ⁽ᵗ⁾n **chæ**dəd frə wyᵊl]
	It was getting later and later.	[it w'z gedding leidr'n **lei**dr]
Or	We had two or three options.	[we hæd tu⁽ʷ⁾r three⁽ʸ⁾**äp**sh'nz]
	No one could see or hear anything.	[nou w'n küd see⁽ʸ⁾r hi**renn**y thing]

Are	The neighbors are complaining again.	[th' neibrzr k'm**play** ningə gen]
	Whose shoes are these?	[hooz **shoozr** theez]
Your	The door's on your left.	[th' door zänyr **left**]
	Are you on your way yet?	[är yu⁽ʷ⁾änyr **way** yet]
One	There's another one later.	[therzə nəthr w'n **leidr**]
	One of them is outside.	[w'n'v'm'z æo⁽ᵗ⁾**side**]
The	The other one's in here.	[thee⁽ʸ⁾əthr w'n zin hir]
	Did he pass the test?	[didee pæss th' **test**]
A	Let's take a cab.	[lets teikə **cæb**]
	What's the tallest building in America?	[wts th' täll'st **bil**ding inəmerəkə]
Of	Would you like a piece of pie?	[Jläikə peesə **pie**]
	They'll be gone for a couple of weeks.	[thell be gän frə couplə **weeks**]
Can	Do you think you can do it?	[dyu thing kyu k'n **du**⁽ʷ⁾'t]
	Can you believe it?!	[k'new b'**lee**vit]
Had	We think he'd never done it before.	[we thing keed never **də**nit b'for]
	They'd always done it that way.	[they däweez **də**nit thæt way]
Would	Why would he tell her?	[wy woody **tel**ler]
	I don't know if he'd agree.	[äi dou nou if heedə **gree**]
Was	Who was on the phone?	[hoo w'zän th' **foun**]
	The drummer was off beat.	[th' drəmr w'zäf **beet**]
What	Let's see what he wants.	[let see wədee **wänts**]
	Who knows what it is?	[hoo nouz w'd**'d'z**]
Some	Some of it got in my eyes.	[s'm'v't gädin my **äiz**]
	Somebody took my place.	[s'mb'dee tük my **pleis**]

Review Exercise 1-54: Intonation and Pronunciation of "That"

Relative Pronoun	The grapes that he bought were sweet.	[th' **greips** the dee bät wr **sweet**]
Conjunction	We hope that you'll be there.	[we houp the chüll **bee** there]
Demonstrative	Don't do that!	[doun⁽ᵗ⁾**du** thæt]
Combination	I know that you'll like that car	[äi **nou** the chüll like thæt **cär**
	that you bought.	the chew bät]

Review Exercise 1-55: Crossing Out Reduced Sounds

Th̶i̶n̶k̶ th̶e̶ Unit̶e̶d̶ **Auto** W̶o̶rk̶e̶rs c̶a̶n̶ beat Cat̶e̶rpill̶a̶r **Inc.** i̶n̶ their b̶i̶tter **contract** battle? Before placing your **bets**, talk to Paul **Branan**, who **can't wait** to cross the **picket** line at Caterpillar's **factory** in East **Peoria**. **Branan**, **recently** laid **off** by a **rubber**-parts plant where he earned **base** pay of **$6.30** an **hour**, lives **one** block from a **heavily** picketed **gate** at the **Cat** complex. **Now** he's applying to replace one of **12,600 workers** who have been on **strike** for the **past** five **months**. "**Seven**teen dollars an **hour** and **they** don't want to **work**?" asks Branan. "**I** don't want to take **another** guy's **job**, but **I'm** hurting, **too**."

Review Exercise 1-56: Reading Reduced Sounds

Th'nk th' Unit'd **Auto** Wrkrs c'n beat Cat'pill'r **Inc.** 'n their b'tter **contract** battle? B'fore plac'ng y'r **bets**, talk t' Paul **Bran'n**, who **can't wait** t' cross th' **p'cket** line 't Cat'pill'r's **factry** 'n East **Peoria**. **Bran'n**, **rec'ntly** laid **off** by' **r'bb**'r-parts plant where he 'rned **base** pay'v **$6.30**'n **hour**, l'ves **w'n** block fr'm' **heav'ly** p'ck't'd **gate** 't th' **Cat** complex. **Now** hes 'pplying t' r'place w'n'v **12,600 wrkrs** who h've b'n on **strike** f'r th' **past** five **m'nths**. "**Sev'n**teen doll'rs 'n **hour** 'nd **they** dont want t' **work**?" asks Bran'n. "**I** dont want t' take '**n'ther** guys **job**, b't **I'm** h'rting, **too**."

Review Exercise 1-57: Phrasing

Statement	**Birds** lay **eggs**.
Clauses	As we all **know**, **birds** lay **eggs**.
Listing	**Birds** lay **eggs**, build **nests**, and hunt for **food**.
Question	Do **birds** lay **eggs**?
Repeated Question	Do **birds** lay **eggs**?!!
Tag Question	**Birds** lay **eggs**, **don't** they?
Tag Statement	**Birds** lay **eggs**, **DON'T** they!
Indirect Speech	He asked if **birds** laid **eggs**.
Direct Speech	"Do **birds** lay **eggs**?" they **inquired**.

Review Exercise 1-60: Tag Endings

1. There's none left, <u>is there</u>! _____
2. That was fun, _____ !
3. You don't have a clue, _____ !
4. He wouldn't forget, _____ ?
5. They can do it over, _____ ?
6. She had to do it, _____ ?
7. She'd rather do it, _____ ?
8. She'd better do it,_____ !
9. She'd never do it,_____ ?
10. She'd never done it, _____ ?

Review Exercise 2-1: Spelling and Pronunciation
Buddy.   Buddy forgot.   He said OK, buddy forgot.   He said OK, but he forgot.

Review Exercise 2-4: Consonant / Vowel Liaison Practice
1. I think he's on his way.   _____
2. He put it in an umbrella stand.   _____
3. We bought it in Italy.   _____

Review Exercise 2-8: Consonant / Consonant Liaison Practice
1. Nick Clark hopes to put ten dollars down.   _____
2. But Tom makes so much juice.   _____
3. Bob's dog got some bones.   _____

Review Exercise 2-9: Vowel / Vowel Liaison Practice
1. Can you see it through to the end?   _____
2. Be available for the other opportunity in my office. _____
3. He always wants to offer to go over it again.   _____

Review Exercise 2-11: T, D, S, or Z + Y Liaison Practice
1. We're glad that your homework's done.   _____
2. Would you help me with this?   _____
3. Do you miss your old friends?   _____
4. Where's your brother?   _____

Review Exercise 2-12: Finding Liaisons and Glides
Think the United **Auto** Workers can beat Caterpillar **Inc.** in their bitter **contract** battle? Before placing your **bets**, talk to Paul **Branan**, who **can't wait** to cross the **picket** line at Caterpillar's **factory** in East **Peoria**. **Branan**, **recently** laid **off** by a **rubber**-parts plant where he earned **base** pay of $6.30 an **hour**, lives **one** block from a **heavily** picketed **gate** at the **Cat** complex. **Now** he's applying to replace one of **12,600 workers** who have been on **strike** for the **past** five **months**. "**Seven**teen dollars an **hour** and **they** don't want to **work**?" asks Branan. "**I** don't want to take **another** guy's **job**, but **I'm** hurting, **too**."

Review Exercise 2-13: Practicing Liaisons

Think the[y]Unite däuto Workers can beat Caterpillr rinc. in their bitter **contract** battle? Before placing your **bets**, talk to Paul **Branan**, who **can't wait** to cross the **picket** ly n't Caterpillar's **fac**tree yineest Pe[y]ori[y]a. **Branan**, **recently** lay däff bya **rubber**-parts plant wheree[y]earned **base** pay'v $6.30[y]a **næ**[w]er, live zw'n block froma **heavily** picketed **gate** a[t]the **Cat** complex. Nowee zapplying to replace w'n'v **12,600 workers** who[w]v binän **strike** for the **past** five **months**. "**Seven**teen dollar sa **næ**[w]er and **they** don't want to **work**?" asks Branan. "**I** don't wan[t]to take **another** guy's **job**, b'dime hurting, **too**."

Review Exercise 3-1: Word-by-Word and in a Sentence

Stressed		Unstressed		
that	thæt	th't	thət	We think th't we can **get** there in time.
than	thæn	th'n	thən	It's **harder** th'n she **thought**.
as	æz	'z	əz	It was'z **flat**'z a **pan**cake.
at	æt	't	ət	We **jumped**'t the **chance**.
and	ænd	'nd	ənd	The **speaker** went on'n **on**.
have	hæv	h'v	həv	How h'v you **been**?
had	hæd	h'd	həd	I wish we h'd **been** there.
can	cæn	c'n	cən	Let me know if you c'n **be** there.

Review Exercise 3-3: Vowel-Sound Differentiation

	æ	ä	ə	ou	a	ε
1.	ask	often	under	over	April	ever
2.	back	ball	bunch	both	baby	bend
3.	cap	cop	cup	cope	cape	kept
4.	dash	dot	does	don't	date	desk
5.	fast	fall	fun	photo	fail	fell

Review Exercise 3-4: Finding the æ, ä, ə Sounds

Think thə United äuto Workers can beat Cæterpillar **Inc**. in their bitter **contract** battle? Before placing your **bets**, talk to Paul **Branan**, who **can't wait** to cross the **picket** line at Caterpillar's **factory** in East **Peoria**. **Branan**, **recently** laid **off** by a **rubber**-parts plant where he earned **base** pay of $6.30 an **hour**, lives **one** block from a **heavily** picketed **gate** at the **Cat** complex. **Now** he's applying to replace one of **12,600 workers** who have been on **strike** for the **past** five **months**. "**Seven**teen dollars an **hour** and **they** don't want to **work**?" asks Branan. "**I** don't want to take **another** guy's **job**, but **I'm** hurting, **too**."

Review Exercise 3-5: Reading the [æ] Sound

Fæst Dæncing Næncy

We plan to have a dance on the last Saturday in January. It's the last chance for a dance. We practice at a dance class with Max and Nancy. Max dances fast, but Nancy dances best. We are happy about the dance, but Max is sad that Sally can't dance. Her ankle is in a cast!

Review Exercise 3-6: Reading the [ä] Sound

Päul's Täll Däughter

Tom watches Paul's tall daughter play softball and volleyball. Paul's daughter is called Molly. Molly starts playing softball in March and ends in August. She plays volleyball in October. Tom is Molly's godfather. They have a lot in common. Tom bought Molly a ball. When Molly saw the ball, she tossed it in the air. "Thanks a lot, Tom!"

Review Exercise 3-7: Reading the [ə] Sound

S'nday 'n M'nday

M<u>o</u>nday is s<u>u</u>ch <u>a</u> w<u>o</u>nderf<u>u</u>l day. B<u>u</u>t S<u>u</u>nday is m<u>u</u>ch more w<u>o</u>nderf<u>u</u>l th<u>a</u>n M<u>o</u>nday! We have so m<u>u</u>ch f<u>u</u>n on S<u>u</u>nday, and we m<u>u</u>st r<u>u</u>n on M<u>o</u>nday. Wh<u>a</u>t tr<u>ou</u>ble … D<u>ou</u>g m<u>u</u>st r<u>u</u>n on S<u>u</u>nday *and* M<u>o</u>nday. D<u>ou</u>g has no f<u>u</u>n.

Review Exercise 4-1: Stressed and Unstressed T

paternal   pattern   critique   critic

Review Exercise 4-3: Rule 1—Top of the Staircase

1. Tell Tina's tailor to take two tucks in the top of Tim's trousers tomorrow.
2. We try and try, but Todd still tells us to try harder.
3. Terry had a tingling in her toes until the doctor took her temperature.

Review Exercise 4-4: Rule 2—Middle of the Staircase

1. What a totally naughty little daughter!   [wədə toudəlee **nä**dee liddle **dä**dr]
2. Matty got a little cottage in the city.   [**mæ**dee gädə liddle **cäd**'j in th' **si**ddee]
3. Letty bought a lot of bottles for Katie.   [**lɛ**dee bädə lädə **bäd**lz fr **kei**dee]

Review Exercise 4-5: Rule 3—Bottom of the Staircase

1. Matt got to put Jim's pet rat back in the cage. [**mæ**⁽ᵗ⁾gä⁽ᵗ⁾t' pü⁽ᵗ⁾ **jimz** pe⁽ᵗ⁾**ræ**⁽ᵗ⁾bæck in th' **keij**]
2. Pat set the date with Kate.   [**pæ**⁽ᵗ⁾se⁽ᵗ⁾th' **dei**⁽ᵗ⁾with **kei**⁽ᵗ⁾]
3. It's not what they went for.   [its **nä**⁽ᵗ⁾wə⁽ᵗ⁾ they **wen**⁽ᵗ⁾ for]

Review Exercise 4-6: Rule 4—"Held T" Before N

1. Whitney saw lightning on the mountain.   [**wi**⁽ᵗ⁾nee sä **li**⁽ᵗ⁾ning än the **mæon**⁽ᵗ⁾n]
2. He was certainly a frightening accountant.   [he w'z sr⁽ᵗ⁾nlee⁽ʸ⁾ə**fri**⁽ᵗ⁾ning ə**kæon**⁽ᵗ⁾n⁽ᵗ⁾]
3. That was a rotten way to shorten the curtain! [thæt w'z'**rä**⁽ᵗ⁾n weid' **shor**⁽ᵗ⁾n th' **kr**⁽ᵗ⁾n]

Review Exercise 4-7: Rule 5—The Silent T

1. We had twenty interviews on May 22.   [we hæd twenny **inn**erviewzän may twenny **sek**'nt]
2. They don't even want a percentage.   [they doe neev'n wänə prsen'j]
3. We took advantage of the interruption.   [we tükəd **væn**'j'v the⁽ʸ⁾innerəpshən]

Review Exercise 4-10: T Combinations in Context

1. But he said that it's OK.   [bədee sed thədit sou **kei**]
2. It's not what you want, but it's what you get. [its nät wəchew **wänt**, bədits wəchew **get**]
3. What a way to get what he wants!   [wədə weidə get wədee **wänts**]

Review Exercise 4-11: Voiced and Unvoiced Sounds with T

paw	pod	pot		bah	bawd	bought
par	pard	part		bar	bard	Bart
pall	palled	palt		ball	balled	Balt

Review Exercise 5-2: Sounds Comparing L with T, D, and N

Beginning				**Middle**			**End**			
lab	nab	tab	dab	Ellie	any	Eddie	bill	bin	bit	bid
lot	not	tot	dot	caller	Conner	cotter	sill	sin	sit	sid
lie	night	tie	die	alley	Annie's	at ease	bowl	bone	boat	bode

Review Exercise 5-3: Final El with Schwa

1	**bill**	2	**bull**	3	**pool**	4	**bail**
	bi-ə-lə		bü-ə-lə		pū-$^{(w)}$ə-lə		bay-$^{(y)}$ə-lə
5	**bell**	6	**peel**	7	**Buell**	8	**pearl**
	bɛ-ə-lə		pee-$^{(y)}$ə-lə		byū-$^{(w)}$ə-lə		pr-rə-lə

Review Exercise 5-4: Many Final Els

1	**bill**	2	**bull**	3	**pool**	4	**bail**
	bi-əlll		bü-əlll		pū-$^{(w)}$əlll		bay-$^{(y)}$əlll
5	**bell**	6	**peel**	7	**Buell**	8	**pearl**
	bɛ-əlll		pee-$^{(y)}$əlll		byū-$^{(w)}$əlll		pr-rəlll

Review Exercise 5-5: Liaise the Ls

1 call him	[cällim]	**2** visible	[vizəbəlᵊ]

Review Exercise 5-7: Silent Ls

1. would   could   should
2. chalk   talk   walk
3. already   always   almost

Review Exercise 5-8: Hold Your Tongue!

Let Larry's little lily leaves fall off.

Review Exercise 5-9: Bill and Ellie

Bill still calls Ellie all the time. He'll really be glad when she calls back, but it may be a while. He slowly dials the telephone for the twelfth time. *Trill, trill, trill.* No luck. Well, Ellie will feel ill when Bill is in the hospital. He might fall from the windowsill. "Ellie? Hello! Are you well?" Saved by the bell!

Review Exercise 5-11: Final L Practice

	üll	äll	æwl	ell	ale	oll	eel	dl
1.	bull	ball	bowel	bell	bale	bowl	Beal	bottle
2.	pull	pall	Powell	pell	pail	pole	peel	poodle
3.	full	fall	foul	fell	fail	foal	feel	fetal

Review Exercise 5-12: A Frontal Lobotomy?

I'd rather have a frontal lobotamy than a bottle in front of me, chortled the gentle little man, or was it the little gentleman? But anyway, it'll take a battle to test his mettle. What'll he do to get a handle on the whole kit and caboodle? I don't want to meddle, but what if he flies off the handle again? Out of luck, that's what!

Review Exercise 5-13: Speed-reading

Repeat the paragraph from Review Exercise 1-55 as quickly as possible.

Review Exercise 5-14: Tandem Reading

Repeat the paragraph from Review Exercise 1-55 along with me.

Review Exercise 6-1: R Location Practice

[g], [gr], Greg, grin, grand, gray, cray, care, core, corner, curl, girl, urban, her, earn, earth, world, were, word

---

Review Exercise 6-2: Double Vowel Sounds with R

	är	**ɛr**	**or**	**eer**	**er**
1	[ä] + [er]	[ɛ] + [ər]	[o] + [ər]	[e] + [ər]	[ər] + [ər]
2	[hä•ərd]	[shɛ•ər]	[mo•ər]	[he•ər]	[wər•ər]
3	hard	share	more	here	were

Review Exercise 6-3: How to Pronounce Troublesome Rs

1.	were	[wər•ər]	3.	world/whirled	[were rolled]	5.	where/wear	[wɛər]
2.	word	[wər•ərd]	4.	wore/war	[woər]			

Review Exercise 6-4: Zbigniew's Epsilon List

embarrass	character	any	vocabulary	said	paragraph
Paris	necessary	says	parallel	guarantee	area

Review Exercise 6-5: R Combinations

	ər	**är**	**ɛr**	**or**	**eer**	**æwr**
1.	earn	art	air	or	ear	hour
2.	hurt	heart	hair	horse	here	how're
3.	were	far	where	wore	we're	power

Review Exercise 6-6: Roy the Rancher

Roy's **car** will a<u>rr</u>ive a<u>r</u>ound **th<u>r</u>ee** in the afte<u>r</u>noon. **Ga<u>r</u>y** will **<u>r</u>est** befo<u>r</u>e they **<u>r</u>ide** a<u>r</u>ound the **<u>r</u>anch** to-gether in the **Fo<u>r</u>d**. **Ga<u>r</u>y**'s a **grape** g<u>r</u>ower in No<u>r</u>the<u>r</u>n **California**, and **<u>R</u>oy**'s a <u>r</u>anche<u>r</u> in **Southe<u>r</u>n** Califor-nia. They we<u>r</u>e **f<u>r</u>iends** in **Pa<u>r</u>is** at the **So<u>r</u>bonne** fo<u>r</u> fou<u>r</u> **yea<u>r</u>s**. <u>R</u>oy and **Ga<u>r</u>y** had an **o<u>r</u>ange** g<u>r</u>ove and an **apple** o<u>r</u>cha<u>r</u>d in **Ba<u>r</u>stow**, but the **o<u>r</u>anges** we<u>r</u>e **ho<u>rr</u>ible** and the **apple** t<u>r</u>ees we<u>r</u>e **wo<u>r</u>se**. They **<u>r</u>oamed** a<u>r</u>ound **Eu<u>r</u>ope** fo<u>r</u> several **yea<u>r</u>s** until Ga<u>r</u>y's **ma<u>rr</u>iage**. He ma<u>rr</u>ied **Sa<u>r</u>ah** in **Bake<u>r</u>sfield** and had fou<u>r</u> **child<u>r</u>en: <u>R</u>achel, <u>R</u>udy, <u>R</u>andy**, and **Ha<u>rr</u>y**. **Ha<u>rr</u>y** was a fai<u>r</u>ly **<u>r</u>ude** boy and he c<u>r</u>eated <u>r</u>athe<u>r</u> a lot of **t<u>r</u>ouble** between Ga<u>r</u>y and **Sa<u>r</u>ah**. **Ga<u>r</u>y** o<u>r</u>de<u>r</u>ed **Ha<u>rr</u>y** to shape **up** o<u>r</u> **fo<u>r</u>get** wo<u>r</u>king in the **ya<u>r</u>d** fo<u>r</u> ext<u>r</u>a **money**. **Ha<u>rr</u>y** said he was **so<u>rr</u>y** and the **group** became **f<u>r</u>iends** again. After a long **sepa<u>r</u>ation**, **Ga<u>r</u>y** hea<u>r</u>d f<u>r</u>om his f<u>r</u>iend, **<u>R</u>oy**. **<u>R</u>oy** was d<u>r</u>iving th<u>r</u>ough **F<u>r</u>esno** and wanted to get **together** with Ga<u>r</u>y's **family**. **Eve<u>r</u>y-one** gathe<u>r</u>ed a<u>r</u>ound the **fi<u>r</u>eplace** to wait for **Ga<u>r</u>y's** old **f<u>r</u>iend**. **Ga<u>r</u>y, Sa<u>r</u>ah, <u>R</u>achel, <u>R</u>udy, <u>R</u>andy**, and **Ha<u>rr</u>y** a<u>r</u>e sitting in a **<u>r</u>ow** nea<u>r</u> the **ga<u>r</u>age**. <u>R</u>oy's **car** will a<u>rr</u>ive a<u>r</u>ound **th<u>r</u>ee** in the afte<u>r</u>noon.

Review Exercise C: Modifying Descriptive Phrases

	Descriptive Phrase	**Modified Description**
1.	It's a black **cat**.	It's a **dark** black **cat**.
2.	It's a scrambled **egg**.	It's a **totally** scrambled **egg**.
3.	It's a fast **car**.	It's a **really** fast **car**.

Review Exercise D: Modifying Set Phrases

	Set Phrase	**Modified Set Phrase**
1.	It's a **wild**cat.	It's a fierce **wild**cat.
2.	It's an **egg** timer.	It's a plastic **egg** timer.
3.	It's a **car** crash.	It's a catastrophic **car** crash.

Review Exercise E: Two- and Three-Word Set Phrases

	Two-Word Set Phrase	**Three-Word Set Phrase**
1.	It's a **wild**cat.	It's a **wild**cat preserve.
2.	It's an **egg** timer.	It's an **egg** timer bell.
3.	It's a **car** crash.	It's a **car** crash report.

Review Exercise F: Three-Word Phrase Summary

Modified Description	Modified Set Phrase	Three-Word Set Phrase
1. a **dark** black **cat**	a fierce **wild**cat	a **wild**cat preserve
2. a **totally** scrambled **egg**	a plastic **egg** timer	an **egg** timer bell
3. a **really** fast **car**	a catastrophic **car** crash	a **car** crash report

---

Review Exercise I: Multiple Modifiers with Set Phrases

Modified Set Phrase	Remodified Set Phrase
1. It's a fierce **wild**cat.	It's an **astonishingly** fierce **wild**cat.
2. It's a plastic **egg** timer.	It's an **old** plastic **egg** timer.
3. It's a catastrophic **car** crash.	It's a **truly** catastrophic **car** crash.

Review Exercise J: Compound Intonation of Numbers

1. How **old** is she?	2. How long has it **been**?	3. How **old** is she?
She's thir**teen**. [thir**téen**]	**Thir**teen **yéars**.	She's **thir**teen years **old**.
She's **thir**ty. [**thír**dy]	**Thir**ty **years**.	She's **thir**ty years **old**.

Review Exercise K: Modifying Three-Word Set Phrases

Three-Word Set Phrase	Modified Three-Word Set Phrase
1. It's a **wild**cat preserve.	It's a new **wild**cat preserve.
2. It's an **egg** timer bell.	It's a loud **egg** timer bell.
3. It's a **car** crash report.	It's a graphic **car** crash report.

Review Exercise L: Three Word Phrase Story—The Amazing Rock Soup

A **tired** young **hiker** was striding through the **thick**, dark **forest** when he came upon a **gnarled** old **crone** standing before a **small** stone **hut** in a **sunny** little **clearing**. "My **poor old stomach** is **really** very **empty**," he thought. "I hope this old **land**lady can spare a little **food**." Sensing what he was about to say, she snapped, "**No**! I have **barely** enough for my**self**!" "My good **woman**," he said, "On the **contrary**! I'd like to cook you a **sumptuously** rich **dinner**...of rock **soup**!" She was **naturally** very **suspicious**, but she let him **in**. He boiled some **clear**, fresh **water**, added **three** clean **rocks**, and hung the **dented** old **kettle** in the old **fire**place. He tasted the **mysterious** liquid **concoction**. "This is truly **delicious**," he declared, "but it would be **so** much **better** with just **one** little **vegetable**." She begrudgingly gave him a **small** limp **carrot** and **two** dry **onions**. "**Yum**," he said happily. "But if **only** ..." **Bit** by bit, he cajoled the lonely **house**wife into making a savory **stew**pot. The two of them **sat** down, **smiled** at each other, and enjoyed a fabulous **dinner** together.

Review Exercise M: Building Up to Five-Word Phrases

1. It's a <u>**house**</u>.	6. It's a <u>**light**</u>house.
2. It's <u>**old**</u>.	7. It's an <u>old</u> <u>**light**</u>house.
3. It's <u>really</u> <u>**old**</u>.	8. It's a <u>**really**</u> old <u>**light**</u>house.
4. It's an <u>old</u> <u>**house**</u>.	9. He's a <u>**light**</u>house keeper.
5. It's a <u>**really**</u> old <u>**house**</u>.	10. He's an <u>old</u> <u>**light**</u>house keeper.
	11. He's a <u>**really**</u> old <u>**light**</u>house keeper.

Review Exercise 7-1: The Thing

<u>This</u> is <u>the</u> <u>thing</u> <u>that</u> <u>they</u> told <u>them</u> about <u>this</u> Thursday. <u>This</u> thing or <u>that</u> thing? <u>This</u> thing. Actually, <u>there</u> are two of <u>them</u>. Both of <u>these</u> <u>things</u> were wi<u>th</u> <u>the</u> <u>three</u> o<u>ther</u> <u>things</u> <u>there</u> in <u>the</u> <u>theater</u>. <u>They're</u> wor<u>th</u> <u>three</u> <u>thousand</u> dollars. Ru<u>th</u> and her mo<u>ther</u> <u>think</u> <u>that</u> <u>they</u> are wor<u>th</u> more <u>than</u> <u>that</u>, <u>though</u>, unless <u>they</u> break, and <u>then</u> <u>they</u> are wor<u>thless</u>. Alto<u>gether</u> wor<u>thless</u> to <u>them</u>. <u>That</u> would bo<u>ther</u> Ru<u>th's</u> bro<u>ther</u>, mo<u>ther</u> and fa<u>ther</u> on <u>their</u> bir<u>thday</u>, <u>the</u> <u>thirtieth</u> of <u>this</u> month. Ru<u>th</u>, E<u>thel</u>, and Be<u>th</u> have a rule of <u>thumb</u> about bir<u>thdays</u>, which is to stay to<u>gether</u>, <u>through</u> <u>thick</u> and <u>thin</u>, whe<u>ther</u> it's wor<u>th</u> it or not. And <u>that's</u> <u>the</u> <u>thing</u>.

Noun Intonation Summary

Rule 1: New Information
Noun Verb **Noun**: **Bob** studies **English**.   Pronoun Verb **Noun**: He studies **English**.

Rule A: Descriptive Phrases

pretty **good**	a good **shot**	a **pretty** good **shot**
really **long**	a long **talk**	**really** very **long**
fairly **rubbery**	a rubber **hose**	a **long** rubber **hose**

Rule B: Compound Nouns

a **snap**shot	a **snap**shot collection
a **talk**show	a **talk**show host
a **rubber** band	a **rubber** band box

a good **snap**shot	a good **snap**shot collection
a funny **talk**show	a funny **talk**show host
a cheap **rubber** band	a cheap **rubber** band box

a **really** good **snap**shot	a **really** good **snap**shot collection
a **super** funny **talk**show	a **super** funny **talk**show host
a **very** cheap **rubber** band	a **very** cheap **rubber** band box

Rule C: Descriptive Phrases with Sentence Balance

The Great **Wall**	pretty **good**
The **Great** Wall of **China**	a **pretty** good **shot**

seven**teen**	four**teen**
seventeen **dollars**	**four**teen **years**
seventeen dollars an **hour**	**four**teen years **old**
seventeen dollars and ten cents an **hour**	**four**teen and a half years **old**

Rule 2: Old Information
Pronoun **Verb** Pronoun: He **studies** it.   Noun **Verb** Pronoun: Bob **studies** it.

Rule 3: Contrast
We need a red **pen**. (*new information*)   We need a **red** pen. (*not a blue one*)

Rule 4: Opinion
I should go **jogging**. (*new info*)—I **should** go jogging … (*opinion indicating the opposite*)
pretty **good** (*new info*)—**pretty** good (*just OK*); I think **so** (*confident*)—I **think** so (*not sure*)

Rule 5: Negation (Can't)

I can do it.	[I k'n **do** it]	(*positive*)	I can do it.	[I **kææn do** it]	(*extra positive*)
I can't do it.	[I **kæn**⁽ᵗ⁾ **do** it]	(*negative*)	I can't do it.	[I **kæn**⁽ᵗ⁾ do it]	(*extra negative*)

Review Exercise 8-1: Comparing [u] and [ü]

u	ü	u	ü
soon	book	Luke	look
cooed	could	wooed	would
shoed	should	tool	took

Review Exercise 8-2: Lax Vowels

e	i	ü	ə	ər
held	hill	hook	hug	her
bet	bit	book	but	burn
kept	kiss	could	cut	curt

Review Exercise 8-4: Bit or Beat? Bid or Bead?

Tense Vowels		Lax Vowels	
beat	bead	bit	bid
seat	seed	sit	Sid
heat	he'd	hit	hid

Review Exercise 8-5: Tense and Lax Vowel Review Exercise

Tense	Lax	
1. even	if	**Even** if it's **raining**, they'll **go**.
2. bean	been	We've been growing **beans**.
3. deal	dill	You made a **deal** for **dill** pickles.

Review Exercise 8-6: Middle "I" List

similar	typical	president	episode	beautiful	ability
animal	chemistry	experiment	security	technical	monitor

Review Exercise 8-10: [ü] Paragraph

You could've pushed, you could've pulled. You should've pushed and pulled, by hook or by crook, to take a good look at that book. It stood a full foot tall, propped up on the cushion at the Book Nook. Now, I'm all shook up, sugar!

Review Exercise 8-11: [u] Paragraph

As a rule, you and Sue Woo are truly too cool—if only you knew how cool you two choose to be at school or at the movies. Lou blew his cool on Tuesday while perusing the newspaper for the truth about who flew the coop from the boot camp, including the lieutenant. Who knew the truth?

Review Exercise 9-1: Mind Your Vees

P	B	F	V	W
Perry	berry	fairy	very	wary
pat	bat	fat	vat	wax
Paul	ball	fall	vault	wall

1. Peter picked a peck of pickled peppers.
2. It's important to provide perfect principles for young people.
3. Hopscotch, lollipops, hoolahoops, and popsicles keep a little nipper happy.
4. Laptop computers put payroll, payables, and spreadsheets at our fingertips.
5. It's impossible to predict population patterns.

1. Betty bought a bit of better butter.
2. Ben believes Bill broke Bob's box.
3. Billions of bagels are being baked in Brooklyn.
4. Babies babble and blow bubbles.
5. Bananas come from Cuba.

1. What were the women doing in the woods?
2. How would I know?
3. When was Willy's worst weekend?
4. Why would we wear warm wool?
5. Where were we when we woke up?

1. <u>F</u>red <u>f</u>orgot to <u>f</u>ry <u>f</u>ish on <u>F</u>riday.
2. <u>F</u>ew <u>f</u>riends <u>f</u>ail to <u>f</u>ight.
3. <u>F</u>reedom <u>f</u>ighters <u>f</u>ight <u>f</u>or <u>f</u>reedom.
4. Only a <u>f</u>ool <u>f</u>eeds <u>f</u>ugu to <u>f</u>riends.
5. <u>F</u>eel <u>f</u>ree to lau<u>gh</u> if it's <u>f</u>unny.

1. It's <u>e</u>vident that <u>V</u>era was <u>v</u>ery <u>v</u>aluable.
2. Cliff Cla<u>v</u>en was a<u>v</u>ailable for e<u>v</u>ery <u>v</u>ersion.
3. The na<u>v</u>y re<u>v</u>oked his <u>v</u>isa for ob<u>v</u>ious reasons.
4. Bea<u>v</u>ers gi<u>v</u>e the en<u>v</u>ironment <u>v</u>ery <u>v</u>aluable dams.
5. Ca<u>v</u>es lea<u>v</u>e me cold, but I lo<u>v</u>e to di<u>v</u>e.

Review Exercise 10-1: S or Z?

s	z	s	z
ice	eyes	dust	does
ace	A's	race	rays
fleece	fleas	muscle	muzzle

Review Exercise 10-2: Sally at the Seashore

It's <u>s</u>o <u>s</u>illy to <u>s</u>ee <u>S</u>ally <u>s</u>ell <u>s</u>eashells at the <u>s</u>eashore. <u>S</u>ally and her <u>s</u>ister, <u>S</u>ue, can <u>s</u>ell <u>s</u>eventy-<u>s</u>ix apie<u>c</u>e every <u>S</u>aturday and <u>S</u>unday in Augu<u>s</u>t and <u>S</u>eptember, but their pri<u>c</u>e mu<u>s</u>t decrea<u>s</u>e or their <u>s</u>ales will <u>s</u>ink.

Review Exercise 10-3: Fuzzy Wuzzy

Fu<u>zz</u>y Wu<u>zz</u>y wa<u>s</u> a bear. Fu<u>zz</u>y Wu<u>zz</u>y had no hair. Fu<u>zz</u>y Wu<u>zz</u>y wa<u>s</u>n't fu<u>zz</u>y, wa<u>s</u> he!

Review Exercise 11-1: Tense Vowels

	æ	æo	ä	i	a	e	u	ou
1.	ask	out	ought	I'm	ape	eel	oops	own
2.	bake	about	boss	bike	bathe	bean	boost	both
3.	camp	cow	cough	kind	case	keep	coop	code

Review Exercise 11-3: Lax Vowels

e	i	ü	ə	ər
wed	which	would	what	work
bet	bit	book	but	burn
kept	kiss	could	cut	curt

Review Exercise 11-7: Compound Nouns and Complex Verbs

invendə
1. The **wily** old **light**house keepers invent a **highly** lucrative **money**-laundering scheme once a season.

invenədə
2. The **wily** old **light**house keepers invented a **highly** lucrative **money**-laundering scheme last year.

zərinvending
3. The **wily** old **light**house keepers're inventing a **highly** lucrative **money**-laundering scheme again.

zəlinvendə
4. The **wily** old **light**house keepers'll invent a **highly** lucrative **money**-laundering scheme if they aren't afraid of being caught and sent to prison.

zədinvendə
5. The **wily** old **light**house keepers'd invent a **highly** lucrative **money**-laundering scheme if they weren't afraid of being caught and sent to prison.

zədəvinvenədə
6. The **wily** old **light**house keepers'd've invented a **highly** lucrative **money**-laundering scheme if they hadn't been afraid of being caught and sent to prison.

zədəvinvenədə
7. The **wily** old **light**house keepers that've invented a **highly** lucrative **money**-laundering scheme are languishing in Club Fed at the moment.

zəvinvenədə

8. The **wily** old **light**house keepers've invented a **highly** lucrative **money**-laundering scheme for the tenth year in a row.

zədinvenədə

9. The **wily** old **light**house keepers had invented a **highly** lucrative **money**-laundering scheme long before multilevel marketing became popular.

zələvinvenədə

10. The **wily** old **light**house keepers'll've invented a **highly** lucrative **money**-laundering scheme by the time they get back from checking their off-shore bank accounts.

zädə invendə

11. The **wily** old **light**house keepers ought to invent a **highly** lucrative **money**-laundering scheme to handle the overflow cash from their many nefarious enterprises.

shüdin vendə

12. The **wily** old **light**house keepers should invent a **highly** lucrative **money**-laundering scheme to stash their ill-gotten gains.

shüdn•nin vendə

13. The **wily** old **light**house keepers shouldn't invent a **highly** lucrative **money**-laundering scheme in this anti-crime climate.

shüdə vinvendə

14. The **wily** old **light**house keepers should've invented a **highly** lucrative **money**-laundering scheme while they were in the witness **protection** plan.

shüdn•nəvin venedə

15. The **wily** old **light**house keepers shouldn't've invented a **highly** lucrative **money**-laundering scheme while they were being monitored by the FBI.

cüdin vendə

16. The **wily** old **light**house keepers could invent a **highly** lucrative **money**-laundering scheme once a year for a hundred years and never run out of ideas.

cüdn•nin vendə

17. The **wily** old **light**house keepers couldn't invent a **highly** lucrative **money**-laundering scheme even if their lives depended on it.

cüdə vinvenədə

18. The **wily** old **light**house keepers could've invented a **highly** lucrative **money**-laundering scheme if they'd had a laptop and a bank account.

cüdn•nəvin venəd suchə

19. Even those **wily** old **light**house keepers couldn't've invented such a **highly** lucrative **money**-laundering scheme without outside help.

mydin vendə

20. The **wily** old **light**house keepers might invent a **highly** lucrative **money**-laundering scheme unless they're kept under house arrest.

mydəvin vendədə

21. The **wily** old **light**house keepers might've invented a **highly** lucrative **money**-laundering scheme while they were waiting for trial.

məssdin vendə

22. The **wily** old **light**house keepers must invent a lot of **highly** lucrative **money**-laundering schemes.

məssdəvin vendədə

23. The **wily** old **light**house keepers must've invented a **highly** lucrative **money**-laundering scheme while they were out on parole.

cənin vent

24. The **wily** old **light**house keepers can invent hundreds of **highly** lucrative **money**-laundering schemes.

kændin vendenee
25. The **wily** old **light**house keepers can't invent any more **highly** lucrative **money**-laundering schemes.

Review Exercise 11-8: Your Own Compound Nouns

On a separate piece of paper, build up your own compound nouns, both subject and object, as on page 140.

Review Exercise 11-9: Your Own Compound Nouns and Complex Verbs

On a separate piece of paper, write out your own sentences as on page 141.

Review Exercise 12-1: Nasal Consonants

	Initial		Middle		Final	
m/b	more	bore	summing	subbing	jam	jab
n/d	nine	dine	Anna	adder	pawn	pod
ng/g	bring each	geese	singer	cigar	ring	rig

Review Exercise 12-2: Ending Nasal Consonants

M	N	NG
rum°	run°	rung°
some	son	sung
hum	hun	hung

Review Exercise 12-3: Reading Nasal Consonant Sounds

Some young men wanted to fling a ring along the rim of the fountain, but we told them to clam up and clean up their game. One was a well-mannered young man with the name Dan Wang. He said, "Yes, ma'am."

Review Exercise 13-1: Throaty Consonants

	Initial	Middle	Final
h	how	rehire	
k	cow	accent	sink
g	go	regard	drag
ng	bring in	thanks	sing
r	row	mirror	car

Review Exercise 13-2: The Letter X

[ks]		[gz]	
excite	[ɛksäit]	example	[əgzæmpᵊl]
extra	[ɛkstrə]	exactly	[əgzæklee]
except	[əksɛpt]	examine	[əgzæmən]
excellent	[ɛksələnt]	exit	[ɛgzit]

Review Exercise 13-3: Reading the H, K, G, NG, and R sounds

Dr. Baxter's exact experience was such that when the good doctor traveled to the Sahara, he inhaled the arid air, picked up his still packed bags, and headed for the bar. It was time to examine the sorry situation, which was exactly the case with Dr. Igor Baxter, an English historian with a peg leg and a unquenchable thirst for Mexican rum. Baxter had had a pair of strange experiences in the area, but he was still game to accomplish his goal in the exiled purgatory of the great, dry Sahara. When he saw that his patients were to be camels, however, he packed up and took off for green England, without a single pang of regret.

Nationality Guides

No matter what language you speak, you will have different sounds and rhythms from a native speaker of American English. These Nationality Guides will give you a head start on what to listen for in American English from the perspective of your own native language. In order to specifically identify what you need to work on, this section can be used in conjunction with the *diagnostic analysis*. The analysis provides an objective rendering of the sounds and rhythms based on how you currently speak, as well as specific guidelines for how to standardize your English; call **(800) 457-4255** for a private consultation.

Each section will cover *intonation*, *word connections*, *word endings*, *pronunciation*, *location of the language in the mouth*, as well as particular difficulties to work through, and solutions to common misperceptions.

Most adult students rely too heavily on spelling. It's now your job to listen for pure sound, and reconcile that to spelling—not the other way around. This is the same path that a native speaker follows.

As you become familiar with the major characteristics and tendencies in American English, you will start using that information in your everyday speech. One of the goals of the diagnostic analysis is to show you what you already know, so you can use the information and skills in English as *transfer skills*, rather than *newly learned skills*. You will learn more readily, more quickly, and more pleasantly—and you will retain the information and use the accent with less resistance.

Read all the nationality guides—you never know when you'll pick up something useful for yourself. Although each nationality is addressed individually, there are certain aspects of American English that're difficult for everyone, in this order:

1. Pitch changes and meaning shifts of intonation
2. Regressive vocalization with a final voiced consonant (*bit/bid*)
3. Liaisons
4. R & L
5. æ ä ə (including the æo in *ow*)
6. Tense & lax vowels (i/ē and ü/ū)
7. Th
8. B & V & W

Ideally, you would have learned intonation before you learned grammar, but since that didn't happen, you can now incorporate the intonation into the grammar that you already know. When you first start listening for intonation, it sounds completely random. It shifts all around even when you use the same words. So, where should you start? In basic sentences with a *noun-verb-noun* pattern, the nouns are usually stressed. Why? Because nouns carry the new information. Naturally, contrast can alter this, but noun stress is the default. Listen to native speakers and you will hear that their pitch goes up on the noun most of the time.

You will, however, also hear verbs stressed. When? The verb is stressed when you replace a noun with a pronoun. Because *nouns are new information* and *pronouns are old information*—and we don't stress old information—the intonation shifts over to the verb. Intonation is the most important part of your accent. Focus on this, and everything else will fall into place with it.

*   *Intonation*
*   *Liaisons*
*   *Word endings*
*   *Pronunciation*
*   *Location in the mouth*
*   *Particular difficulties*

Nouns generally indicate new information and are stressed.

***Pronouns** indicate old information and are unstressed.*

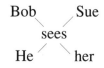

The four "ma" tones of Mandarin Chinese

ma^1 ——

ma^2 ╱

ma^3 ╲╱

ma^4 ╲

Chinese Intonation Summary

1. *Say the four ma's.*
2. *Write them out with the appropriate arrows.*
3. *Replace the stressed word in a sentence with each of the four ma's.*
4. *Decide which one sounds best.*
5. *Put the stressed word back in the sentence, keeping the tone.*

Chinese

Intonation

There are several immediately evident characteristics of a Chinese accent. The most notable is the lack of speech music, or the musical intonation of English. This is a problem because, in the English language, *intonation* indicates meaning, new information, contrast, or emotion. Another aspect of speech music is *phrasing*, which tells if it is a statement, a question, a yes/no option, a list of items, or where the speaker is in the sentence (introductory phrase, end of the sentence, etc.). In Chinese, however, a change in tone indicates a different vocabulary word.

In English, Chinese speakers have a tendency to increase the *volume* on stressed words, but otherwise give equal value to each word. This atonal volume-increase will sound aggressive, angry, or abrupt to a native speaker. When this is added to the tendency to lop off the end of each word, and almost no word connections at all, the result ranges from choppy to unintelligible.

In spite of this unpromising beginning, Chinese students have a tremendous advantage. Here is an amazingly effective technique that radically changes how you sound. Given the highly developed tonal qualities of the Chinese language, you are truly a "pitch master." In order for you to appreciate your strength in this area, try the four *ma* tones of Mandarin Chinese. (Cantonese is a little more difficult since it has eight to twelve tones and people aren't as familiar with the differentiation.) These four tones sound identical to Americans — *ma, ma, ma, ma.*

Take the first sentence in Exercise 1-5 *It sounds like **rain*** and replace *rain* with *ma¹.* Say *It sounds like ma¹.* This will sound strangely flat, so then try *It sounds like ma².* This isn't it either, so go on to *It sounds like ma³* and *It sounds like ma⁴.* One of the last two will sound pretty good, usually *ma³.* You may need to come up with a combination of *ma³* and *ma⁴,* but once you have the idea of what to listen for, it's really easy. When you have that part clear, put *rain* back in the sentence, keeping the tone:

It sounds like *ma³.*
It sounds like *rain³.*

If it sounds a little short (*It sounds like ren*), **double** the sound:

It sounds like ray^3 een.

When this exercise is successful, go to the second sentence, *It **sounds** like rain* and do the same thing:

It *ma³* like rain.
It *sounds³* like rain.

Then, contrast the two:

It sounds like *rain³.*
It *sounds³* like rain.

From this point on, you only need to periodically listen for the appropriate *ma,* substituting it in for words or syllables. You don't even need to use the rubber band since your tonal sophistication is so high.

The main point of this exercise is to get you listening for the tone shifts in English, which are very similar to the tone shifts in Chinese. The main difference is that Americans use them to indicate stress, whereas in Chinese, they are fully different words when the tone changes.

A simple way to practice intonation is with the sound that American children use when they make a mistake—***uh**-oh*. This quick note shift is completely typical of the pattern, and once you have mastered this double note, you can go on to more complex patterns. Because Chinese grammar is fairly similar to English grammar, you don't have to worry too much about word order.

uh

oh

Liaisons

All of the advantages that you have from *intonation* are more than counterbalanced by your lack of *word connections*. The reason for this is that Chinese characters (words or parts of words) start with consonants and end with either a vowel or a nasalized consonant, *n* or *ng*. There is no such thing as a final *t*, *l*, or *b* in Chinese. To use an example we've all heard of, *Mao Tse Tung*. This leads to several difficulties:

- ❏ No word endings
- ❏ No word connections
- ❏ No distinction between final voiced or unvoiced consonants.

It takes time and a great deal of concentration, but the lack of word endings and word connections can be remedied. Rather than force the issue of adding on sounds that will be uncomfortable for you, which will result in overpronunciation, go with your strengths — notice how in *speech*, but not *spelling*, Americans end their words with vowel sounds and start them with consonants, just as in Chinese! It's really a question of rewriting the English script in your head that you read from when you speak.

Liaisons or *word connections* will force the final syllable to be pronounced by pushing it over to the beginning of the next word, where Chinese speakers have no trouble — not even with *l*.

Written English	Chinese Accent	American (with Liaisons)
Tell him	teo him	tellim
Pull it out	puw ih aw	pü li dout

Because you are now using a natural and comfortable technique, you will sound smooth and fluid when you speak, instead of that forced, exaggerated speech of people who are doing what they consider unnatural. It takes a lot of correction to get this process to sink in, but it's well worth the effort. Periodically, when you speak, write down the exact sounds that you made, then write it in regular spelling, so you can *see* the Chinese accent and the effect it has on meaning (*puw ih aw* has no meaning in English). Then convert the written English to spoken American (*pull it out* changes to *pü li dout*) to help yourself rewrite your English script.

When you don't use liaisons, you also lose the underlying hum that connects sentences together. This *coassonance* is like the highway and the words are the cars that carry the listener along.

The last point of intonation is that Chinese speakers don't differentiate between voiced and unvoiced final consonants — *cap* and *cab* sound exactly the same. For this, you will need to go back to the staircase. When a final consonant is voiced, the vowel is lengthened or doubled. When a final consonant is unvoiced, the vowel is short or single.

Additionally, the long *a* before an *m* is generally shortened to a short ɛ. This is why the words *same* and *name* are particularly difficult, usually being pronounced *sem* and *nem*. You have to add in the second half of the sound. You need *nay + eem* to get *name*. Doubled vowels are explained on page 3.

Unvoiced   *Voiced*

Pronunciation

The most noticeable nonstandard pronunciation is the lack of final *l*. This can be corrected by either liaisons, or by adding a tiny schwa after it (l^uh or lᵊ) in order to position your tongue correctly. This is the same solution for *n* and *ng*.

Like most other nationalities, Chinese students need to work on *th* and *r*, but fortunately, there are no special problems here.

The remaining major area is [ā], [ɛ], and [æ], which sound the same. *Mate, met, mat* sound like *met, met, met*. The [ɛ] is the natural sound for the Chinese, so working from there, you need to concentrate on Chapters 3 and 11. In the word *mate*, you are hearing only the first half of the [ɛi] combination, so double the vowel with a clear *eet* sound at the end (even before an unvoiced final consonant). Otherwise, you will keep saying *meh-eht* or *may-eht*.

a   It frequently helps to know exactly how something would look in your own language—and in Chinese, this entails characters. The characters on the left are the sounds needed for a Chinese person to say both the long *i* as in *China* and the long *a* as in *made* or *same*. Read the character, and then put letters in front and in back of it so you are reading half alphabet, half character. An *m* in front and a *d* in back of the first character will let you read *made*. A *ch* in front and *na* in back of the second character will produce *China*. It's odd, but it works.

L   A word that ends in *~ail* is particularly difficult for Chinese speakers since it contains both the hard [ɛi] combination and a final *l* (Chapter 5). It usually sounds something like *feh-o*. You need to say *fail* as if it had three full syllables —*fay-yə-l*ᵒ.

u, v, f, w   Another difficulty may be *u, v, f,* and *w*. The point to remember here is that *u* and *w* can both be considered *vowels* (i.e., they don't touch anywhere in the mouth), whereas *v* and *f* are *consonants* (your upper teeth touch your lower lip). *u*, as in *too* or *use* should be no problem. Similar to *u*, but with a little push of slightly rounded lips is *w*, as in *what* or *white*. The letters *f* and *v* have basically the same sound, but *f* is unvoiced and *v* is voiced. Your lower lip should come up a little to meet your top teeth. You are not biting down on the outside of your lip here; the sound is created using the inside of your lower lip. Leave your mouth in the same position and make the two sounds, both voiced and unvoiced. Practice words such as *fairy, very,* and *wary.*

Long A

Long I

There is another small point that may affect people from southern mainland China who use *l* and *n* interchangeably. This can be corrected by working with *l* words and pinching the nose shut. If you are trying to say *late* and it comes out *Nate*, hold your nose closed and the air will be forced out through your mouth.

æ The *æ* sound doesn't exist in Chinese, so it usually comes out as *ä* or *ε*, so *last* sounds like *lost* or *name* sounds like *nem*. You need to work on Chapter 3, which drills this distinctively American vowel.

ä Because of spelling, the *ä* sound can easily be misplaced. The *ä* sound exists in Chinese, but when you see an *o*, you might want to say [o], so *hot* sounds like *hoht* instead of *haht*. Remember, most of the time, the letter *o* is pronounced *ah*. This will give you a good reference point for whenever you want to say *ä* instead of [o]; astr<u>o</u>nomy, c<u>ä</u>ll, l<u>ä</u>ng, pr<u>ä</u>gress, etc.

o Conversely, you may pronounce the letter *o* as *ä* or *ə* when it should be an *o*, as in *only, most, both*. Make sure that the American *o* sounds like *ou: ounly, moust, bouth*.

ə The schwa is typically overpronounced based on spelling. Work on Chapter 1, Intonation, and Chapter 3, Pronunciation. If your intonation peaks are strong and clear enough, then your valleys will be sufficiently reduced as well. Concentrate on smoothing out and reducing the valleys and *ignore spelling!*

ü The [ü] sound is generally overpronounced to *ooh*. Again, spelling is the culprit. Words such as *smooth, choose,* and *too* are spelled with 2 *o*'s and are pronounced with a long *u* sound, but other words such as *took* and *good* are spelled with 2 *o*'s but are pronounced halfway between *ih* and *uh*; [tük] and [güd].

i In most Chinese dictionaries, the distinction between *i* and *ē* is not made. The *ē* is generally indicated by [i:], which causes problems with final consonants, and the *i* sound is overpronounced to *eee*. Practice these four sounds, remembering that *tense vowels* indicate that you tense your lips or tongue, while *lax vowels* mean that your lips and tongue are relaxed and the sound is produced in your throat. *Unvoiced* final consonants *(t, s, k, p, ch, f)* mean that the vowel is short and sharp; *voiced* final consonants *(d, z, g, b, j, v)* mean that the vowel is doubled. Work on Bit or Beat? Bid or Bead? in Chapter 8.

r Chinese speakers usually pronounce American *r* as *ä* at the end of a word (*car* sounds like *kaaah*) or almost a *w* in the beginning or middle (*grow* sounds like *gwow*). The tongue should be curled back more, and the *r* produced deep in the throat.

th If you pronounce *th* as *t* or *d* (depending if it's voiced or unvoiced), then you should allow your tongue tip to move about a quarter of an inch forward, so the very tip is just barely between your teeth. Then, from this position you make a sound similar to *t* or *d*.

n Chinese will frequently interchange final *n* and *ng*. The solution is to add a little schwa at the end, just like you do with the *el*. This will make the tongue position more apparent, as you can see on page 89.

sh Some people pronounce the *sh* in a particularly Chinese-sounding way. It seems that the tongue is too curled back, which changes the sound. Make sure that the tongue is flat, the tongue tip is just at the ridge behind the top teeth, and that only a thin stream of air is allowed to escape.

Final Consonants One of the defining characteristics of Chinese speech is that the final consonants are left off (*hold* sounds like *ho*). Whenever possible, make a liaison with the following word. For example, *hold* is difficult to say, so try *hold on = hol dän*. Pay particular attention to Chapter 2.

t American English has a peculiar characteristic in that the *t* sound is, in many cases, pronounced as a *d*. Work on Chapter 4.

Location of the Language

Chinese, like American English, is located in the *back of the throat*. The major difference between the two languages is that English requires that the speaker use the *tongue tip* a great deal: *l*, *th*; and final *t*, *d*, *n*, *l*.

Japanese

Intonation

Although Chinese and Japanese are both Asian languages and share enormously in their written characters, they are opposites in terms of intonation, word-endings, pronunciation, and liaisons. Whereas the Chinese stress every word and can sound aggressive, Japanese speakers give the impression of stressing no words and sounding timid. Both impressions are, of course, frequently entirely at odds with the actual meaning and intention of the words being spoken. Chinese speakers have the advantage of *knowing* that they have a tonal language, so it is simply a question of transferring this skill to English.

Japanese, on the other hand, almost always insist that the Japanese language "has no intonation". Thus, Japanese speakers in English tend to have a picket fence intonation | | | | | | | | | | | | | | | |. In reality, the Japanese language does express all kinds of information and emotion through intonation, but this is such a prevalent myth that you may need to examine your own beliefs on the matter. Most likely, you need to use the rubber band extensively in order to avoid volume increases rather than on changing the pitch.

One of the major differences between English and Japanese is that there is a fixed word order in English—a verb grid—whereas in Japanese, you can move any word to the head of a sentence and add a topic particle (*wa* or *ga*). Following are increasingly complex verbs with adverbs and helping verbs. Notice that the positions are fixed and do *not* change with the additional words.

	auxillary	negative	perfect auxillary	adverb	passive	continuous	main verb
Draw!							Draw!
He draws.							draws.
He does draw.	does						draw.
He is drawing.	is						drawing.
He is not drawing.	is	not					drawing.
He is not always drawing.	is	not		always			drawing.
He is not always being drawn.	is	not		always	being		drawn.
He has not always been drawn.	has	not		always	been		drawn.
He has not always been being drawn.	has	not		always	been	being	drawn.
He will not have always been being drawn.	will	not	have	always	been	being	drawn.

Liaisons

Whereas the Chinese drop word endings, Japanese totally overpronounce them. This is because in the katakana syllabary, there are the five vowels sounds, and then consonant-vowel combination. In order to be successful with word connections, you need to think only of the final consonant in a word, and connect that to the next word in the sentence. For example, for *What time is it?* instead of *Whato täimu izu ito?* connect the two *t*'s, and let the other consonants move over to connect with the vowels, *w' täi mi zit?* Start with the held *t* in Chapter 4 and use that concept for the rest of the final consonants.

Written English	The only way to get it is to practice all of the time.
American accent	Thee$^{(y)}$only way də geddidiz də præctisälləv th' time.
Japanese accent	Zä ondee weh tsu getto itto izu tsu pudäctees odu obu zä taimu.

Pronunciation

æ The *æ* doesn't exist in Japanese; it usually comes out as *ä*, so *last* sounds like *lost*. You need to raise the back of your tongue and drop your jaw to produce this sound. Work on Chapter 3, which drills this distinctively American vowel.

ä The *ä* sound is misplaced. You have the *ä* sound, but when you see an *o*, you want to say *o*, so *hot* sounds like *hohto* instead of *haht*. Here's one way to deal with it. Write the word *stop* in katakana—the four characters for *su + to + hold + pu*, so when you read it, it sounds like *stohppu*. Change the second character from *to* to *ta*: *su + ta + hold + pu*, it will sound like *stop*. This will give you a good reference point for whenever you want to say *ä* instead of *o*; *imp*o*ssible, c*a*ll, l*o*ng, pr*o*blem*, etc.

o You may pronounce the letter *o* as *ä* or *ə* when it should be an *o*, as in *only, most, both*. Make sure that the American *o* sounds like *ou*: *ounly, moust, bouth*. This holds true for the diphthongs as well—*oi* sounds like *ou-ee*.

t<u>ou</u>n	t<u>o</u>ne	n<u>ou</u>t	n<u>o</u>te	h<u>ou</u>m	h<u>o</u>me
<u>ou</u>nli	<u>o</u>nly	c<u>ou</u>l	c<u>oa</u>l	j<u>ou</u>k	j<u>o</u>ke

Another way to develop clear strong vowels instead of nonstandard hybrids is to understand the relation between the American English spelling system and the Japanese katakana sounds. For instance, if you're having trouble with the word *hot*, say *ha, hee, hoo, heh, hoh* in Japanese, and then go back to the first one and convert it from *ha* to *hot* by adding the held *t* (Chapter 4). Say *hot* in Japanese, *atsui*, then add an *h* for *hatsui* and then drop the *-sui* part, which will leave *hot*.

ə The schwa is typically overpronounced, based on spelling. Concentrate on smoothing out and reducing the valleys and *ignore spelling!*

ü Distinguishing tense and lax vowels is difficult, and you'll have to forget spelling for *ū* and *ü*. They both can be spelled with *oo* or *ou*, but the lax vowel *ü* should sound much closer to *i* or *uh*. If you say *book* with a tense vowel, it'll sound like *booque*. It should be much closer to *bick* or *buck*.

i Similarly, you need to distinguish between *e* and *i*, as in *beat* and *bit*, on page 123. Also, tone down the middle *i* in the multisyllabic words on page 125; otherwise, *similar* [sim'lr] will sound like [see-mee-lär]. Most likely, you overpronounce the lax vowel *i* to *eee*, so that *sit* is mispronounced as *seat*. Reduce the lax *i* almost to a schwa; *sit* should sound like *s't*. In most Japanese dictionaries, the distinction between *i* and *ē* is not made. Practice the four sounds— *bit, beat, bid, bead*—remembering that *tense vowels* indicate that you tense your lips or tongue, while *lax vowels* mean that your lips and tongue are relaxed and the sound is produced in your throat. *Unvoiced* final consonants (*t, s, k, p, ch, f*) mean that the vowel is short and sharp; *voiced* final consonants (*d, z, g, b, j, v*) mean that the vowel is doubled. Work on Bit or Beat? Bid or Bead? in Chapter 8.

	single	double
tense	beat	bead
lax	bit	bid

The Japanese R = The American T

ベリ　バラ　ビラ	Be<u>tt</u>y bought a bi<u>t</u> of
アイ　バラ　バイク	I bough<u>t</u> a bike.
クディ　ドゥイッ	Coul<u>d</u> he do it?
ウィ　アラ　ゴウ	We ought to go.

アイ　ニーダ　ラァダ　タイム	I need a lot of time.
マイ　マロウ	my motto
ミリン	meeting
アイム　ナラン　タイム	I'm not on time.

The Japanese *r* is a consonant. This means that it touches at some point in the mouth. Japanese speakers usually trill their *r*s (tapping the ridge behind the top teeth), which makes it sound like a *d* to the American ear. The tongue should be curled back, and the *r* produced deep in the throat—*not* touching the top of the mouth. The Japanese pronunciation of *r* is usually just an *ä* at the end of a word (*car* sounds like *caaah*) or a flap in the beginning or middle (*area* sounds like *eddy-ah*)

l   Japanese speakers often confuse the *el* with *r* or *d*, or drop the schwa, leaving the sound incomplete.

th   The *th* sound is mispronounced *s* or *z*, depending if it is voiced or unvoiced.

v   *v* is mispronounced either as a simple *bee*, or if you have been working on it, it may be a combination such as *buwee*. You need to differentiate between the four sounds of *p/b/f/v*. The plosives *b/p* pop out; the sibilants *f/v* slide out. *b/v* are voiced; *f/p* are unvoiced. *b/v* are the *least* related pair. The root of the problem is that you need a good, strong *f* first. To the American ear, the way the Japanese say *Mount Fuji* sounds like *Mount Hooji*. Push your bottom lip up with your finger so that it is *outside* your top teeth and make a sharp popping sound. Practice these sounds:

F	V	B	F	V	B
fat	vat	bat	ferry	very	berry
face	vase	base	effort	ever	Ebber
fear	veer	beer	foul	vowel	bowel

Once you have the *f* in place, simply allow your vocal cords to vibrate and you will then have a *v*.

	unvoiced	voiced
plosive	P	B
sibilant	F	V

w   The *w* is erroneously dropped before *ü*, so *would* is shortened to *ood*. Since you can say *wa, wi, wo* with no problem, use that as a starting point; go from *waaaaa, weeeeeee, woooooo* to *wüüüüüü*. It's more a concept problem than a physical one.

n   Japanese will frequently interchange final *n* and *ng*. Adding the little schwa at the end will clear this up by making the tongue position obvious, as on page 89.

z   *z* at the beginning of a word sounds like *dz* (*zoo* sounds like *dzoo*). For some reason, this is a tough one. In the syllabary, you read *ta, chi, tsu, teh, toh* for unvoiced and *da, ji, dzu, de, do* for voiced. Try going from unvoiced *sssssue* to *zzzzzzzoo*, and don't pop that *d* in at the last second.

179

si   The *si* combination is mispronounced as *shi*, so *six* comes out as *shicks*. Again, this is a syllabary problem. You read the *s* row as *sa, shi, su, seh, soh*. You just need to realize that since you already know how to make a hissing *s* sound, you are capable of making it before the *i* sound.

Location of the Language

Japanese is more *forward* in the mouth than American English, and more like Spanish except there is much *less lip movement*.

Spanish

Intonation

Spanish-speaking people (bearing in mind that there are 22 Spanish-speaking countries) tend to have strong intonation, but it's usually toward the end of a phrase or sentence. It is very clear sometimes in Spanish that a person is taking an entire phrase pattern and imposing it on the English words. This can create a subtle shift in meaning, one that the speaker is completely unaware of. For example,

Spanish	English with a Spanish Pattern	Standard English Pattern
Quiero comer *álgo*.	I want to eat *sóme*thing.	I want to *éat* something.

This is a normal stress pattern in Spanish, but it indicates in English that either you are willing to settle for less than usual or you are contrasting it with the possibility of *nothing*.

Spanish has five pure vowels sounds—*ah, ee, ooh, eh, oh*—and Spanish speakers consider it a point of pride that words are clearly pronounced the way they are written. The lack of the concept of schwa or other reduced vowels may make you overpronounce heavily in English. You'll notice that I said the *concept* of schwa—I think that every language has a schwa, whether it officially recognizes it or not. The schwa is just a neutral vowel sound in an unstressed word and at some point in quick speech in any language, vowels are going to be neutralized.

Liaisons

In Spanish, there are strong liaisons — *el hombre* sounds like *eh lombre*, but you'll probably need to rewrite a couple of sentences in order to get away from word-by-word pronunciation. Because consonant clusters in Spanish start with an epsilon sound (*español* for *Spanish*, *especial* for *special*), this habit carries over into English. Rewriting expressions to accommodate the difference will help enormously.

With Epsilon	Rewritten	With Epsilon	Rewritten
I estudy	ice tudy	excellent espeech	excellence peech
in espanish	ince panish	my especialty	mice pecialty
their eschool	theirss cool	her espelling	herss pelling

Word Endings

In Spanish, words end in a vowel (*o* or *a*), or the consonants *n, s, r, l, d*. Some people switch *n* and *ng* (*I käng hear you*) for either *I can hear you* or *I can't hear you*. Another consequence is that final consonants can get dropped in English, as in *short* (shor) or *friend* (fren).

Pronunciation

With most Spanish speakers, the *s* is almost always unvoiced, *r* is trilled, *l* is too short and lacks a schwa, *d* sounds like a voiced *th*, and *b* and *v* are interchangeable. Spanish speakers also substitute the *ä* sound whenever the letter *a* appears, most often for *æ, ä* and *ə*. Bear in mind that there are six different pronunciations for the letter *a* as on page 142. Knowing these simple facts will help you isolate and work through your difficulties.

The Spanish S = The American S, But...

In Spanish, an *s* always sounds like an *s*. (In some countries, it may be slightly voiced before a voiced consonant such as in *mismo*.) In English, a final ~*s* sounds like *z* when it follows a voiced consonant or a vowel (*raise* [raz], *runs* [rənz]). The most common verbs in English end in the *z* sound—*is*, *was*, *does*, *has*, etc. Double the preceding vowel and allow your vocal cords to vibrate.

The Spanish R = The American T

Beri bara bira	Betty bought a bit of	ai nira lara taim	I need a lot of time.
Ai! Caracol!	I caught a cold.	mai marou	my motto
Curi du it?	Could he do it?	mirin	meeting
ui ara gou	We ought to go.	aim naran taim	I'm not on time.

In Spanish, *r* is a consonant. This means that it touches at some point in the mouth. Spanish speakers usually roll their *r*s (touching the ridge behind the top teeth), which makes it sound like a *d* to the American ear. The tongue should be curled back, and the *r* produced deep in the throat—*not* touching the top of the mouth. The Spanish pronunciation of *r* is usually the written vowel and a flap *r* at the end of a word (*feeler* is pronounced like *feelehd*) or a flap in the beginning or middle (*throw* sounds like *tdoh*). In English, the pronunciation of *r* doesn't change if it's spelled *r* or *rr*.

The -ed Ending

You may have found yourself wondering how to pronounce *asked* or *hoped*; if you came up with *as-ked* or *ho-ped*, you made a logical and common mistake. There are three ways to pronounce the -*ed* ending in English, depending what the previous letter is. If it's voiced, -*ed* sounds like *d*: *played* [pleid]. If it's unvoiced, -*ed* sounds like *t*: *laughed* [læft]. If the word ends in *t* or *d*, -*ed* sounds like *əd*: *patted* [pædəd].

The Final T

The *t* at the end of a word should not be heavily aspirated. Let your tongue go to the *t* position, and then just stop. It should sound like [häˈ], not [hä], or [häch], or [häts].

The Spanish D = The American Th (voiced)

The Spanish *d* in the middle and final positions is a fricative *d* (*cada* and *sed*). If you are having trouble with the English *th*, substitute in a Spanish *d*. First, contrast *cara* and *cada* in Spanish, and then note the similarities between *cara* and *caught a*, and *cada* and *father*.

> *cada*   *father*   *beid*   *bathe*

The Spanish of Spain Z or C = The American Th (unvoiced)

The letters *z* and *c* in most Spanish-speaking countries sound like *s* in English (not in Andalusia, however). The *z* and *c* from Spain, on the other hand, is equivalent to the American unvoiced *th*. When you want to say *both* in English, say *bouz* with an accent from Spain.

> *bouz*   *both*   *gracias* *grathias*   *uiz*   *with*

The Spanish I = The American Y (not j)

In most Spanish-speaking countries, the *y* and *ll* sounds are equivalent to the American *y*, as in *yes* or in liaisons such as *the(y)other one*.

> *Jes, I jelled at jou jesterday* can be heard in some countries such as Argentina.
> *hielo*   *yellow (not jello)*   *ies*   *yes*   *iu*   *you*

The Doubled Spanish A Sound = The American O, All or AW Spelling

Because of spelling, the *ä* sound can easily be misplaced. The *ä* sound exists in Spanish, but it is represented with the letter *a*. When you see the letter *o*, you pronounce it [o], so *hot* sounds like *hoht* instead of *haht*. Remember, most of the time, the letter *o* is pronounced *ah*. You can take a sound that already exists in Spanish, such as *jaat* (whether it means anything or not) and say it with your native accent— *jaat* with a Spanish accent more or less equals *hot* in English. This will give you a good reference point for whenever you want to say *ä* instead of *o*; *astronomy, call, long, progress*, etc. Focus on Chapter 3, differentiating *æ, ä, ə*.

| *jaat* | *hot* | *caal* | *call* | *saa* | *saw* |

The Spanish O = The American OU

You may pronounce the letter *o* as *ä* or *ə* when it really should be an *o*, as in *only, most, both*. Make sure that the American *o* sounds like [ou], *ounly, moust, bouth*. This holds true for the diphthongs as well—*oi* sounds like *ou-ee*.

| *ounli* | *only* | *joup* | *hope* | *nout* | *note* |

æ The *æ* sound doesn't exist in Spanish, so it usually comes out as *ä*, so *last* sounds like *lost*. You need to work on Chapter 3, which drills this distinctively American vowel.

ə The schwa is typically overpronounced, based on spelling. Work on Chapter 1 Intonation and Chapter 3 Pronunciation. If your intonation peaks are strong and clear enough, then your valleys will be sufficiently reduced as well. Concentrate on smoothing out and reducing the valleys and *ignore spelling!*

ü The [ü] sound is generally overpronounced to *ooh*. Again, spelling is the culprit. Words such as *smooth, choose* and *too* are spelled with two *o*'s and are pronounced with a long *u* sound, but other words such as *took* and *good* are spelled with two *o*'s but are pronounced halfway between *ih* and *uh*; [tük] and [güd].

i Spanish speakers overpronounce the lax vowel *i* to *eee*, so *sit* comes out as *seat*. In most Spanish dictionaries, the distinction between *i* and *ē* is not made. Practice the four sounds— bit, beat, bid, bead— remembering that *tense vowels* indicate that you tense your lips or tongue, while *lax vowels* mean that your lips and tongue are relaxed and the sound is produced in your throat. *Unvoiced* final consonants (*t, s, k, p, ch, f*) mean that the vowel is short and sharp; *voiced* final consonants (*d, z, g, b, j, v*) mean that the vowel is doubled. Work on Bit or Beat? Bid or Bead? in Chapter 8. Reduce the soft [i] to a schwa; *sit* should sound like *s't*.

	single	double
tense	beat	bead
lax	bit	bid

Also, watch out for cognates such as *similar*, pronounced [see-mee-lär] in Spanish, and [si•m'•lr] in American English. Many of them appear in the Middle "I" List on page 125.

l The Spanish *l* lacks a schwa, leaving the sound short and incomplete to the American ear. Contrast similar words in the two languages and notice the differences.

Written	Pronounced	Spanish
ball	*bä-uhl*	*bal*

v A Spanish speaker usually pronounces *v* and *b* the same (*I have trouble with my bowels* instead of *I have trouble with my vowels*). You need to differentiate between the four sounds of *p/b/f/v*. The plosives *b/p* pop out; the sibilants *f/v* slide out. *b/v* are voiced; *f/p* are unvoiced. *b/v* are the *least* related pair. Push your bottom lip up with your finger so that it is *outside* your top teeth and make a sharp popping sound. Practice these sounds:

F	V	B		F	V	B
fat	*vat*	*bat*		*ferry*	*very*	*berry*
face	*vase*	*base*		*effort*	*ever*	*Ebber*
fear	*veer*	*beer*		*foul*	*vowel*	*bowel*

Once you have the *f* in place, simply allow your vocal cords to vibrate and you will then have a *v*.

	unvoiced	voiced
plosive	P	B
sibilant	F	V

n   The final *n* is often mispronounced *ng—meng* rather than *men*. Put a tiny schwa at the end to finish off the *n*, menᵊ, as explained on page 89.

w   The *w* sound in Spanish can sound like a *gw* (*I gwould do it*). You need to practice *g* in the throat and rounding your lips for *w*. You can also substitute in a Spanish *u*, as in *will* [uil].

h   The Spanish *h* is silent, as in *hombre*, but Spanish speakers often use a stronger fricative than Americans would. The American *h* is equivalent to the Spanish *j*, but the air coming out shouldn't pass through a constricted throat—it's like you're steaming a mirror—*hat, he, his, her, whole, hen*, etc. In some Spanish-speaking countries, the *j* is fricative and in others it is not. Also, there are many words in which the *h* is completely silent, as in *hour, honest, herb*, as well as in liaisons with object pronouns such as *her* and *him* (*tell her* sounds like *teller*).

ch   In order to make the *ch* sound different from the *sh*, put a *t* in front of the *ch*. Practice the difference between *wash* [wäsh] and *watch* [wätch], or *sharp* [shärp] and *charm* [chärm].

p   The American *p* is more strongly plosive than its Spanish counterpart. Put your hand in front of your mouth—you should feel a strong burst of air. Practice with *Peter picked a peck of pickled peppers*.

j   In order to make a clear *j* sound, put a *d* in front of the *j*. Practice *George* [djordj].

There was a woman from Spain who used to say, "Es imposible que se le quite el acento a uno," pronouncing it, "Esh imposhible que se le quite el athento a uno." In her particular accent, *s* sounded like *s*, which would transfer quite well to standard American English. What it also means is that many people claim it is impossible to change the accent. For clarification, see page v.

Location of the Language
Spanish is very far forward with much stronger use of the lips.

Indian

Intonation
Of the many and varied Indian dialects (Hindi, Telugu, Punjabi, etc.), there is a common intonation transfer to English—sort of a curly, rolling cadence that flows along with little relation to meaning. It is difficult to get the average Indian student to change pitch. Not that people are unwilling to try or difficult to deal with; on the contrary, in my experience of working with people from India, I find them incredibly pleasant and agreeable. This is part of the problem, however. People agree in concept, in principle, in theory, in every aspect of the

matter, yet when they *say* the sentence, the pitch remains unchanged.

I think that what happens is that, in standard American English, we raise the pitch on the beat, Indians drop their pitch on the beat. Also, the typical Indian voice is much higher pitched than Americans are accustomed to hearing. In particular, you should work on the voice quality exercise on page 94.

Of the three options *(volume, length, pitch)*, you can raise the volume easily, but it doesn't sound very good. Since volume is truly the least desirable and the most offensive to the listener, and since pitch has to be worked on over time, lengthening the stressed word is a good stopgap measure. Repeating the letter of a stressed word will help a lot toward changing a rolling *odabah odabah odabah* intonation to something resembling peaks and valleys.

The oooonly way to geeeeeeedidiz to prææææææææǽæktis all of the time.

One thing that works for pitch is to work on the little sound that children make when they make a mistake, "uh-oh!" The first sound is on a distinctly higher level than the second one, and since it's a nonsense syllable, it's easier to work with.

Since so much emotion is conveyed through intonation, it's vital to work with the various tone shifts, *Intonation and Attitude*, as seen on page 128.

It's necessary to focus on placing the intonation on the correct words (nouns, compound nouns, descriptive phases, etc.), as well as contrasting, negating, listing, questioning, and exclaiming.

Intonation is also important in numbers, which are typically difficult for Indian speakers. There are both intonation and pronunciation between 13 and 30. The number **13** should sound like **thr-*teen***, while **30** sounds like ***thr*-dee**; **14** is **for-*teen***, and **40** is *for*-**dee**

Liaisons

Liaisons shouldn't be much of a problem for you once the pattern is pointed out and reinforced.

Pronunciation

One way to have an accent is to leave out sounds that should be there, but the other way is to put in sounds that don't exist in that language. Indians bring a rich variety of voiced consonants to English that contribute to the heavy, rolling effect.

t　For the initial *t* alone, there are eight varieties, ranging from plosive to almost swallowed. In American English, *t* at the top of a staircase is a sharp *t*, and *t* in the middle is a soft *d*. Indians tend to reverse this, using the plosive British *t* in the middle position (wa*t*er) and a *t*-like sound in the beginning. (*I need two* sounds like *I need doo*). The solution is to substitute *your th*—it will sound almost perfect (*I need thoo* sounds just like *I need two*). Another way is to separate the *t* from the rest of the word and whisper it. **T + aim = time**. Bit by bit, you can bring the whispered, sharply plosive *t* closer to the body of the word. A third way is to imagine that it is actual *ts*, so you are saying *tsäim*, which will come out sounding like *time*.

T	**D**	**T**	**D**
tennis	*Dennis*	*ten*	*den*
time	*dime*	*to*	*do*

The final *t* is typically too plosive, and should be held just at the position before the air is expelled.

p　This is similar to the initial *t*, in that you probably voice the unvoiced *p* so it sounds like a *b*. Start with the *m*, progress to the *b*, and finally whisper the *p* sound.

M	**B**	**P**	**M**	**B**	**P**
men	*Ben*	*pen*	*mull*	*bull*	*pull*
mail	*bail*	*pail*	*mossy*	*bossy*	*possible*
met	*bet*	*pet*	*mile*	*bile*	*pile*

æ The *æ* sound usually sounds like *ä*. You might refer to *the last class*, but it will sound like *the lost closs*. You should raise the back of your tongue, and make a noise similar to that of a lamb.

ä Because of spelling, the *ä* sound can easily be misplaced. The *ä* sound exists in the Indian languages, but is represented with the letter *a*. When you see the letter *o*, you pronounce it *o*, so *John* sounds like *Joan* instead of *Jahn*. Remember, most of the time, the letter *o* is pronounced *ah*. You can take a sound that already exists in your language, such as *tak* (whether it means anything or not) and say it with your native accent— *tak* with an Indian accent more or less equals *talk* in English. This will give you a good reference point for whenever you want to say *ä* instead of *o*; astr<u>o</u>nomy, c<u>a</u>ll, l<u>o</u>ng, pr<u>o</u>gress, etc. Focus on Chapter 3, differentiating *æ, ä, ə*.

| h<u>aa</u>t | h<u>o</u>t | c<u>aa</u>l | c<u>a</u>ll | s<u>aa</u> | s<u>aw</u> |

o You may pronounce the letter *o* as *ä* or *ə* when it really should be an *o*, as in *only, most, both*. Make sure that the American *o* sounds like *ou*, *ounly, moust, bouth*. This holds true for the diphthongs as well—[oi] sounds like *ou-ee*.

| <u>ou</u>nli | <u>o</u>nly | h<u>ou</u>p | h<u>o</u>pe | n<u>ou</u>t | n<u>o</u>te |

r Indians tend to have a British *r*, which means that it is either a flap at the beginning or middle of a word or it is reduced to *ä* at the end of a word. You need to understand that the American *r* is not a consonant (i.e., it doesn't touch at any two points in the mouth)—it is much closer to a vowel in that the tongue curls back to shape the air flow.

th The American *th*, both voiced and unvoiced, usually sounds like a *d* when said by an Indian speaker, *thank you* sounds like *dank you*. Also you must distinguish between a voiced and an unvoiced *th*. The voiced ones are the extremely common, everyday sounds—*the, this, that, these, those, them, they, there, then*; unvoiced are less common words—*thing, third, Thursday, thank, thought*.

v Indians usually reverse *v/w*: *These were reversed* ➡ *Dese ver reversed*. It should be a simple thing to simply reverse them back, but for some reason, it's more problematic than that. Try substituting in the other word in actual sentences.

> *He vent to the store.*   *He closed the went.*
> *I'll be back in a vile.*   *It was a while attack.*

Think of the *w*, a "double *u*", as a "single *u*"; so in place of the *w* in *want*, you'd pronounce it *oo-änt*. There can be NO contact between the teeth and the lips for *w*, as this will turn it into a consonant. Feel the *f/v* consonants, and then put *oo~* in place of the *w* (*oo~ile* for *while*). Conversely, you can substitute *ferry* for *very* so that it won't come out as *wary*. Because of the proximity of the consonants, *f* and *v* are frequently interchanged in English (belief/believe, wolf/wolves). Consequently, *It was ferry difficult* is easier to understand than *It was wary difficult*. Practice Ex. 9-1 to distinguish among *p/b, f/v* and *w*.

F	**V**	**W**	**F**	**V**	**W**
fence	*vent*	*went (oo-ent)*	*first*	*verse*	*worse (oo-rs)*
face	*vase*	*waste (oo-aste)*	*file*	*vile*	*while (oo-ile)*

l The *l* is too heavy, too drawn out, and is missing the schwa component.

Location of the Language

Far forward and uttered through rounded lips.

Russian

Intonation

Russian intonation seems to start at a midpoint, and then cascades down. The consequence is that it sounds very downbeat. You definitely need to add a lilt to your speech—more peaks, as there're already *plenty* of valleys. To the Russian ear, English can have a harsh, almost metallic sound due to the perception of nasal vibrations in some vowels. This gives a clarity to American speech that allows it to be heard over a distance. When Russian speakers try to imitate that "loudness" and clarity, without the American speech music, instead of the intended pronunciation, it can sound aggressive. On the other hand, when Russians do not try to speak "loud and clear," it can end up sounding vaguely depressed.

Liaisons

Word connections should be easy since you have the same fluid word/sound boundaries as in American English. The phrase [dosvedänyə] sounds like *dos vedanya*, whereas you know it as *do svedanya*. It won't be difficult to run your words together once you realize it's the same process in English.

Pronunciation

Although you have ten vowels in Russian, there are quite a few other vowels out there waiting for you.

æ The [æ] sound doesn't exist in Russian, so *last* is demoted to the lax ε, *lest*. In the same way, Russian speakers reduce *actually* to *ekchually*, or *matter* to *metter*. Drop your jaw and raise the back of your tongue to make a noise like a goat: *æ*! Work on Chapter 3, which drills this distinctively American vowel.

ä The [ä] sound exists in Russian, but is represented with the letter *a*. Bear in mind that there are six different pronunciations of the letter *a*, as you can see on page 142. Because of spelling, the *ä* sound can easily be misplaced. When you see the letter *o*, you pronounce it *o*, so *job* sounds like *jobe* instead of *jääb*. Remember, most of the time, the letter *o* is pronounced *ah*. Take a sound that already exists in Russian, such as *baab* (whether it means anything or not) and say it with your native accent. *baab* with a Russian accent more or less equals *Bob* in English. This will give you a good reference point for whenever you want to say *ä* instead of *o*; *bi̲ology*, *c̲all*, *lo̲ng*, *pro̲blem*, etc. Focus on Chapter 3, differentiating *æ*, *ä*, *ə*.

o Conversely, you may pronounce the letter *o* as *ä* or *ə* when it really should be an *o*, as in *only*, *most*, *both* (which are exceptions to the spelling rules). Make sure that the American *o* sounds like [ou], *ounly*, *moust*, *bouth*. This holds true for the diphthongs as well—*oi* should sound like *ou-ee*.

toun	t<u>o</u>ne	nout	n<u>o</u>te	h<u>ou</u>m	h<u>o</u>me
<u>ou</u>nli	<u>o</u>nly	c<u>ou</u>l	c<u>o</u>al	OK	<u>ou</u>kei

ə The schwa is often overpronounced to *ä*, which is why you might sound a little like Count Dracula when he says, *I vänt to säck your bläd* instead of *I wänt to sək your bləd*. Don't drop your jaw for the neutral schwa sound; it's like the final syllable of *spasiba* [sp'sibə], not [sp'sibä]. Similarly, in English, the schwa in an unstressed syllable is completely neutral; *famous* is not [fay-moos], but rather [fay-m's].

ü Distinguishing tense and lax vowels is difficult, and you'll have to forget spelling for *u* and *ü*. They both can be spelled with *oo* or *ou*, but the lax vowel *ü* should sound much closer to *i* or *uh*. If you say *book* and *could* with a tense vowel, it'll sound like *booque* and *cooled*. It should be much closer to *bick* or *buck*.

i Similarly, you need to distinguish between *ee* and *i*, as in *beat* and *bit* (page 123), as *his big sister* is mispronounced as *heez beeg seester* or with the [y], *hyiz byig systr*. Frequently, Russian speakers transpose these two sounds, so while the lax vowel in *his big sister* is overpronounced to *heez beeg seester*, the tense vowel in *She sees Lisa*, is relaxed to *shi siz lissa*. Also, tone down the middle *i* in the multisyllabic words on page 125; otherwise, *similar* [sim'lr] will sound like [see-mee-lär].

-y Russian speakers often mispronounce the final *-y* as a short *-i*, so that *very funny* sounds like *verə funnə*. Extend the final sound out with three e's: *vereee funneee*.

The Russian R = The American T

The Cyrillic *r* is a consonant. This means that it touches at some point in the mouth. Russian speakers usually roll their *r*s (touching the ridge behind the top teeth), which makes it sound like a *d* to the American ear. The American *r* is not really a consonant anymore—the tongue should be curled back, and the *r* produced deep in the throat—*not* touching the top of the mouth. The Russian pronunciation of *r* is usually the written vowel and a flap *r* at the end of a word (*feeler* sounds like *feelehd*) or a flap in the beginning or middle (*throw* sounds like *tdoh*).

бэ́ри ба́ра би́ра	Betty bought a bit of	а́ин и́ра ла́ра та́им	I need a lot of time.
ай ба́ра ба́ик	I bought a bike.	ма́и ма́роу	my motto
уэ́ира сэ́кен	Wait a second.	ми́рин	meeting
уй а́ра го́у	We ought to go.	а́ин на́ран та́им	I'm not on time.
юв га́ра пэ́ира гэ́рит	You've got to pay to get it.	бю́рафли	beautifully

Another major point with the American *r* is that sometimes the preceding vowel is pronounced, and sometimes it isn't. When you say *wire*, there's a clear vowel plus the *r*—wy•r; however, with *first*, there is simply no preceding vowel. It's *frst, not feerst,* (Ex. 6-2 and 6-3).

t At the beginning of a word, the American *t* needs to be more plosive—you should feel that you are "spitting air." At the end of the word, it is held back and not aspirated.

eh One of the most noticeable characteristics of a Russian accent is the little *y* that is slipped in with the *eh* sound. This makes a sentence such as *Kevin has held a cat* sound like *Kyevin hyes hyeld a kyet*. This is because you are using the back of the tongue to "push" the vowel sound out of the throat. In English, you need to just allow the air to pop through directly after the consonant, between the back of the tongue and the soft palate: k•æ, not k•yæ.

h Another strong characteristic of Russian speech is a heavily fricative *h*. Rather than closing the back of the throat, let the air flow unimpeded between the soft palate and the back of your tongue. Be sure to keep your tongue flat so you don't push out the little *y* mentioned above. Often, you can simply drop the *h* to avoid the whole problem. For *I have to*, instead of *I hhyef to*, change it to *I y'v to*.

v The v is often left unvoiced, so the common word *of* sounds like *oaf*. Allow your vocal cords to vibrate.

sh There are two *sh* sounds in Russian, ш and щ. The second one is closer to the American *sh*, as in щиу́з for *shoes*, not шуз.

th You may find yourself replacing the voiced and unvoiced *th* sounds with *t/d* or *s/z*, saying *dä ting* or *zä sing* instead of *the thing*. This means that your tongue tip is about a half inch too far back on the alveolar ridge (the gum ridge behind the teeth). Press your tongue against the *back* of the teeth and try to say *dat*. Because of the tongue position, it will sound like *that*.

-ing Often the *-ing* ending is not pronounced as a single *ng* sound, but rather as *n* and *g*, or just *n*. There are three nasals, *m* (lips), *n* (tongue tip and alveolar ridge), and *ng* (soft palate and the back of the tongue). It is not a hard consonant like *g*, but rather a soft nasal.

French

Intonation

The French are, shall we say, a linguistically proud people. More than working on accent or pronunciation; you need to "believe" first. There is an inordinate amount of psychological resistance here, but the good thing is that, in my experience, you are very outspoken about it. Unlike the Japanese, who will just keep quiet, or Indians, who agree with everything with sometimes no discernible change in their speech patterns, my French students have quite clearly pointed out how difficult, ridiculous, and unnatural American English is.

If the American pattern is a stairstep, the Gallic pattern is a fillip at the end of each phrase.

*He*llo, *my* name is Pierre. I live in *Par*is.   Al*lo*, my name is *Pierre*. I live in Par*ee*. I ride the sub*way*.

Liaisons

The French either invented liaisons or raised them to an art form. You may not realize, though, that the rules that bind your phrases together, also do in English. Just remember, in French, it is spelled *ce qu'ils disent*, but you've heard it pronounced colloquially a thousand times, *skidiz*!

Pronunciation

th In French, the *tee aitch* is usually mispronounced *s* or *f*, as in *sree* or *free* for *three*.

r The French *r* is in the same location as the American one, but it is more like a consonant. For the French *r*, the back of the tongue rasps against the soft palate, but for the American *r*, the throat balloons out, like a bullfrog.

æ The *æ* sound doesn't exist in French, so it usually comes out as *ä* or *ɛ*; consequently, *class* sounds like *cläss*, and *cat* sounds like *ket*. The *in-* prefix, however, sounds like a nasalized æ. Say *in* in French, and then denasalize it to *æd*. Work on Chapter 3, which drills this distinctively American vowel.

ə The schwa is typically overpronounced, based on spelling. Work on Chapter 1, for the rhythm patterns that form this sound, and Chapter 3, for its actual pronunciation. If your intonation peaks are strong and clear enough, then your valleys will be sufficiently reduced as well. Concentrate on smoothing out and reducing the valleys and *ignore spelling!*

ü The *ü* sound is generally overpronounced to *ooh*, which leads to *could* being mispronounced as *cooled*. Again, spelling is the culprit. Words such as *smooth, choose,* and *too* are spelled with two *o*'s and are pronounced with a long *u* sound, but other words such as *look* and *took* are spelled with two *o*'s but are pronounced halfway between *ih* and *uh*; *lük* and *tük*. *Leuc* and *queuc* with a French accent are very close.

i French speakers overpronounce the lax vowel *i* to *eee*, so *sit* comes out like *seat*. Reduce the soft *i* to a schwa; *sit* should sound like *s't*. In most French dictionaries, the distinction between *i* and *ē* is not made. Practice the four sounds—*bit, beat, bid, bead*—remembering that *tense vowels* indicate that you tense your lips or tongue, while *lax vowels* mean that your lips and tongue are relaxed, and the sound is produced in your throat. *Unvoiced* final consonants (*t, s, k, p, ch, f*) mean that the vowel is short and sharp; *voiced* final consonants (*d, z, g, b, j, v*) mean that the vowel is doubled. Work on Bit or Beat? Bid or Bead? in Chapter 8.

	single	double
tense	beat	bead
lax	bit	bid

Also, watch out for cognates such as *typique/typical*, pronounced [tee•peek] in French, and [ti•p'•kl] in American English. Many of them appear in the Middle "I" List on page 125.

ä Because of spelling, the *ä* sound can easily be misplaced. The *ä* sound exists in French, but is represented with the letter *a*. When you see the letter *o*, you pronounce it *o*, so *lot* sounds like *loht* instead of *laht*. Remember, most of the time, the letter *o* is pronounced *ah*. You can take a sound that already exists in French, such as *laat* (whether it means anything or not) and say it with your native accent—*laat* with a French accent more or less equals *lot* in English.This will give you a good reference point for whenever you want to say *ä* instead of *o*; *astronomy*, *call*, *long*, *progress*, etc. Focus on Chapter 3, differentiating *æ*, *ä*, *ə*.

    h<u>aa</u>t   h<u>o</u>t   c<u>aa</u>l   c<u>all</u>   s<u>aa</u>   s<u>aw</u>

o On the other hand, you may pronounce the letter *o* as *ä* or *ə* when it really should be an *o*, as in *only*, *most*, *both*. Make sure that the American *o* sounds like [ou], *ounly*, *moust*, *bouth*. This holds true for the diphthongs as well—*oi* sounds like *o-u-ee*.

    <u>ou</u>nli   <u>o</u>nly   l<u>ou</u>n   l<u>oa</u>n   n<u>ou</u>t   n<u>o</u>te

h French people have the most fascinating floating *h*. Part of the confusion comes from the *hâche aspiré*, which is totally different from the American *aitch*. Allow a small breath of air to escape with each *aitch*.

in~ The nasal combination *in~* and *~en* are often pronounced like *æñ* and *äñ*, so *interesting* [**in**tr'sting] sounds like *æñteresting*, and enjoy [ɛn**joy**] and *attention* [ətɛnshən] sound like *äñjoy* and *ätäñseeõn*.

Location in the Mouth
Very far forward, with extensive use of the lips.

German
Intonation
Germans have what Americans consider a stiff, rather choppy accent. The great similarity between the two languages lies in the two-word phrases, where a **hót** dog is food and a *hot **dóg*** is an overheated chihuahua. In German, a *thimble* is called a ***finger**hut*, literally a *finger hat*, and a *red hat* would be a *rote **hut***, with the same intonation and meaning shift as in English.

Liaisons
German word connections are also quite similar to American ones. Consider how *In einem Augenblick* actually is pronounced *ineine maugenblick*. The same rules apply in both languages.

Pronunciation
j A salient characteristic of German is the unvoicing of *j*, so you might say *I am Cherman* instead of *I am German*. Work with the other voiced pairs (*p/b*, *s/z*, *k/g*) and then go on to *ch/j* while working with J words such as *just*, *Jeff*, *German*, *enjoy*, *age*, etc.

w Another difference is the transposing of *v* and *w*. When you say *Volkswagen*, it most likely comes out *Folksvagen*. It works to rewrite the word as *Wolksvagen*, which then will come out as we say *Volkswagen*. A Germany student was saying that she was a *wisiting scholar*, which didn't make much sense—say *wisiding* with a German accent — it'll sound like *visiting* in American English.

th In German, the *tee aitch* is usually pronounced *t* or *d*.

r The German *r* is in the same location as the American one, but it is more like a consonant. For the German *r*, the back of the tongue rasps against the soft palate, but for the American *r*, the throat balloons out, like a bullfrog.

æ The *æ* sound doesn't exist in German, so it usually comes out as *ä* or *ε*, so *class* sounds like *cläss*, You need to work on Chapter 3, which drills this distinctively American vowel.

ə The schwa is typically overpronounced, based on spelling. Work on Chapter 1, for the rhythm patterns that form this sound, and Chapter 3, for its actual pronunciation. If your intonation peaks are strong and clear enough, then your valleys will be sufficiently reduced as well. Concentrate on smoothing out and reducing the valleys and *ignore spelling!*

ü The *ü* sound is generally overpronounced to *ooh*, which leads to *could* being mispronounced as *cooled*. Again, spelling is the culprit. Words such as *smooth, choose,* and *too* are spelled with two *o*'s and are pronounced with a long *u* sound, but other words such as *look* and *took* are spelled with two *o*'s but are pronounced halfway between *ih* and *uh*; *lük* and *tük*.

i German speakers overpronounce the lax vowel *i* to *eee*, so *sit* comes out like *seat*. Reduce the soft *i* to a schwa; *sit* should sound like *s't*. In most German dictionaries, the distinction between *i* and *ē* is not made. Practice the four sounds—*bit, beat, bid, bead*—remembering that *tense vowels* indicate that you tense your lips or tongue, while *lax vowels* mean that your lips and tongue are relaxed, and the sound is produced in your throat. *Unvoiced* final consonants (*t, s, k, p, ch, f*) mean that the vowel is short and sharp; *voiced* final consonants (*d, z, g, b, j, v*) mean that the vowel is doubled. Work on Bit or Beat? Bid or Bead? in Chapter 8.

	single	double
tense	beat	bead
lax	bit	bid

Also, watch out for words such as *chemical/Chemikalie*, pronounced [ke•mi•kä•lee•eh] in German, and [kɛmək³l] in American English. Many of them appear in the Middle "I" List on page 125.

ä Because of spelling, the *ä* sound can easily be misplaced. The *ä* sound exists in German, but is represented with the letter *a*. When you see the letter *o*, you pronounce it [o], so *lot* sounds like *loht* instead of *laht*. Remember, most of the time, the letter *o* is pronounced *ah*. You can take a sound that already exists in German, such as *laat* (whether it means anything or not) and say it with your native accent—*laat* with a German accent more or less equals *lot* in American English. This will give you a good reference point for whenever you want to say *ä* instead of *o*; *astronomy, call, long, progress,* etc. Focus on Chapter 3, differentiating *æ, ä, ə*.

  haat *hot*   *caal* *call*   *saa* *saw*

o German speakers tend to use the British *o*, which sounds like *εo* rather than the American *ou*. Make sure that the American *o*, in *only, most, both,* sounds like *ou, ounly, moust, bouth*. This holds true for the diphthongs as well—*oi* sounds like *o-u-ee*.

  ounli *only*   *houp* *hope*   *nout* *note*

Korean

Intonation

While English is a stress-timed language, Korean is a syllable-timed language. Korean is more similar to Japanese than Chinese in that the pitch range of Korean is also narrow, almost flat, and not rhythmical. Many Korean speakers tend to stress the wrong word or syllable, which changes the meaning in English (*They'll sell fish* and *They're selfish*.) Korean speakers tend to add a vowel to the final consonant after a long vowel: *b/v* (*babe/beibu* and *wave/weibu*), *k/g* (*make/meiku* and *pig/pigu*), and *d* (*made/meidu*.) **Koreans** also insert a vowel after *sh/ch/j* (*wash/washy, church/churchy, bridge/brijy*), and into consonant clusters (*bread/buredu*). It is also common problem to devoice final voiced consonants, so that *dog* can be mispronounced as either *dogu* or *dock*. All this adversely influences the rhythm patterns of spoken English. The different regional intonation patterns for Korean interrogatives also affect how questions come across in English. In standard Korean, the intonation goes up for both *yes/no* questions and *wh* questions (who?, what?, where?, when?, why?); in the Kyungsang dialect, it drops for both; and in the Julla dialect, it drops and goes up for both. In American English, the intonation goes up for *yes/no*, and drops down for *wh* questions.

Word Connections

Unlike Japanese or Chinese, word connections are common in Korean. The seven final consonants (*m, n, ng, l, p, t, k*) slide over when the following word begins with a vowel. Although a *t* between two vowels in American English should be voiced (*latter/ladder* sound the same) a frequent mistake Korean speakers make, however, is to also voice *k* or *p* between two vowels, so *back up, check up,* and *weekend* are mispronounced as *bagup, chegup,* and *weegend*; and *cap is* sounds like *cab is*. Another liaison problem occurs with a plosive consonant (*p/b, t/d, k/g*) just before a nasal (*m, n, ng*)—Koreans often nasalize the final consonant, so that *pick me up* and *pop music* sound like *ping me up* and *pom music*.

Pronunciation

l/r At the beginning of a word or in a consonant cluster, *l* and *r* are confused, with both being pronounced like the American *d*, which can be written with the letter *t* (*glass* or *grass* sound like either *gurasu* or *gudasu*, and *light* or *right sound* like *raitu* or *daitu*). The final *r* is usually dropped (*car/kaa*).

f The English *f* does not exist in Korean, so people tend to substitute a *p*. This leads to words such as *difficult* sounding like *typical* to the American ear. When a Korean speaker says a word from the **F** column, it's likely to be heard by Americans as being from the **P** column.

F	P		F	P		F	P
difficult	typical		coffee	copy		half and	happen
calf	cap		deaf	tape		Steph	step
left	leapt		cough	cop		laugh	lap
often	open		fat	pet		informant	important
stuff	stop		after	apter		fossil	possible
enough	and up		friend	planned		free	pre~

æ The exact *æ* sound doesn't exist in Korean; it's close to *ɛ*, so *bat* sounds like *bet*. You need to raise the back of your tongue and drop your jaw to produce this sound. Work on Chapter 3, which drills this distinctively American vowel.

ä The *ä* sound is misplaced. You have the *ä* sound when you laugh *hahaha* 하하하, but when you see an *o*, you want to say [o], as in *hohoho* 호호호, so *John* sounds like *Joan* instead of *Jähn*. If you're having trouble with the word *hot*, say *ha* 하 in Korean, and then add a very slight *t*.

o   You may pronounce the letter *o* as *ä* or *ə* when it really should be an *o*, as in *only, most, both*. Make sure that the American *o* sounds like *ou: ounly, moust, bouth*. This holds true for the diphthongs as well—*oi* sounds like *o-u-ee*.

toun	*tone*	*nout*	*note*	*houm*	*home*
ounli	*only*	*coul*	*coal*	*jouk*	*joke*

ə   The schwa is typically overpronounced, based on spelling. Concentrate on smoothing out and reducing the valleys and *ignore spelling!*

ü   Distinguishing tense and lax vowels is difficult, and you'll have to forget spelling for *u* and *ü*. They both can be spelled with *oo* or *ou*, but the lax vowel *ü* should sound much closer to *i* or *uh*. If you say *book* with a tense vowel, it'll sound like *booque*. It should be much closer to *bick* or *buck*.

i   Similarly, you need to distinguish between *e* and *i*, as in *beat* and *bit*, as on page 123. Tone down the middle *i* in multisyllabic words, as on page 125, otherwise, *beautiful* [**byoo**•d'•fl] will sound like [byoo-tee-fool]. Most likely, you overpronounce the lax vowel *i* to *eee*, so *sit* is overpronounced to *seat*. Reduce the soft *i* to a schwa; *sit* should sound like *s't*. In most Korean dictionaries, the distinction between *i* and *ē* is not made. Practice the four sounds—*bit, beat, bid, bead*—remembering that *tense vowels* indicate that you tense your lips or tongue, while *lax vowels* mean that your lips and tongue are relaxed and the sound is produced in your throat. *Unvoiced* final consonants (*t, s, k, p, ch, f*) mean that the vowel is short and sharp; *voiced* final consonants (*d, z, g, b, j, v*) mean that the vowel is doubled. Work on Bit or Beat? Bid or Bead? in Chapter 8.

	single	double
tense	beat	bead
lax	bit	bid

The Korean R = The American T

The Korean *r* is a consonant. This means that it touches at some point in the mouth. Korean speakers usually trill their *r*s (tapping the ridge behind the top teeth), which makes it sound like a *d* to the American ear. The tongue should be curled back, and the *r* produced deep in the throat—*not* touching the top of the mouth. The Korean pronunciation of *r* is usually just an *ä* at the end of a word (*car* sounds like *caaah*) or a flap in the beginning or middle (*area* sounds like *eddy-ah*).

베리 바라비라	Betty bought a bit of	아이 니랄라라 타임	I need a lot of time.
아이 카라콜드	I caught a cold.	마이 마로우	my motto
쿠리 두잇	Could he do it?	미링	meeting
위 아라 고우	We ought to go.	아임 나란 타임	I'm not on time.

th   The *th* sound is often mispronounced as a strong *s* or *d* depending if it is voiced or unvoiced as in *thing* [ssing], or *that* [dat].

Answer Key

Exercise 1-4: Sentence Intonation Test
1. **Sam** sees **Bill**.
2. She **wants** one.
3. **Betty** likes **English**.
4. They **play** with them.
5. **Children** play with **toys**.
6. **Bob** and I call you and **Bill**.
7. You and **Bill** read the news.
8. It **tells** one.
9. **Bernard** works in a **restaurant**.
10. He **works** in one.
11. He **sees** him.
12. **Mary** wants a **car**.
13. She **likes** it.
14. They **eat** some.
15. Len and **Joe** eat some **pizza**.
16. We **call** you.
17. You **read** it.
18. The **news** tells a **story**.
19. **Mark** lived in **France**.
20. He **lived** there.

Exercise 1-15: Application of Stress
Hello, **my** name is_____. I'm taking American Ac**c**ent Train-ing. There's a **lot** to learn, but I **hope** to make it as en**joy**able as possible. I should pick **up** on the American into**na**tion pattern pretty **eas**ily, although the **only** way to **get** it is to **prac**tice all of the time. I use the **up** and down, or **peaks** and valleys, intonation more than I **used** to. I've been paying attention to **pitch, too**. It's like **walk**ing down a **stair**case. I've been **talk**ing to a lot of A**mer**icans lately, and they tell me that I'm **eas**ier to under**stand**. An**y**way, I could go **on** and on, but the im**por**tant thing is to **listen** well and sound **good**. **Well**, what do you **think**? **Do I**?

Exercise 1-17: Staircase Intonation Practice
Hello,   my   Accent
      name   Training.
      is   There's
        I'm   a
          taking
            American
lot   hope   enjoyable
  to   to   as
    learn,   make   possible.
      but   it   I
        I   as   should
                    pick
up   intonation   easily,
  on   pattern   although
    the   pretty   the
      American
only   get   practice
  way   it   all
    to   is   of
        to   the
                    time.

Exercise 1-23: Syllable Count Test
1. 1a	1. 3d	1. 4d	1. 4c	1. 4b	13. 3b
2. 1b	2. 4f	2. 3b	2. 4b	2. 4a	14. 3b
3. 3d	3. 2a	3. 3c	3. 2a	3. 3c	15. 4b
4. 4d	4. 2b	4. 3b	4. 2b	4. 4b	16. 4c
5. 3d	5. 3d	5. 2a	5. 3bcd	5. 4f	17. 3a
6. 4e	6. 4f	6. 2ab	6. 3a	6. 3d	18. 4d
7. 4d	7. 3b	7. 2ab	7. 4b	7. 4f	19. 4b
8. 2a	8. 3d	8. 3b	8. 3d	8. 4d	20. 4c
9. 2a	9. 4e	9. 3b	9. 4d	9. 4b	21. 4b
10. 3c	10. 4f	10. 4d	10. 4c	10. 4e	
11. 4f	11. 4b	11. 3b	11. 4a	11. 3c	
12. 4e	12. 4e	12. 3c	12. 4b	12. 3b	

Exercise 1-29: Making Set Phrases
1. a **chair**man
2. a **phone** book
3. a **house** key
4. a **base**ball
5. a **door** bell
6. the **White House**
7. a **movie** star
8. the **Bullet** train
9. a **race** car
10. a **coffee** cup
11. a **wrist**watch
12. a **beer** bottle
13. a **high** chair
14. a **hunting** knife
15. a **dump** truck
16. a **jelly**fish
17. a **love** letter
18. a **thumb**tack
19. a **lightning** bolt
20. a **pad**lock

Exercise 1-35: Contrast of Compound Nouns
1. The **White** House
2. a white **house**
3. a **dark**room
4. a dark **room**
5. Fifth **Avenue**
6. **Main** Street
7. a main **street**
8. a hot **dog**
9. a **hot** dog
10. a **baby** blanket
11. a baby's **blanket**
12. a baby **bird**
13. a **black**bird
14. a black **bird**
15. a **green**house
16. a green **house**
17. a green **thumb**
18. a **parking** ticket
19. a one-way **ticket**
20. an unpaid **ticket**
21. **convenience** store
22. convenient **store**
23. to pick **up**
24. a **pickup** truck
25. six years **old**
26. a **six-year-old**
27. six and a **half**
28. a **sugar** bowl
29. a wooden **bowl**
30. a large **bowl**
31. a **mixing** bowl
32. a **top** hat
33. a nice **hat**
34. a straw **hat**
35. a **chair**person
36. **Ph.D.**
37. **IBM**
38. **MIT**
39. **USA**
40. **ASAP**
41. a **door**knob
42. a glass **door**
43. a locked **door**
44. **ice** cream
45. I **scream**.
46. elemen**tary**
47. a lemon **tree**
48. **Water**gate
49. the back **gate**
50. the final **year**
51. a **year**book
52. United **States**
53. New **York**
54. **Long** Beach
55. Central **Park**
56. a raw **deal**
57. a **deal** breaker
58. the bottom **line**
59. a **bottom** feeder
60. a new **low**

Exercise 1-36: Description and Set Phrase Test
1. He's a **nice guy**.
2. He's an **American** guy from San **Francisco**.
3. The **cheerleader** needs a **rubber** band to hold her **ponytail**.
4. The executive **asst.** needs a **paper** clip for the **final report**.
5. The **law** student took an **English** test in a **foreign country**.
6. The **policeman** saw a **red car** on the **freeway** in Los **Angeles**.
7. My old **dog** has **long ears** and a **flea** problem.
8. The new **teacher** broke his **coffee** cup on the **first day**.
9. His **best friend** has a **broken cup** in his **other office**.
10. Let's play **football** on the **weekend** in New **York**.
11. "**Jingle** Bells" is a nice **song**.
12. Where are my **new shoes**?
13. Where are my **tennis** shoes?
14. I have a **headache** from the **heat** wave in South **Carolina**.
15. The **newlyweds** took a long **walk** in **Long Beach**.
16. The **little dog** was sitting on the **sidewalk**.
17. The **famous athlete** changed clothes in the **locker** room.
18. The **art** exhibit was held in an **empty room**.
19. There was a **class reunion** at the **high** school.
20. The **headlines** indicated a **new policy**.
21. We got **on line** and went to americanaccent **dot com**.
22. The **stock** options were listed in the **company directory**.
23. All the **second**-graders were out on the **playground**.

Exercise 1-48: Regular Transitions of Adj. and Verbs
1. You need to *insert* a paragraph here on this newspaper *insert*.
2. How can you *object* to this *object*?
3. I'd like to *present* you with this *present*.
4. Would you care to *elaboreit* on his *elabor't* explanation?
5. The manufacturer couldn't *recall* if there'd been a *recall*.
6. The religious *convert* wanted to *convert* the world.
7. The political *rebels* wanted to *rebel* against the world.
8. The mogul wanted to *record* a new *record* for his latest artist.
9. If you *perfect* your intonation, your accent will be *perfect*.
10. Due to the drought, the fields didn't *produce* much *produce* this year.
11. Unfortunately, City Hall wouldn't *permit* them to get a *permit*.

12. Have you heard that your *associ't* is known to *associeit* with gangsters?
13. How much do you *estimeit* that the *estim't* will be?
14. The facilitator wanted to *separeit* the general topic into *sepr't* categories.

Exercise 1-51: Extended Listening Practice
1. I'd like to have it at eight, if at all possible.
   [äi•dläik•tə•hæ•vi•də•dɛit•i•fə•däll•pä•sə•bəl]
2. I'm afraid it's back-ordered.
   [äi•m'•frei•dits•bæ•kor•drd]
3. Let's go over it again.
   [lets•go•wou•vr•ri•də•gɛn]
4. Try to put it off for another hour.
   [träi•də•pwü•di•däff• fr•rə•nə•thr•ræ•wr]
5. Talk it over with the other operator.
   [tä•ki•dou•vr•with•thee•yə•thr•rä•pr•ray•dr]
6. The accounts have all been updated.
   [thee•yə•kæon•tsə•väll•bi•nəp•dei•dəd]
7. Send them a fax about the problem.
   [sen•də•mə•fæk•sə•bæo⁽ᵗ⁾•thə•prä•bləm]
8. Don't even think about it!
   [dou•nee•vən•thing•kə•bæo•dit]
9. We hope he'll OK it.
   [we•hou•pi•lou•kɛi•yit]
10. He'll really put you on the spot if you make a mistake.
    [hill•ri•lee•pwü•choo•wän•thə•spä•di•fiu•mei•kə•mis•teik]

Exercise 1-60: Tag Endings
1. isn't he	8. will you	15. hadn't we	22. did I
2. can't he	9. doesn't he	16. wouldn't we	23. will I
3. does she	10. don't we	17. hasn't it	24. don't you
4. didn't they	11. haven't we	18. could you	25. aren't you
5. do you	12. didn't we	19. won't you	26. don't you
6. is it	13. didn't we	20. shouldn't he	27. did you
7. aren't I	14. hadn't we	21. shouldn't he	28. isn't it

Exercise 2-4: Consonant / Vowel Liaisons
1. ree donly	6. se lit
2. fä läff	7. ta kout
3. fällo wə pän	8. fa də way
4. cə min	9. sik so
5. cä lim	10. eh may

Exercise 2-8: Consonant / Consonant Liaisons
1. busine sdeal	6. someplan znee dluck
2. credi⁽ᵗ⁾check	7. che⁽ᶜᵏ⁾cashing
3. the topfile	8. let⁽ᵗ⁾themma⁽ᵏ⁾conditions
4. sellnine newcars	9. hadthe
5. sitdown	10. bothdays

Exercise 2-9: Vowel / Vowel Liaisons
1. go⁽ʷ⁾ɛnywhere	6. do⁽ʷ⁾äi
2. so⁽ʷ⁾änest	7. I⁽ʸ⁾æskt
3. through⁽ʷ⁾är	8. to⁽ʷ⁾open
4. you⁽ʷ⁾är	9. she⁽ʸ⁾äweez
5. he⁽ʸ⁾iz	10. too⁽ʷ⁾äffen

Exercise 2-11: T, D, S, or Z Liaisons
1. dijoo	6. tisshue
2. hoozhier	7. gächer
3. jesjer	8. wherzhier
4. jesjer	9. c'ngræjəlationz
5. misshue	10. hæjer

Exercise 2-12: Finding Liaisons and Glides
Hello, **my** name is_____. I'm taking American **A**ccent Training. There's a **lot** to learn, but **I hope** to make it as enjoyable as possible. I should pick **up** on the⁽ʸ⁾American intonation pattern pretty⁽ʸ⁾easily, although the⁽ʸ⁾only way to **get** it is to **prac**tice all of the time. I⁽ʸ⁾use the⁽ʸ⁾**up** and down, or **peaks** and valleys, intonation more than I⁽ʸ⁾**used** to. I've been paying **a**ttention to **pitch, too.** It's like **walking** down a **stair**case. I've been **talking** to⁽ʷ⁾a lot of **A**mericans lately, and they tell me that **I'm ea**sier to⁽ʷ⁾understand. **Any**way, I could go⁽ʷ⁾**on** and on, but the⁽ʸ⁾**impor**tant thing is to **lis**ten well and sound **good. Well**, what do you **think**? **Do**⁽ʷ⁾I?

Exercise 2-16: Liaison Staircases

Exercise 3-2: Finding [æ], [ä] and [ə] Sounds
Hello, **my** name is_____. I'm taking əmerəcən **æc**sənt Training. There's ə **lät** tə learn, bət I **hope** tə make ət əs ənjoyəbələs pässəbəl. I should pick əp än the əmerəcən əntənashən pættern pretty **ea**səly, ä⁰lthough the **only** way tə **get** ət əs tə **prac**təss ä⁰ll əv thə time. I use the **əp** ənd down, ər **peaks** ənd vælleys, intənashən mōre thən I **used** to. I've been paying əttenshən tə **pitch, too.** It's like **wälk**ing down ə **stair**case. I've been **tälk**ing to ə lät əf əmerəcans lately, ənd they tell me thət **I'm ea**sier tə əndər**stænd. Any**way, I could go **än** ənd än, bət the impor**tant** thing əs tə **lis**sən we⁰ll ənd sound **good. We⁰ll**, whət də yə **think**? **Do** I?

Exercise 4-12: Finding American T Sounds
Hello, **my** name is_____. I'm taking American **A**ccen⁽ᵗ⁾ Training. There's a **lo**⁽ᵗ⁾to learn, bud **I hope** to make id as enjoyable as possible. I should pick **up** on the American intonation paddern priddy **ea**sily, although the **only** way də **ged**dis də **prac**tice all of the time. I use the **up** and down, or **peaks** and valleys, intonation more than I **use**⁽ᵗ⁾to. I've been paying attention to **pitch, too.** It's like **walk**ing down a **stair**case. I've been **talk**ing to a läddəv **A**mericans la⁽ᵗ⁾ely, and they tell me the dime **ea**sier də under**stand. Any**way, I could go **on** and on, bu⁽ᵗ⁾ the impor⁽ᵗ⁾n⁽ᵗ⁾ thing is də **lis**sen well and sound **good. Well**, wha⁽ᵈ⁾do you **think**? **Do** I?

Exercise 5-6: Finding L Sounds

He<u>ll</u>o, **my** name is_____. I'm taking American **A**ccent Training. There's a **lot** to <u>l</u>earn, but I **hope** to make it as en<u>j</u>oyab<u>l</u>e as possib<u>l</u>e. I should pick **up** on the American into<u>n</u>ation pattern pretty ea<u>sil</u>y, although the on<u>l</u>y way to **get** it is to **prac**tice a<u>ll</u> of the time. I use the **up** and down, or **peaks** and va<u>ll</u>eys, intonation more than I **used** to. I've been paying attention to **pitch, too**. It's <u>l</u>ike **walk**ing down a **stair**-case. I've been **talk**ing to a <u>l</u>ot of **A**mericans late<u>l</u>y, and they te<u>ll</u> me that I'm **ea**sier to under**stand**. **Any**way, I could go **on** and on, but the im**por**tant thing is to <u>l</u>isten we<u>ll</u> and sound **good**. **We**<u>ll</u>, what do you **think**? **Do** I?

Exercise 6-7: Finding the R Sound

Hello, **my** name is_____. I'm taking Ame<u>r</u>ican **A**ccent T<u>r</u>aining. The<u>r</u>e's a **lot** to lea<u>r</u>n, but I **hope** to make it as en<u>j</u>oyable as possible. I should pick **up** on the Ame<u>r</u>ican intonation pattern p<u>r</u>etty easily, although the **only** way to **get** it is to **prac**tice all of the time. I use the **up** and down, o<u>r</u> **peaks** and valleys, intonation mo<u>r</u>e than I **used** to. I've been paying attention to **pitch, too**. It's like **walk**ing down a **stair**-case. I've been **talk**ing to a lot of **A**mericans lately, and they tell me that I'm **ea**sie<u>r</u> to unde<u>r</u>**stand**. **Any**way, I could go **on** and on, but the im**por**tant thing is to **lis**ten well and sound **good**. **Well**, what do you **think**? **Do** I?

Review Exercise B: Intonation Review Test

1. Los **Angeles**	11. **every**thing
2. paper **bag**	12. **moving** van
3. **lunch** bag	13. new **paper**
4. **convenience** store	14. **news**paper
5. convenient **store**	15. glass **eyes**
6. **home**work	16. **eye**glasses
7. good **writer**	17. high **chair**
8. apple **pie**	18. **high**chair
9. **pine**apple	19. **base**ball
10. all **things**	20. blue **ball**

Exercise 7-2: Targeting the TH Sound

Hello, **my** name is_____. I'm taking American **A**ccent Training. <u>Th</u>ere's a **lot** to learn, but I **hope** to make it as enjoyable as possible. I should pick **up** on <u>th</u>e American intonation pattern pretty easily, al<u>th</u>ough <u>th</u>e **only** way to **get** it is to **prac**tice all of <u>th</u>e time. I use <u>th</u>e **up** and down, or **peaks** and valleys, intonation more <u>th</u>an I **used** to. I've been paying attention to **pitch, too**. It's like **walk**ing down a **stair**-case. I've been **talk**ing to a lot of **A**mericans lately, and <u>th</u>ey tell me <u>th</u>at I'm **ea**sier to under**stand**. **Any**way, I could go **on** and on, but <u>th</u>e im**por**tant <u>th</u>ing is to **lis**ten well and sound **good**. **Well**, what do you **think**? **Do** I?

Exercise 8-8: Finding Reduced Sounds

Hello, **my** name is_____. I'm taking American **A**ccent Training. There's a **lot** to learn, but I **hope** to make it as enjoyable as possible. I shüd pick **up** on the American in-tonation pattern pretty **ea**sily, although the **only** way to **get** it is to **prac**tice all of the time. I ūse the **up** and down, or **peaks** and valleys, intonation more than I **used** tū. I've been paying attention to **pitch**, tū. It's like **walk**ing down a **stair**-case. I've been **talk**ing tū a lot of **A**mericans lately, and they tell me that I'm **ea**sier tū understand. **Any**way, I cüd go **on** and on, but the im**por**tant thing is to **lis**ten well and sound güd. **Well**, what do you **think**? D̄ū I?

Exercise 9-3: Finding V Sounds

Hello, **my** name is_____. I'm taking American **A**ccent Training. There's a **lot** to learn, but I **hope** to make it as

enjoyable as possible. I should pick **up** on the American intonation pattern pretty ea<u>s</u>ily, although the **only** way to **get** it is to **prac**tice all o<u>f</u> the time. I use the **up** and down, or **peaks** and <u>v</u>alleys, intonation more than I **used** to. I'<u>v</u>e been paying attention to **pitch, too**. It's like **walk**ing down a **stair**-case. I'<u>v</u>e been **talk**ing to a lot o<u>f</u> **A**mericans lately, and they tell me that I'm **ea**sier to under**stand**. **Any**way, I could go **on** and on, but the im**por**tant thing is to **lis**ten well and sound **good**. **Well**, what do you **think**? **Do** I?

Exercise 10-5: Finding S and Z Sounds

Hello, **my** name i<u>z</u>_____. I'm taking American **Ac**<u>s</u>ent Training. There'<u>z</u> a **lot** to learn, but I **hope** to make it a<u>z</u> enjoyable a<u>z</u> po<u>ss</u>ible. I should pick **up** on the American intonation pattern pretty ea<u>z</u>ily, although the **only** way to **get** it i<u>z</u> to **prac**ti<u>s</u>e all of the time. I u<u>z</u>e the **up** and down, or **peak**<u>s</u> and valley<u>z</u>, intonation more than I u<u>s</u>ed to. I've been paying attention to **pitch, too**. It'<u>s</u> like **walk**ing down a **stair**-ca<u>s</u>e. I've been **talk**ing to a lot of **A**merican<u>z</u> lately, and they tell me that I'm **ea**<u>z</u>ier to under**stand**. **Any**way, I could go **on** and on, but the im**por**tant thing i<u>z</u> to **li**<u>s</u>ten well and <u>s</u>ound **good**. **Well**, what do you **think**? **Do** I?

Exercise 11-2 and 11-4: Finding Tense (a, e, æ) and Lax Vowel Sounds (i, ə)

Hello, my n<u>a</u>me *is*_____. I'm t<u>a</u>k*i*ng əmerəcən **æk**sənt Tr<u>a</u>ini*ng*. Th<u>e</u>re's ə **lot** tə learn, bət I **hope** tə m<u>a</u>ke *it* əs ɛn<u>joy</u>əb'l əs possəbəl. I should p<u>i</u>ck əp on th<u>e</u> əmerəcən *i*ntə<u>na</u>shən pættern pr*i*tty <u>ea</u>səly, although th<u>e</u> **only** w<u>a</u>y tə **get** *it i*s tə **pr**æctəs all əv thə time. I use th<u>e</u> **up** ən dæon, or **peak**s ən vælleys, *i*ntənashən more thən I **used** to. I've b*i*n pay*i*ng əttenshən tə **pitch, too**. *i*t's like **walk**ing dæon ə **st**ɛrcase. I've b*i*n **talk**ing to ə lot əv əmerəcəns lately, ənd thay tell m<u>e</u> thət I'm **ea**sier tə onderstænd. ɛnyw<u>a</u>y, I could go **on** ənd on, bət th<u>e</u> *i*mport'nt th*i*ng *i*s to **li**stən well ənd sæond **good**. **We**ll, whət d' you **think**? **Do** I?

Exercise 12-4: Finding [n] and [ng] Sounds

Hello, **my** name is_____. I'm taki<u>ng</u> America<u>n</u> **Accen**t Traini<u>ng</u>. There's a **lot** to lear<u>n</u>, but I **hope** to make it as e<u>n</u>joyable as possible. I should pick **up** o<u>n</u> the America<u>n</u> i<u>n</u>to<u>n</u>ation patter<u>n</u> pretty **ea**sily, although the **on**ly way to **get** it is to **prac**tice all of the time. I use the **up** a<u>n</u>d dow<u>n</u>, or **peaks** a<u>n</u>d valleys, i<u>n</u>to<u>n</u>ation more tha<u>n</u> I **used** to. I've bee<u>n</u> payi<u>ng</u> atte<u>n</u>tio<u>n</u> to **pitch, too**. It'<u>s</u> like **walk**i<u>ng</u> dow<u>n</u> a **stair**-case. I've bee<u>n</u> **talk**i<u>ng</u> to a lot of **A**merica<u>n</u>s lately, a<u>n</u>d they tell me that I'm **ea**sier to u<u>n</u>derstand. **A**<u>n</u>yway, I could go **o**<u>n</u> a<u>n</u>d o<u>n</u>, but the im**por**ta<u>n</u>t thi<u>ng</u> is to **li**ste<u>n</u> well a<u>n</u>d sou<u>n</u>d **good**. **Well**, what do you **thi**<u>n</u>k? **Do** I?

Exercise 13-4: Glottal Consonant Practice

He<u>l</u>lo, **my** name is_____. I'm taking America<u>n</u> **A**ccent T<u>r</u>aining. There's a **lot** to lear<u>n</u>, but I **h**ope to ma<u>k</u>e it as enjoyable as possible. I should pic<u>k</u> **up** on the Ame<u>r</u>ican intonation patter<u>n</u> pretty **ea**sily, although the **only** way to **get** it is to **prac**tice all of the time. I use the **up** and down, o<u>r</u> **peak**<u>s</u> and valleys, intonation mo<u>r</u>e than I **used** to. I've been payi<u>ng</u> attention to **pitch, too**. It's li<u>k</u>e **walk**ing down a **stair**-case. I've been **talk**ing to a lot of **A**mericans lately, and they tell me that I'm **ea**sie<u>r</u> to under**stand**. **Any**way, I could go **on** and on, but the im**por**tant thing is to **lis**ten well and sound **good**. **Well**, what do you **think**? **Do** I?

Review Section Answer Key

Review Ex. 1-4: Sentence Intonation Test
1. They **took** it.
2. **Mary** had a **baby**.
3. **Louis** talked on the **phone**.
4. We **forgot** about it.
5. She **had** one.
6. Sam **called** him.
7. The **dogs** howled at the **moon**.
8. Did you **order** any?
9. We **noticed** her.
10. The **books** fell on the **floor**.

Review Ex. 1-29: Making Set Phrases
1. a **box** car
2. a **baby**-sitter
3. a **palm** tree
4. a **crab** cake
5. a **tea** cup
6. a **bottle** opener

Review Ex. 1-35: Contrast of Compound Nouns
1. a dark **room**
2. a **dark**room
3. an **antique** shop
4. an **antique** dealer
5. an antique **chair**
6. a new **video**
7. the **video** store
8. a **coffee** table
9. hot **coffee**
10. a **coffee**pot
11. a **chemistry** set
12. a chemical **reaction**
13. a sixth **sense**
14. six **cents**
15. a **sixth** grader
16. the sixth **grade**
17. long **hair**
18. a **hair**dresser
19. a **hair**cut
20. the wrong **station**
21. a **police** station
22. a **radio** station
23. **orange** juice
24. a **guitar** case
25. an electric **guitar**
26. trick **photography**
27. a **photo**-op
28. a **wedding** ceremony
29. a beautiful **ceremony**
30. a **wedding** cake

Review Ex. 1-36: Description and Set Phrase Test
1. The **schoolkids** took the **subway** down**town** for their **field** trip on urban **living**.
2. Our **local sheriff** had a **bumper sticker** on his **back bumper**.
3. The **homeowners** thought they had to pay **property** taxes to the federal **government**.
4. There were **small tremblors** after the **earthquake** in San **Francisco**.
5. The **Geology** Club went on a **camping** trip to Mount **Hood**.
6. The **award ceremony** at the **Hilton Hotel** lasted for two **hours**.
7. Bob **Smith** took his **surfboard** out on a **stormy day** near **Diamond** Head.
8. The **boy scouts** pitched their **pup tents** on the **mountaintop** in the **pouring rain**.
9. It's a **little late** to ask the **baby-sitter** to stay over**night**.
10. The **sixth** graders were reading **comic** books and drinking **chocolate milk**.

Review Ex. 1-48: Adjective and Verb Transitions
1. Would you please *alterneit* seats with the other *altern't*?
2. They signed a *contract* in order to *contract* their services.
3. Who could *object* to *progress*?
4. The unidentified flying *object progressed* slowly across the night sky.
5. We need a written *estim't* in order to *estimeit* the payment.

Review Ex. 1-51: Extended Listening Practice
1. We think he's got to get over it.
   we•thing•keez•gä•də•ge•do•vr•rit
2. Does anyone know how to get a line of credit?
   də•ze•nee•wən•no•hæo•də•ge•də•ly•nə•kre•dət
3. They should try to show them how to use the Internet.
   thay•shüd•try•də•sho•wəm•hæo•də•yuz•thee•ʸi•nr•net

Review Ex. 1-60: Tag Endings
1. is there
2. wasn't it
3. do you
4. would he
5. can't they
6. didn't she
7. wouldn't she
8. hadn't she
9. would she
10. had she

Review Ex. 2-4: Cons. / Vowel Liaison Practice
1. I thing kee zä ni zway.
2. He pü di di n' n'mbrella stand.
3. We bä di di nid'lee.

Review Ex. 2-8: Cons. / Cons. Liaison Practice
1. Ni⁽ᵏ⁾Clar kopest' pu⁽ᵗ⁾tendollar zdown.
2. Bu⁽ᵗ⁾Tommake⁽ˢ⁾so muchjuice.
3. Bob zdo⁽ᵍ⁾go⁽ᵗ⁾somebones.

Review Ex. 2-9: Vowel / Vowel Liaison Practice
1. Can you see⁽ʸ⁾it through to the⁽ʸ⁾end?
2. Be⁽ʸ⁾available for the⁽ʸ⁾other opportunity⁽ʸ⁾in my⁽ʸ⁾office.
3. He⁽ʸ⁾always wants to⁽ʷ⁾offer to go⁽ʷ⁾over it again.

Review Ex. 2-11: T, D, S, or Z Liaison Practice
1. We're glad the cher homework's done.
2. Wüjou help me with this?
3. Do you missher old friends?
4. Where zhier brother?

Review Ex. 2-12: Finding Liaisons and Glides
Think the United **Auto** Workers can beat Caterpillar **Inc.** in their bitter **contract** battle? Before placing your **bets**, talk to Paul **Branan**, who **can't wait** to cross the **picket** line at Caterpillar's **factory** in East **Peoria**. **Branan**, **recently** laid **off** by a **rubber**-parts plant where he earned **base** pay of $6.30 an **hour**, lives **one** block from a **heavily** picketed **gate** at the **Cat** complex. **Now** he's applying to replace one of **12,600 workers** who have been on **strike** for the **past** five **months**. "**Seventeen** dollars an **hour** and **they** don't want to **work**?" asks Branan. "I don't want to take **another** guy's **job**, but **I'm** hurting, **too**."

Review Ex. 3-4: Finding the æ, ä, ə, and d Sounds
Think thə Unidəd **ädo** Workers cən beat Cædəpillar **Inc.** in their bidder **cäntræct** bædəl? Bəfore placing your **bets**, tälk tə Päl **Brænən**, who **cæn't wait** tə cräss thə **pickət** line ət Cædəpillar's **fæctory** in East **Peoriə. Brænən**, **resəntly** laid **äff** by ə **rəbber**-pärts plænt where he earned **base** pay əf $6.30 ən **hæor**, lives **wən** bläck frəm ə **heavəly** pickədəd **gate** ət thə **Cæt** cämplex. **Næo** he's əpplying tə rəplace wən əf **twelve** thæosand six həndrəd **workers** who həve been än **strike** for thə **pæst** five **mənths**. "**Sevənteen** dällrs ən **hæor** ənd **they** don't wänt tə **work**?" æsks **Brænən**. "**I** don't wänt tə take **ənəthr** guy's **jäb**, bəd **I'm** hurding, **too**."

Index